THE COMMUNICATION SKILL

COMMUNICATING
WITH
CUSTOMERS

Baden
EUNSON

JOHN WILEY & SONS
BRISBANE • NEW YORK • CHICHESTER • TORONTO • SINGAPORE

First published 1995 by
JOHN WILEY & SONS
33 Park Road, Milton, Qld 4064

Offices also in Sydney and Melbourne

Typeset in 10.5/13 pt Garamond

© Baden Eunson 1995

National Library of Australia
Cataloguing-in-Publication data

Eunson, Baden.
    Communicating with customers.

    Bibliography.
    Includes index.
    ISBN 0 471 33562 2.

    1. Customer service. 2. Customer relations.
    3. Communication. I. Title.
    (Series: Communication skills (Milton, Qld.)).

658.812

All rights reserved. Unless a specific instruction is given to do otherwise, no part of this publication may be reproduced, stored in a retrieval system, or transmitted in any form or by any means, electronic, mechanical, photocopying, recording, or otherwise, without the prior permission of the publisher.

Edited by Bookmark Co. Pty Ltd

Cover illustration and cartoons by Mike Spoor

Printed in Hong Kong

10 9 8 7 6 5 4 3 2 1

CONTENTS

Preface v

1. **Customers, Providers and Communication** 1
   Customers and providers 1
   Muddling through some models of communication 2

2. **The Service Society** 4
   The rise of the service society 5
   Customer service: why it's so important, and why it's so hard to find 6
   Customer service: what goes wrong 11
   Communication skills: the tip of the iceberg 15
   Talking points: You don't say? What people say about customers and providers 18

3. **Non-verbal Communication** 20
   Head movements 21
   The face 22
   Eye contact 23
   Voice 24
   Smell 24
   Gesture 24
   Posture 25
   Orientation 26
   Touching 26
   Clothing and adornment 27
   Personal space/territoriality 29
   Environment 31
   Time and cultural context 33
   Talking points: You don't say? More of what people say about customers and providers 36

4. **Transactional Analysis: The Games Customers (and Providers) Play** 38
   Transactional analysis: the background 38
   Ego states 39
   Strokes: what you stroke is what you get 43
   Transactions: complementary, crossed and ulterior strokes 46
   May I see your licence, please? 50
   The games people play 52
   Time structuring: filling in time between birth and death 59
   Roles: the drama triangle 61
   Life positions 64
   TA: the practical payoffs for communicating with customers 64
   Talking points: using TA to ensure the customer pays 65
   TA: the overview 67
   Talking points: communicating with customers: a survival kit 68

5. **Assertively Communicating with Customers** 70
   Assessing your assertiveness 70
   Assertive and non-assertive behaviours 72
   Four styles of behaviour 74
   Self-talk 78
   Being assertive: some verbal skills 79
   Rights of the customer and the provider 82
   Talking points: You don't say? More of what people say about customers and providers 85

6. **Establishing Rapport with Customers: Neurolinguistic Programming** 87
   Neurolinguistic programming: modes of perception 87
   Representational systems 87
   Chunking up, chunking down 91
   Talking points: bad communication and non-communication in the service encounter in Australia 93

7. **Listening, Questioning and Complaints: Using Feedback to Improve Service** 95
   Listening: why should you bother 95
   Listening: what is it? 97
   Listening, gender and power 99
   Listening and non-verbal communication 100
   Listening: not-so-remote sensing 100
   Active listening 103
   Bad listening habits 103
   Questioning 105
   Complaints, feedback and strategic listening 106
   Talking points: customer listening in the AMP 108
   Talking points: how to handle customer complaints 109

8. **Communicating on the Telephone** 112
   The pros and cons of telephone communication 112
   The telephone: know the basics 114
   More technology 115
   Answering the telephone 116
   Placing calls 118
   Working on the telephone: a performing art 120
   The chamber of telephone horrors: what *not* to do on the phone 121
   Talking points 125

9. **Communicating with Customers: The Overview** 127
   Making communication easier 127
   Talking points: comments about customer service 129
   Talking points: customers from hell: scenes from a newsagency 130

Endnotes 131

Reference list 142

Index 161

PREFACE

. . . .

We all have experiences of being customers. We know that, as individuals, we are special, and that, as customers, we want to be treated that way — as special people, not ordinary people. The experience of many of us in many situations, however, is of very ordinary customer service. Customer dissatisfaction seems to be more prevalent than customer satisfaction.

Happily, this situation can be reversed, particularly if service providers learn more about the art of communicating with customers, which by an amazing coincidence, is the name of this book.

In *Communicating with Customers*, we will consider the background to the rise of the service society, and we will gain a greater understanding of customers by considering facets of non-verbal communication, listening, questioning and feedback skills, and telephone skills. We will see what we can learn about customers from three models of human behaviour — those of transactional analysis, assertiveness training, and neurolinguistic programming.

Other books in this series also contain specific insights into communicating with customers: *Writing at Work* (writing effective letters), *Writing in Plain English* (ensuring that policies, forms and other documents are easily understood) and *Negotiation Skills* (perceiving the customer–provider encounter as a negotiating or haggling situation).

Throughout this book you will find numerous exercises to help you build your skills. More information about specific points in the text is contained in numbered endnotes at the back of the book. If you wish to read still further in this area, a large and up-to-date reference list is also provided.

BADEN EUNSON

1 CUSTOMERS, PROVIDERS, AND COMMUNICATION

CUSTOMERS AND PROVIDERS

In this book we will be examining just what goes on when a customer or client meets a provider. 'Provider' is a general term, covering just about anyone who sells or provides a good or a service.[1] Some examples of customers, or clients,[2] and providers are shown below.

Customer/client	Provider
shopper	salesperson
patient	doctor
buyer	seller
electricity consumer	clerk in billing section of electricity company
client	lawyer
client	hairdresser
prisoner	prison officer
computer user	person on telephone hot line of computer hardware company
prospective customer	insurance salesperson
tourist	tour guide
hotel guest	member of hotel staff
aircraft passenger	airline steward
taxpayer	analyst in taxation office
car owner	mechanic

In such examples, customers are necessarily external to the organisations where the providers work. Some organisations, however, find it useful to talk about *internal* customers — individuals, groups, departments, branches or divisions within an organisation that depend upon the output of other individuals, groups, departments, branches or divisions also within that organisation (see pp. 10, 133).

Providers often communicate with customers face to face, but there are numerous other channels of communication, such as:

telephone	pre-paid complaints forms
newsletters	trade fairs
postcards	exhibitions
progress reports	shopping centre displays
brochures	video complaint booths
market research surveys	toll-free hot lines/telephone complaint/inquiry/advice lines
electronic data interchange	
advertising	suggestion boxes
media releases	industry/community grapevines/rumour mills
environment, e.g., store layout, interior design	
	focus groups
customer panels/councils	follow-up phone calls to customers who leave
customer visits/inspections	
customer briefings	graffiti boards/electronic graffiti facilities on computer network
dining out	
networking	

MUDDLING THROUGH SOME MODELS OF COMMUNICATION

The dynamics of communication in the encounter between a customer, or client, and a provider can be quite complex. In *Communicating with Customers*, we will examine a number of models of such communication. These models are those of:

- non-verbal communication
- transactional analysis
- assertiveness training
- neurolinguistic programming
- listening, questioning and feedback skills.

All of these models may provide insights into communication which occurs face to face, over the telephone, or in print.

It is not only customers who communicate, of course: in learning about such models of communication, we will learn about the communication patterns of providers as well. Providers and customers are not two separate species: we are all customers *and* providers as we undertake different roles throughout our lives.

We can react to these models in a number of ways as shown below.

Reaction 1	The models represent eternal truths and, as such, are full of blinding insights into human behaviour, thus allowing providers to more honestly communicate with customers.
Reaction 2	The models comprise empty 'psychobabble', or psychological nonsense and, as such, have nothing to tell us about human behaviour.
Reaction 3	The models comprise empty 'psychobabble', but can be dangerous to the extent that some people believe that they work.
Reaction 4	The models are powerful and evil behavioural technologies, and can be used by providers to manipulate customers, and — not incidentally — create a world in which honest communication becomes impossible, or at least impossible to recognise.

You may react in any of these four ways — or a fifth or sixth or seventh way. The truth about the models presented for you here probably draws from more than one — and possibly all — of the reactions or world views. The models themselves are sometimes consistent with each other, but often they are inconsistent with each other. Perhaps the best way to view such models is to see yourself as the customer, strolling through the supermarket of models or ideas — you can pick and choose, as you see fit, testing them against your own sense of what is real, what is plausible.

There are all kinds of customers. Many providers fear dealing with angry or complaining customers — 'customers from hell'. Yet the negative behaviour of such customers can be analysed, understood and worked with by applying models of behaviour and communication, and the insights gained from the feedback given to us by such customers can, in fact, be very helpful, as we will see in a later section (p. 106).

Some communication and behavioural models — when introduced into the workplace — have been used for manipulative ends.[3] Perhaps the best way to neutralise such potential for manipulation is to bring such models or ideas into the public domain, so that all — not just a few — can see them. This book is part of that process.

Before we look in detail at these models, however, we need to consider the context in which the customer-provider encounter occurs. Chapter two — The Service Society — provides us with that context.

2 THE SERVICE SOCIETY

Why has customer service become such a big issue in recent times? To a considerable extent, this has been because society has been undergoing changes, and these changes have led to new values and behaviour patterns. Let's consider the historical context of these changes.

Services are different from goods in that goods are tangible or solid artefacts or things, while services are usually intangible processes. Over historical time, most economies seem to follow a particular sequence:

Agricultural society   Manufacturing society   Services society

Time ⟶

Key
☐ Tertiary Industry
▨ Secondary Industry
▪ Primary Industry

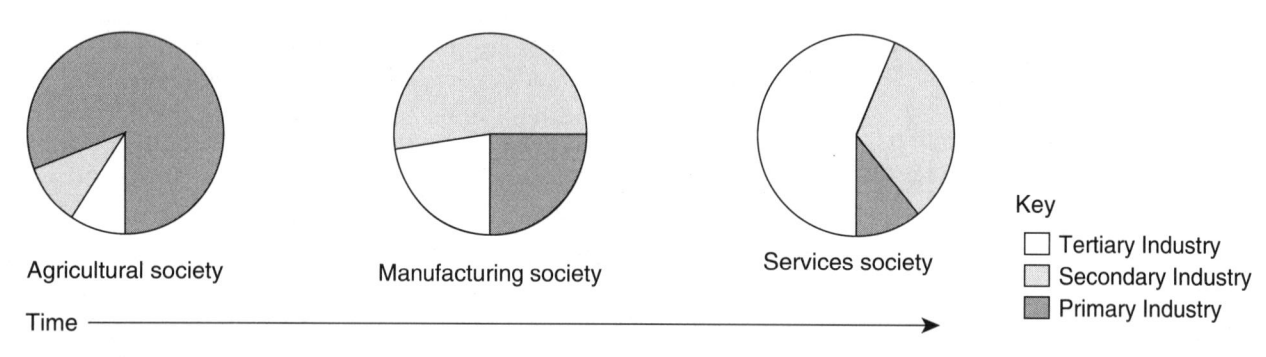

Figure 2.1: Changing patterns of work: proportions of labour force in various industries
(Source: Eunson [1987:7]. Reproduced with permission.)

In traditional societies, prior to the innovation of large-scale manufacture of goods, the majority of the workforce was — and in some parts of the world is — engaged in primary or extractive industries: growing crops, raising domesticated animals, fishing and mining. In Western countries, in the eighteenth and nineteenth centuries, the Industrial Revolution saw the development of the first large-scale manufacturing industries. Manufacturing or secondary industry is concerned with processing the raw materials derived from primary industries. Typical manufacturing industries are iron and steel, chemicals, automobiles, textiles, clothing, footwear and food processing.

Where did the labour come from to staff the emergent manufacturing industries in Western countries undergoing the Industrial Revolution? A substantial part of this new work force came from the old agricultural work force: mechanisation and automation of processes and economies of scale in production meant that there were fewer jobs to be found in the primary or extractive industries. Thus, in an agricultural society, the majority of the work force were employed in primary industry, while in a manufacturing society, the majority of the work force were employed in secondary industry.

THE RISE OF THE SERVICE SOCIETY

A similar change began to creep up on Western societies in the middle of the twentieth century. Mechanisation and automation and economies of scale began to cut a swathe through secondary industry employment, while at the same time tertiary or services industries began to flourish. Typical service industries are insurance, banking, education, media, medicine, welfare, religion and government. In the post-industrial or services society, the majority of people are employed in tertiary industries.

This model of development, initially confined to Euro-American societies, seems to have become the global norm, striven after by almost all societies. Whether it is the ideal model — economically, politically, socially, ecologically, psychologically or spiritually — remains to be seen. Nevertheless, the dynamic processes operating have produced a situation in the services society wherein most of the work force delivers services, rather than goods.[4]

Table 2.1 shows a useful model for analysing service industries. In a very real sense, a hairdressing salon, a schoolroom, an insurance office and a warehouse are all 'service factories'[5] — they are the locations where services are created, and also delivered to the customer.

Table 2.1: Understanding the nature of the service act

What is the nature of the service act?	Who or what is the direct recipient of the service?	
	People	**Possessions**
Tangible actions	Services directed at people's bodies	Services directed at physical possessions
	Passenger transportation Health care Lodging Beauty salons Physical therapy Fitness centres Restaurants/bars Haircutting Funeral services	Freight transportation Repair and maintenance Warehousing/storage Janitorial services Retail distribution Laundry and dry cleaning Refuelling Landscaping/lawn care Disposal/recycling
Intangible actions	Services directed at people's minds	Services directed at intangible assets
	Advertising/PR Arts and entertainment Broadcasting/cable TV Management consulting Education Information services Music concerts Psychotherapy Religion Voice telephone	Accounting Banking Data processing Data transmission Insurance Legal services Programming Research Securities investment Software consulting

(Source: Lovelock, Christopher (1994:4). *Product Plan: How Product and Service = Competitive Advantage*. McGraw-Hill. Reproduced with permission of McGraw-Hill.)

Because service workers spend most of their time dealing with people rather than things, this necessarily places a premium upon communication skills. Does this mean, by the way, that people working in primary and manufacturing industries have no need to communicate with other people, such as their customers? Far from it. How is it possible for communication *not* to take place in circumstances such as:

- a farmer discussing the quality of a crop with a cooperative organisation manager
- managers of a mine negotiating sales of coal with managers of an electric power station
- an automobile retailer telephoning a car manufacturer to pass on complaints about a new model
- a technician working on a washing machine manufacturer's 'hot line', advising a machine owner on how to fix a basic fault
- a pharmaceutical company trying to persuade the public that a new drug is safe.

Whether the communication in such circumstances is effective or not is another matter, of course. Nevertheless, this simple point begins to emerge: whether a person works in a primary/extractive, a secondary/manufacturing or a tertiary/service industry, such a person ultimately is a provider who serves a customer. Customer service, in other words, isn't just the preserve of service industries: it has a vital role to play in *all* industries, and a vital part of customer service is communication. (See also note 8, p. 132.)

CUSTOMER SERVICE: WHY IT'S SO IMPORTANT, AND WHY IT'S SO HARD TO FIND

Let's consider the forces driving towards the provision of quality service, and the forces undermining or weakening such provision (see table 2.2).

Customer service and management specialists often point out, that for today's and tomorrow's organisations, customer service is no longer a luxury,

Table 2.2: Provision of quality customer service — driving and restraining factors

Factors driving towards quality customer service	Factors restraining quality customer service
The service advantage — decline of traditional competitive strengths, e.g., technology	Deregulation
Blurring of goods and services	Short-term financial planning
Co-destiny relationships	'Too much growth, too little maintenance' philosophy
New data on value of customer service	Reactive, tactical status quo
Emergence of proactive, strategic service model — 'moments of truth'	Have-a-nice-day-itis: smiles, not systems
Job and organisational redesign: the inverted pyramid and internal customers	Poor job and organisational design
New emphasis on skills training	Role conflict
Consumer activism	Emotional labour burnout

or an add-on feature — it is vital to the survival of those organisations. Until recent historical times, an organisation could count on things such as technology to make their products stand out from the products of their competitors. ('If our competitor makes a 4 kW widget, and we make a quicker, quieter 6 kW widget, then our competitor's customers will desert them and come to us.') Technical improvements, in other words, allowed organisations to *differentiate* their products from those of their competitors.

This, however, is no longer true: any product innovation is usually copied by competitors within a short space of time, and thus uniqueness is only temporary.[6] Also, the phenomenon of *convergence* means that unique new products — cars, insurance policies, hairstyles — are copied rapidly, and most products offered by competing organisations end up looking the same. How then can an organisation make its product *different* from those of its competitors? The 'great differentiator' is, in fact, the service an organisation can offer.[7]

In an economy's mass-manufacturing phase, the emphasis is upon mass-produced, cheap, simple goods. The encounter between a customer and provider tends to be a once-only affair — at the moment of purchase — and there are no major encounters thereafter, except to maintain the purchased good should it require maintenance. Some economic analysts have suggested that the high-wage, advanced industrial Western economies, in an attempt to stay ahead of the lower-wage, emergent industrial economies, may have to move beyond mass manufacturing to precision-manufactured, custom-tailored and technology-intensive items in the same and some related industrial areas — for example, computer hardware and software, special chemicals and drugs, lasers, ceramics, fibre-optic cables, custom-made synthetics, speciality steels and precision castings. Many of these products require custom designing and ongoing servicing, upgrading and consultancy, and thus the distinction between what is a good and what is a service begins to blur.[8] In such situations, customer service becomes extremely important.

Many creators of goods and services have begun to establish much closer relationships with organisations that supply them with component parts and raw materials. These closer relationships have been nurtured because of the growing popularity of the Japanese-inspired Just In Time (JIT) manufacturing philosophy. In JIT, an organisation can dispense with, or greatly reduce its reliance upon, expensive inventories and quality inspections of incoming parts and materials, with anything required arriving at the point of assembly 'just in time'. This can only occur if there is excellent communication and coordination with suppliers. Thus buyers and sellers, customers and providers, become partners in strategic alliances or enter into a 'co-destiny'.

Recent research in a number of countries has revealed much about the nature of consumer dissatisfaction. Some points to emerge from this research are shown in the following box.

> **Some facts about customers**
> - Only 4 per cent of customers ever complain; some simply suffer in silence, while most simply go elsewhere.
> - People who stop buying from or dealing with a particular business do so because:
>   — 1 per cent die
>   — 3 per cent move away
>   — 5 per cent seek alternatives or develop other business interests
>   — 9 per cent begin doing business with the competition
>   — 14 per cent are dissatisfied with the product or service
>   — 68 per cent are upset with the treatment they have received.
> - It is six times more expensive to acquire a new customer than it is to retain an old one.
> - Happy customers, or customers who have their complaints satisfactorily resolved, will tell three to five people. One study revealed that one unhappy customer told eleven other people, who in turn told five other people (a negative-word-of-chain of 1 + 11 + 55 = 67 people).
> - Between 54–70 per cent of customers who complain will nevertheless continue to be customers if their complaint is resolved to their satisfaction.
> - Organisations which provide superior customer service can charge more, create greater profits and achieve greater market share, because customers will generally pay a premium for superior customer service.

(Source: adapted from Lovelock [1994], Gerson [1992], and Morgan [1989].)

Such data reveal good news and bad news: the bad news is that dissatisfaction is much greater than most organisations suspect or indeed have the ability to detect; the good news however, is that an effective customer service program can not only undo the damage but give organisations a strategic advantage over competition.

But how can customer complaints lead to a major re-think in organisations? In many organisations, customer service, in the past, has been ignored or else given a marginalised role. Lip-service was paid to it, but decision-makers tended to give most attention to 'the real issues' — long-range strategy, industrial relations, exchange rates, advertising, and so on. Yet a new perspective has been emerging in recent years: without customers, organisations die, and the only way most customers encounter an organisation is via many 'moments of truth' with front-line personnel — the people on the counters or on the telephones. Customers judge the entire organisation in those moments of truth, and unless top decision-makers begin to pay attention to this, they are missing the point and will be soon out of a job.[9] In this new perspective, customer service shifts from being a reactive process, taking place at the lower or tactical levels ('take care of complaints and shut them up'), to being a proactive or forward-thinking process, taking place at the upper or strategic levels ('listen to the customer and plan accordingly').* This has meant that some organisations now *actively seek out complaints from customers*, so that the information in such complaints can be fed back into the planning process — the planning of prevention, rather than of just cure (see p. 106).

Following from this, new models of the design of organisations and the jobs within them began to emerge. Such designs have a critical impact upon the motivation (or demotivation) of people who work in organisations.[10] The traditional organisation was a tall pyramid (figure 2.2.(a)).

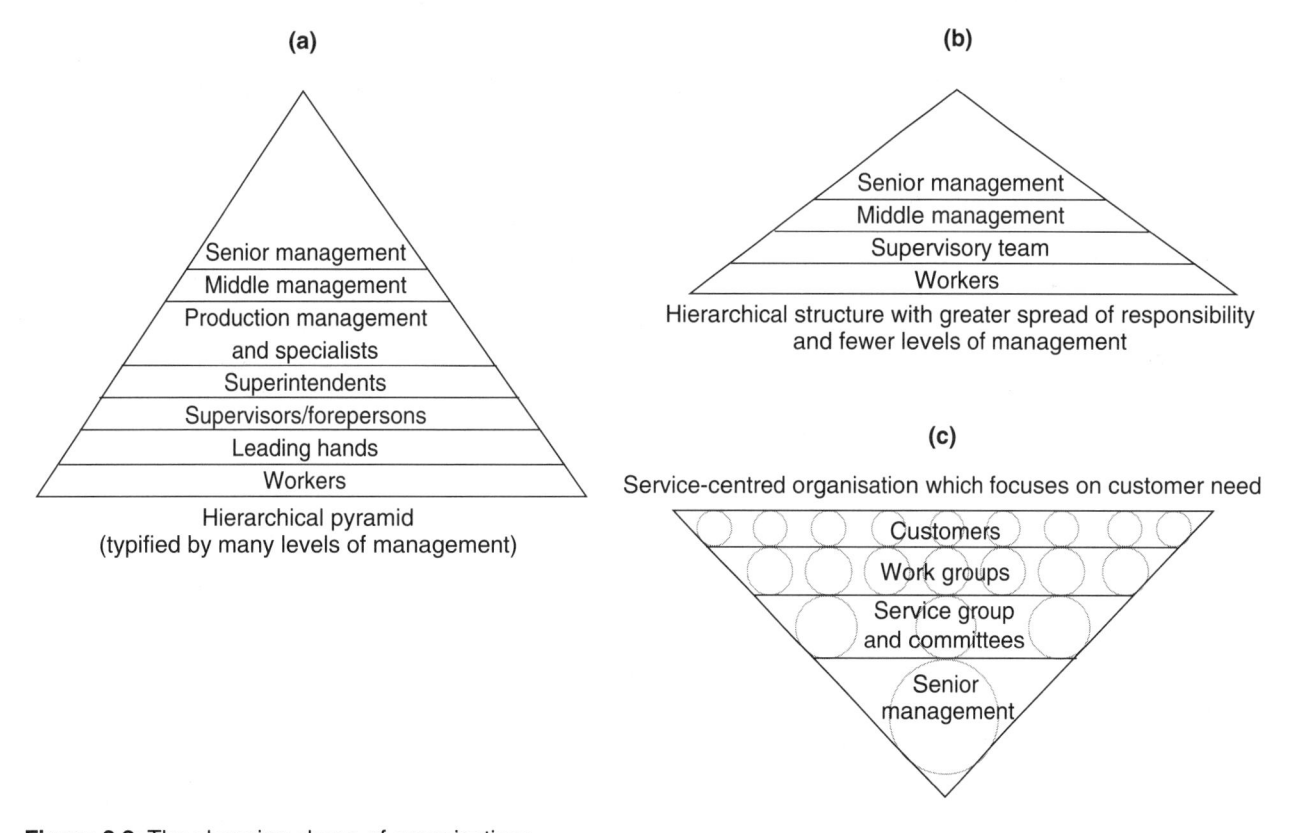

Figure 2.2: The changing shape of organisations

(Source: McPhee and McNicol [1992]. Reproduced with permission of the authors.)

---

* Note, for example, the extract from a strategic planning document of an insurance company, p. 108.

Decision-makers were safely enthroned at the top, and there were many levels of decision-making between the top and the bottom layers. Organisational theorists began to suggest there were problems with this type of structure, such as:
- The tall structure slowed down communication up and down the pyramid.
- Several layers in the middle performed the primary function of shifting information up and down the pyramid, but such a function was becoming redundant as computers enabled data to flow directly from action centres at the bottom to decision-makers at the top.
- Decision-makers at the top were too far removed from the action, and often made decisions that were too late or were based upon inaccurate information.
- Workers at the bottom of the pyramid were imprisoned in narrow job designs; expected only to perform simplified tasks with robot-like repetitiveness, their experience and problem-solving abilities were rarely called upon.
- The structure was totally inward-looking: it did not acknowledge the strategic importance of customer–front-line staff encounters, and did not incorporate the needs and wishes of customers into the heart of the planning process.

As a result of this, the organisational pyramid was first flattened (figure 2.2(b)). This meant 'downsizing', or the removal of many middle-management personnel, the widening of spans of control* of many managers and supervisors, and the implementation of work teams.[11]

The next and final step (figure 2.2(c)) was to reconceptualise or re-think the pyramid as being an inverted or upside-down one: in this organisation, the primary focus is upon the customer, and then the front-line staff, rather than upon the high-status decision-makers at the apex of the pyramid. The opinions of the customer are plugged into the heart of the decision-making process, while the front-line employees undergo a substantial transformation.** Before, such front-line staff had been the lowest of the low — with low wages, no or little information about the rest of the organisation and their role within it, and no or little power to make decisions and solve problems to better serve the customer. Such front-line staff in this new organisational model now become well paid, or at least better paid, become supplied with maximum information about the organisation, and are empowered to make decisions and solve problems in ways that were previously restricted to supervisory and managerial personnel.[12]

In fact, the concept of 'customer' undergoes a transformation: if the output of one work area is the input for another work area, then the second work area is in fact, 'the customer' for the first area, and needs to be treated with the same care as 'external' customers.[13]

Thus customer relations mirror employee relations — if the latter is bad, so is the former; if the latter is good, so is the former. Openly and effectively communicating with customers, then, depends in the first instance upon top-level management communicating openly and effectively with front-line providers (table 2.3).

---

* A span of control refers to the number of subordinates that report to a given manager or supervisor. In a tall organisation, spans of control are narrow (e.g., five employees report to one supervisor at one level; five supervisors report to one manager at the next level), while in flat organisations, spans of control are large (e.g., twenty to thirty employees might report to one supervisor; twenty to thirty supervisors might report to one manager or general manager).

** Note the cycles of success and failure, pp. 13–14.

Table 2.3: Linkages between communication within the organisation and communication with customers

Management to employee	Employee to customer
What are your problems and how can I help solve them?	How may I be of assistance to you?
We want you to know what is happening in our organisation, so here is what is going on.	I am capable of helping you because I am in the know.
Each of us is in the company, so we all share accountability for what happens around here.	I am empowered to help you and take pride in my ability to do so.
We treat each other with professional respect.	I have respect for you as the individual you are.
We stand behind each other's decisions and support each other.	You can count on me and my company to deliver on our promises.

(Source: Desatnick [1987: 21–22].)

These role changes for providers, particularly front-line staff, mean that there is a great need for training in technical and communication skills. This is necessarily expensive, but is undertaken by successful organisations, who see such programs as cheap when compared with the alternative of failure.

Finally, there has been a considerable growth in consumer activism in the past few decades, which has forced organisations to lift their game. This activism derives partly from large and well-resourced organisations, and partly from increasingly assertive individuals.[14] In other words, many customers are saying 'We're as mad as hell and aren't going to take any more!' Organisations with poor customer service, and with little intention of improving such service, ignore such activism at their peril.

CUSTOMER SERVICE: WHAT GOES WRONG

These, then, are the factors that have driven organisations to lift their game in relation to customer service. Why then does bad service still exist? It exists because there have also been numerous factors at play which have restrained or undermined the provision of quality customer service.

More competition among providers does not always spell good news for customers. Substantial deregulation in a number of American industries (banking, airlines, telecommunications) has coincided with a dramatic rise in customer complaints made to those industries. Competitive pressures sometimes seem to lead to cuts in cost and staff, with existing staff becoming demotivated by continual pressure to improve productivity.[15]

Competitive pressures have also led many managers to adopt a short-term financial planning approach, which often means that customer service — where payoffs tend to occur in the medium to long term — is the first activity to get cut. This, to say the least, is counterproductive.[16]

Organisations often subscribe to a 'too much growth, too little maintenance' philosophy: there is a greater emphasis upon obtaining new customers via extensive sales and marketing than there is upon looking after existing customers via customer service. This approach also brings with it the danger of over-committing the organisation to servicing all customers, when, in fact, it does not have the facility to do so. Such an approach causes customer dissatisfaction all around, and also ignores the basic economics of new customers versus old customers (see p. 8).[17]

Old habits die hard, and many organisations see no need to change to the new model of customer service as a proactive, strategic consideration. Instead, they keep customer relations as a reactive, tactical function, wherein there is a separate, low-level complaints department, which is usually the organisation's 'Siberia'.

When such organisations decide that 'something must be done about customer service', they usually settle for the have-a-nice-day-itis syndrome, wherein it is assumed that improved communication skills by themselves will solve problems. This has been called the 'smiles, not systems' approach.[18] Communication skills by themselves are of no use in situations where, for example:

- a nurse has no hospital beds available and is confronted by an angry, bleeding patient
- a department store salesperson is confronted by an angry customer when the computerised cash register system is down for the third time that day
- a waiter talks amicably to customers, knowing that half the menu is not available
- a car dealer with a full order book has no cars available because of industrial relations problems at the factory.

Systems, facilities and technical backup have to be there for the front-line provider to satisfy the customer.

Organisations with such poor customer-service practices usually have poor job and organisational designs in place: not for them the job and organisational redesign that goes with the new paradigm of customer service as a strategic, proactive activity. Such redesign involves inverting the organisational pyramid, empowering front-line staff, paying them better, and keeping them totally informed, rather than keeping them in the dark. Managers may feel that such changes are quite unnecessary, too expensive, and too threatening, but such attitudes may mean that their organisation will be locked into a cycle of service failure (figure 2.3). This cycle is, in fact, a double cycle, involving both employees and customers, with reciprocal feedbacks; it is not the customer who fails, however, but the provider organisation.

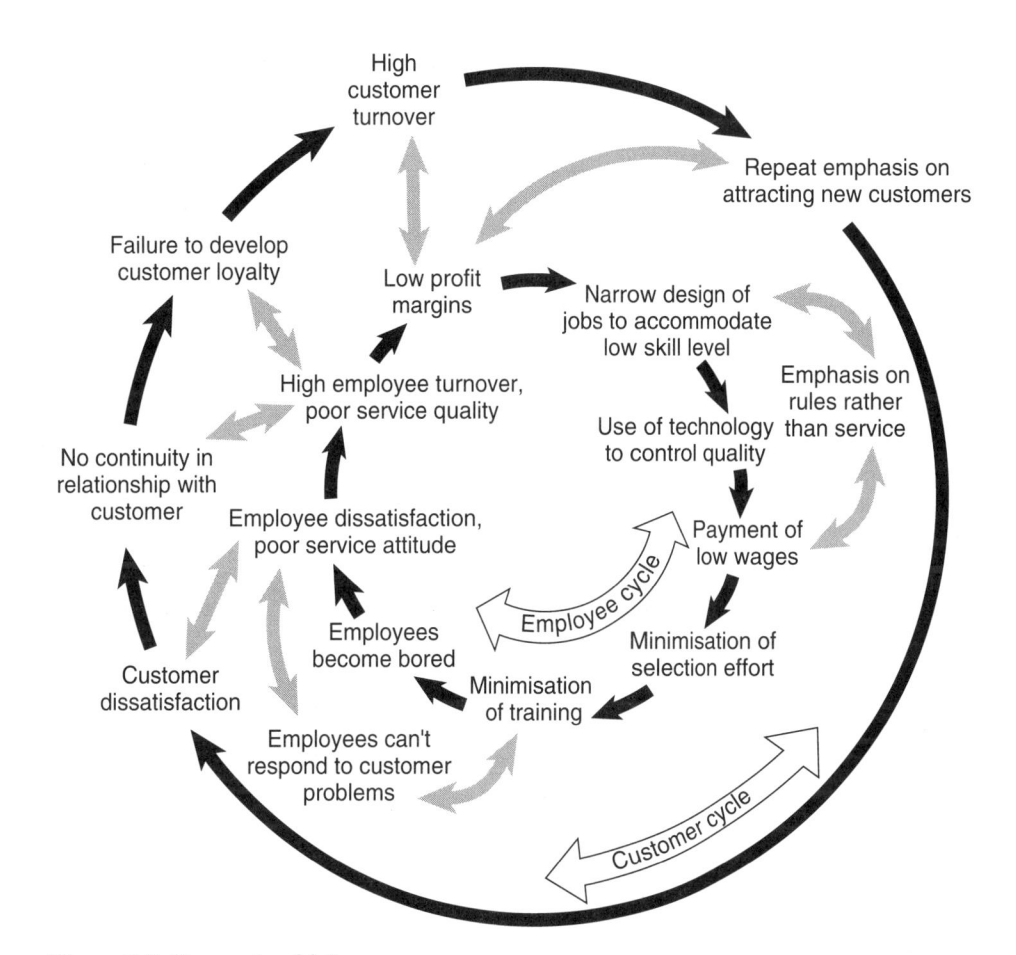

Figure 2.3: The cycle of failure

(Source: Reprinted from 'Breaking the cycle of failure in services' by Leonard L. Schlesinger and James L. Heskett, *Sloan Management Review*, Spring (1991:18). By permission of the publisher. Copyright (1991) by the Sloan Management Review Association. All rights reserved.)

This failure cycle is characterised by:
- managers trying to cut costs by hiring low-wage, low-skill labour
- managers trying to control quality by using systems/technology instead of allowing employees freedom to solve problems as they arise
- managers skimping on selection and training
- demotivated employees giving poor service
- employees leaving, depressing profits.

It doesn't have to be this way, of course. The alternative is the cycle of success (figure 2.4).

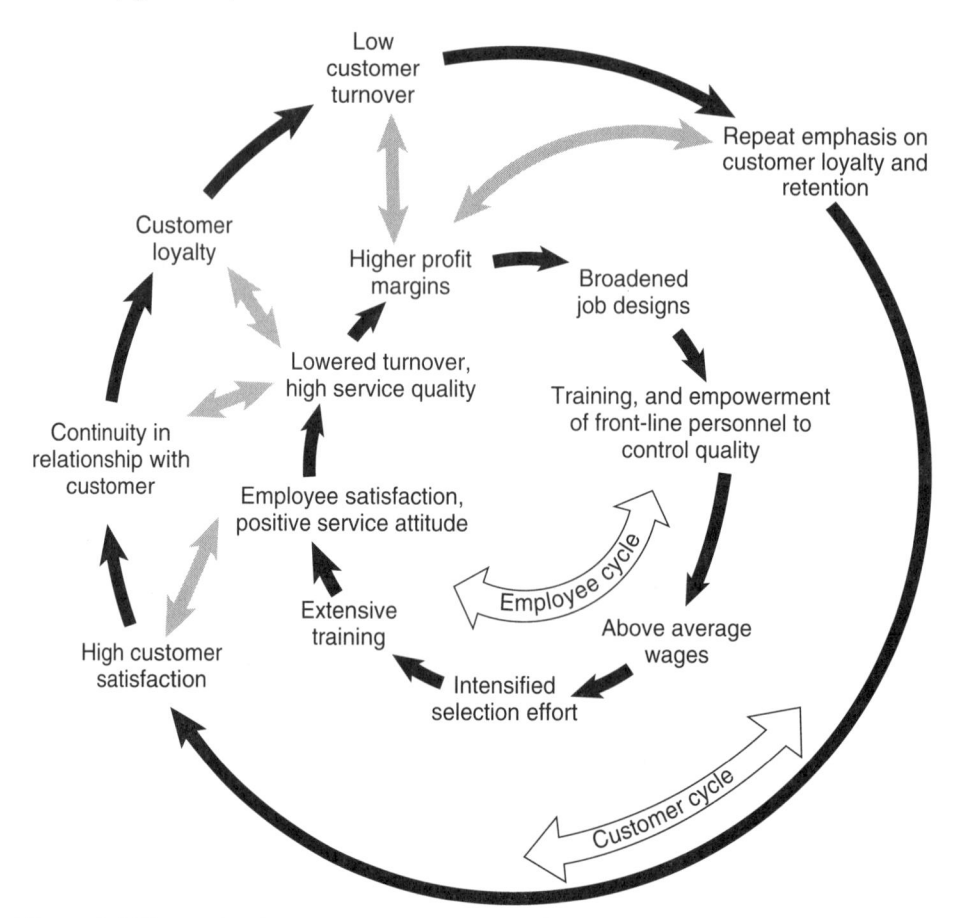

Figure 2.4: The cycle of success

(Source: Reprinted from 'Breaking the cycle of failure in services' by Leonard L. Schlesinger and James L. Heskett, *Sloan Management Review*, Spring (1991:20). By permission of the publisher. Copyright (1991) by the Sloan Management Review Association. All rights reserved.)

This cycle, in fact, reflects the proactive, strategic job and organisational designs we have just considered (p. 10). It's more expensive in the short run, but much cheaper in the medium to long run. Managers who insist on sticking with the cycle of failure, in spite of this, rationalise their mistakes with stock excuses and self-fulfilling prophecies — for example:
- You can't find good (or any) people today.
- People just don't want to work today.
- To get good people would cost too much and you can't pass on these cost increases to customers.
- It's not worth training our front-line people when they leave you so quickly.
- High turnover is simply an inevitable part of our business. You've got to learn to live with it.[19]

The failure cycle produces the 'McJobs' some futurists have warned about — low-paid and with little or no career structure to motivate people,[20] motivation being the essence of quality communication and service. People will not put much passion and sincerity into 'have a nice day' if there is nothing in it for them. Service jobs can be just as frustrating and demeaning — or just as fulfilling and exciting — as jobs anywhere — if they are designed well.[21]

Figure 2.5: Down and out in the service society — Doonesbury's pessimistic view of 'McJobs'. © Universal Press Syndicate.

Another factor undermining the delivery of quality service is the role conflict experienced by many front-line providers. For many people 'service' means 'servility'.[22] They see the role of provider as little better than that of a servant or a slave, who is required to grovel to the customer. Indeed, quite a few 'customers from hell' seem to share that view. Under such circumstances, some providers may feel, in order to preserve their human dignity, that they should react by giving little or no emotional response to the customer, or else by going on the offensive and being passively or overtly hostile to the customer. Thus the offensiveness of bad service is often merely defensiveness in another guise. This, of course, has much to do with the bad job and organisational designs we have just been considering.

Finally, we need to consider the nature of the labour provided in the provider role. Providers increasingly do not have to contribute physical labour, but instead have to contribute what has been called 'emotional labour'.[23] Front-line providers have to continually smile, show empathy, listen and solve problems (see pp. 95–111). Unlike other people in their organisations who work 'behind the scenes', front-line providers are continually in the public view, and thus may find it difficult or inappropriate to express normal human conditions such as tiredness, frustration, boredom and anger. Headaches, hangovers, being distracted by personal problems, and simply being left alone seem unimaginable luxuries to some providers. This is stressful, and may lead to feelings of burnout. Such basic human needs need to be factored into job and organisational designs.

COMMUNICATION SKILLS: THE TIP OF THE SERVICE ICEBERG

In *Communicating with Customers*, we consider a number of models of communication as they occur in the customer–provider encounter. As we have seen, however, communication skills are only part of the total picture. If customer service can be conceptualised as an iceberg, the communication skills component is the most visible, but there are other components beneath the surface, such as technical skills, motivation, job and organisational design, and systems backup (figure 2.6).

In organisations which provide excellent customer service, this behind-the-scenes support is an unremarkable fact. In organisations which have a few (or a lot of) problems in providing customer service, the point needs emphasising. 'Smiles, not systems' may be better than nothing at all, but such a partial approach can never be adequate and will probably be self-defeating.

Communication skills

Technical skills

Motivation

Job design

Organisational design

Systems backup

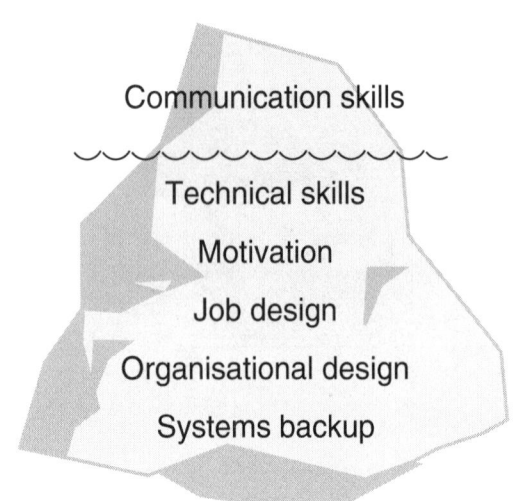

Figure 2.6: The customer service 'iceberg'

Maybe you work in an organisation that has some problems in delivering quality customer service. The concepts developed in this chapter may help you to diagnose the problems your organisation has in this area. Maybe there is a strong need for training in communication and technical skills. Maybe more attention needs to be paid to motivation and job/organisational design problems. Maybe the entire systems/technical backup/facilities situation is in a bad way. How can you best communicate your diagnosis to others more powerful than yourself? You may find it useful to use a communication tool such as the wish list (table 2.4) and send it to decision-makers. Others you work with may also like to complete a copy of the wish list. If your organisation is open and receptive to new ideas, there will be no problems associated with identifying yourself on the wish list. If things are less than ideal, however, you may prefer to remain anonymous, pointing out to those addressed that this lack of openness is in itself a problem.

In this chapter, we have established a context for the customer–provider encounter. In the next chapter, we shall examine the underlying non-verbal aspects of communication between customers and providers, and then proceed in other chapters to examine a number of communication models that are relevant to that encounter.

ACTIVITIES

1. Think of another two factors that drive towards the provision of quality customer service. Write brief notes about these factors.
2. Think of another two factors that might restrain the provision of quality customer service. Write brief notes about these factors.
3. Identify one organisation that is locked into the cycle of failure, and one organisation that is locked into the cycle of success. Write brief notes comparing the two.
4. Draw a diagram of an organisation, showing the sequence of internal customers, and the relationship of the organisation with its external customers.
5. In many organisations, it would be very difficult to implement wish lists because of certain barriers. What might some of these barriers be?

Table 2.4: A wish list

	WISH LIST		
To			
From			
✓	I feel confident enough to give my name, which is .... I work		
	I do not feel confident about giving my name. Doesn't this suggest something about the level of openness and effectiveness around here? This comes from the general area of..		
I/We will give 100 per cent of my/our effort to our customers, but this won't be enough unless we can do the job properly by giving our customers what they want.			
Item No.	**Customers want**	**We have got**	**Change needed**
If you are not empowered to effect these changes, please pass this wish list along to others in the hierarchy.			

TALKING POINTS

YOU DON'T SAY? What people say about customers and providers

The public be damned.

William H. Vanderbilt

When it was a flop, British Airways used to hire on the basis of technical competence, and encouraged employees to focus on pleasing the bureaucracy of the organisation instead of its customers. The new, privatised British Airways screens first for people who enjoy working with customers. The technical stuff comes later.

'You have to get people who enjoy treating people as individuals and who are prepared to accept responsibility for delivering what the customer wants,' says British Airways' Michael Bruce.

Peter Glen

It's far better for an organisation to yank its head out of the sand and to open its eyes to face complaints and complainers than it is to pull a cloak of smugness around its shoulders. Dissatisfied customers are going to strike back, eventually. The company that is aware of complaints will be equipped to take action to prevent the consequences of the complaints ...

Instead of maintaining barriers to complaining, make it easy for customers to complain. Make it as easy as a bad habit. Then the company might discover a flaw in corporate policy or performance that otherwise would be left to alienate large numbers of customers or clients for months — or years. The function of a complaint service is to find wounds in the body corporate and to dress them before gangrene sets in and causes loss of a limb or an organ — a product line, an entire market — or an entire company ... Marva McArthur of Waddell & Reed Services in Kansas City says: 'When we've turned unhappy customers around, they've said something like, "Say, what about this other mutual fund that I've heard you've come out with?" We make more sales.'

John Tschohl and Steve Franzmeier

Rudeness is the weak man's imitation of strength.

Eric Hoffer

Despite these concerted efforts (in early twentieth-century Australia) to cultivate a loyal female clientele, retailers frequently encountered opposition and resistance from women customers. The same desires and demands for satisfaction that were publicly legitimated by the new culture of consumption were often expressed in ways that retailers and their sales assistants found inappropriate or unmanageable. The 'difficult customer' became a stock figure in trade literature. The amount of attention she received, and the intensity of the hostility she provoked, indicates a strong antipathy, largely but not exclusively based on class differences between sales workers and shoppers of the same sex. Saleswomen bitterly resented, and often successfully resisted, customers' apparently thoughtless demands, complaints, ignorance, and lack of consideration. Whether or not female shoppers actually behaved in this way, retail managers turned the stereotype of the difficult shopper to their best advantage. By invoking the spectre of the recalcitrant shopper, retailers deflected potential employee unrest, which may otherwise have been aimed at themselves, towards a common female enemy on the other side of the counter. Manufacturing the difficult customer as a distinctly female personality type, one which most women would find hard to avoid, was an attempt to police women's activities within the store.

Gail Reekie

Companies in which employees are committed to customer satisfaction goals also have good upward and downward communication channels. They view communication as an essential process, since it is the means by which all members of the company are brought together for a common purpose.

Critical to this communication process is the dissemination of information that educates every employee about the company's markets, the needs of these markets, and how the company compares to its competition in meeting customer expectations. Victor Kiam, owner and president of the Remington Shaver Company (of 'I liked the company so much I bought it' fame), believes communication is so important that he stops the company's production line to talk with employees about company results. Four times a year, he delivers a status report to his employees on the company's performance. The production line is closed down at a down time cost of $10,000. But, as Kiam observes, 'You can't turn out good product if the people who make it don't have a stake in its success.'

William A. Band

What's the danger of giving away too much? Are you worried about having an oversatisfied customer? That's not much of a worry. You can forget about an oversatisfied customer, but an unsatisfied customer is one of the most expensive problems you can have ... the danger is not that employees will give away too much. It's that they won't give away anything — because they don't dare.

Jan Carlzon

They have the money, you want it.
They have the perception, you cause it.
You know what it's like, you've lived it.
You know what needs doing, so do it.

John Guaspari

Customers perceive service in their own unique, idiosyncratic, emotional, irrational, end-of-the-day and totally human terms. Perception is all there is!

Tom Peters

We communicate with our customers via leaflets and posters and information boards in the shops, and they can communicate with us through the suggestion boxes to be found in every shop. We don't just pay lip service to their views — six members of staff work full-time cataloguing their suggestions and replying to them. In addition, we hold regular forums, when we open up a shop from six till nine in the evening and invite customers to come and tell us what they like, what they don't like, and what products they would like to see added to the range. It has always been Body Shop policy to find out what customers want by simply asking them, a concept thought to be eccentric in the retail trade ...

On our customer-care course we encouraged staff to treat customers as potential friends, to say hello, smile, make eye contact and to offer advice if it was wanted, to thank them and always to invite them back. I have often thought we could learn a lot from the Americans in this area. The British are cynical and dismissive of American social behaviour, of the constant 'Have a nice day' that follows you wherever you go. Personally, I like it — no matter how evidently insincere, it helps to break down barriers and establishes personal contact, which is more and more important in an increasingly impersonal world.

Anita Roddick

3
NON-VERBAL COMMUNICATION

Body language or non-verbal communication is a vital part of the communication that takes place between customers and providers.

Providers must be aware of the non-verbal communication of customers, but should also be aware that they themselves are sending non-verbal messages to customers. Non-verbal messages can reinforce verbal messages, or they can contradict them. When the verbal and non-verbal channels of communication contradict one another (when they are not 'congruent'), it is often wiser to believe the non-verbal message rather than the verbal. This is because people can control what they say, but they cannot always control what they 'say' non-verbally.

It has become almost a cliché to say that non-verbal communication is more important than verbal communication. Based upon some early research in the area,[24] it has become commonplace to argue that when a person communicates, the following is what happens.

- Only about 7–10 per cent of the message is conveyed through words.
- About 20 per cent is conveyed via vocal pitch, emphasis, and related factors.
- About 70 per cent is conveyed by gesture, posture and related factors.

These figures have proved to be very useful learning tools for those people who have tended to over-emphasise the power of words at the expense of all modes of communication — they provide a shock, which leads to a re-think, which in turn leads to a more balanced view of the total communication process. Although the figures are appropriate for some circumstances, however, they are not appropriate for all; words are simply more important than that. Indeed, once you become more aware of the power of non-verbal communication, you can re-think your perceptions so that you are not overwhelmed by it, and thus concentrate more upon the verbal communication taking place.

Individual examples of non-verbal communication — a gesture, a posture, an item of clothing — do not mean much in isolation. They have to be seen in context, within the totality of other instances of non-verbal and verbal communication. Be careful, in other words, of leaping to hasty generalisations of the 'knowing all about this body language stuff lets me read people's minds' variety.

Body language is not the same as non-verbal communication. Body language usually refers to gestures, postures, eye contact and so on, but non-verbal communication refers not only to bodily behaviour but also to things beyond the body — for example, the clothing worn by provider and customer, the environment in which the service encounter takes place, and the use of time by provider and customer. The various aspects of this wider concept of non-verbal communication are shown in figure 3.1. Let's now consider how this model of non-verbal communication helps to explain just what it is that goes on in the service encounter.

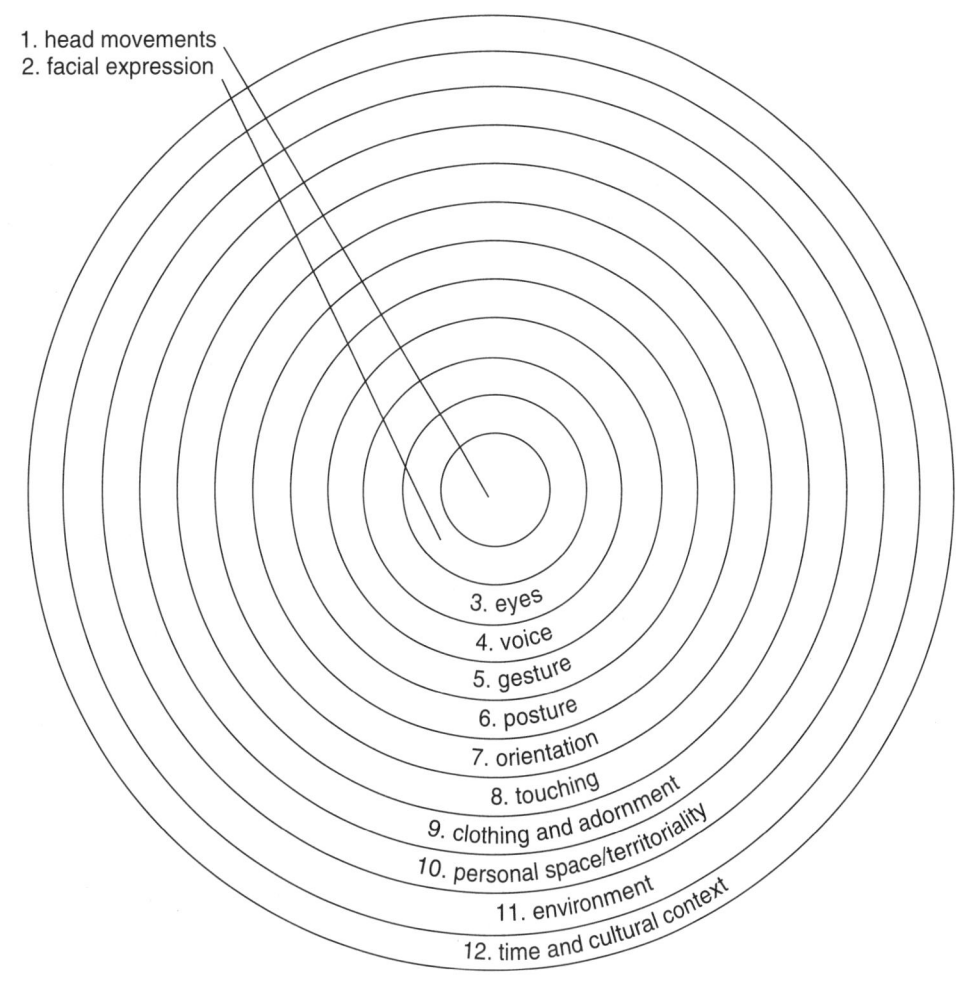

1. head movements
2. facial expression
3. eyes
4. voice
5. gesture
6. posture
7. orientation
8. touching
9. clothing and adornment
10. personal space/territoriality
11. environment
12. time and cultural context

Figure 3.1: A model of non-verbal communication

(Source: adapted with permission from Eunson [1987: 100].)

HEAD MOVEMENTS

When a person tilts his or her head on one side, it can mean a number of things, depending upon context. It can mean that the person is being reflective, and is concentrating upon listening to you, or it can mean that the person is aggressive towards you. The person's facial expression will normally confirm just what emotional state is being revealed.

Head nodding usually shows agreement, and is a shortened version of the up-and-down 'yes' signal which is found in most cultures throughout the world. Nodding is a way in which listeners can give feedback to speakers and, depending upon the intensity of the nodding, that feedback can mean anything from, 'Yes, I'm still awake' to 'I think you're fantastic'. Nodding is often accompanied by friendly grunts or backchannelling such as, 'Uh huh', 'Mmm', 'Mm ... hmmm'. A customer who nods often as a provider is talking is usually a good sign, and a provider can in turn build rapport with that customer by nodding and backchannelling while the customer talks.

Shaking the head from side to side usually means 'no' in most cultures, and slight, as opposed to obvious, nodding may suggest negativity on the part of the nodder.

THE FACE

We convey many emotions via the face, but it is also notable that facial expression is one of the types of non-verbal communication that is most easily controlled. Whether a person is deceiving us or not is difficult to detect merely by studying that person's face.[25]

An immobile face can mean that a person is simply not very good at expressing emotion,[26] or else it may mean that the person is, or believes he or she is, a powerful person. Powerful people tend to have less mobile and more controlled facial expressions than those with less power around them. In comparison with those with less power, more powerful people also tend to look at others less, touch others more, interrupt others more, and invade others personal space more often.[27] When a customer makes his or her face more immobile, or stiffens his or her expression (and possibly also his or her body), then it may be a signal to a provider that the topic under discussion is proving to be an uncomfortable one, and should be dropped in favour of another.[28]

Perhaps the key part of facial non-verbal communication in the customer–provider encounter is the mouth, particularly as a vehicle for smiling (figure 3.2). Smiling can create rapport very quickly, and most of us respond to a smile — but the smile has to be genuine, and not forced. As we saw in chapter 1 (p. 15), service providers are particularly prone to 'smile burnout': service provision is 'emotional labour', demanding that providers give not only of their muscles and minds but also of their emotions. Because of this, burnt-out providers can only muster a plastic smile, or perhaps no smile at all. 'Smile burnout' does not happen all that often to providers who genuinely like working with people, and who have full backup from the system around them (p. 12).

¡SMILE DAMMIT SMILE!

Anita's 20 second crash course in Customer Care:

Never treat customers as enemies, approach them as potential friends.
Think of customers as guests, make them laugh.
Acknowledge their presence within 30 seconds:
smile, make eye contact, say hello.
Talk to them within the first 3 minutes.
Offer product advice where appropriate.
Smile. Always thank customers and invite them back ...
TREAT CUSTOMERS AS YOU'D LIKE TO BE TREATED!

'I think loneliness is a time bomb ticking away in our society, especially in the shopping malls. Anyone who can figure a way of reducing loneliness, either through their stores or their marketing, will have a business that will thrive forever...'   Anita Roddick

'Good customer care has to be our top priority: The Body Shop firmly believes that, as we head towards the next century, our survival is based on the fact that we must be special to our customers.   Anita Roddick

Figure 3.2: Smile, dammit, smile: training sheet given to staff at the Body Shop chain (Source: Roddick [1992: 147]. Reproduced with permission.)

EYE CONTACT

To look at someone can imply a number of things. In Euro-American cultures, to 'look someone in the eye' is a sign of directness and honesty, and thus breaking eye contact may imply anxiety and deception, as may increased rates of blinking.[29] In contrast, in other cultures, such as the Japanese, Hispanic, Black American and West African, to look someone in the eye may imply confrontation and disrespect.[30] There is considerable potential here for inter-cultural misunderstanding.

Even within cultures such as the British, American and Australian, breaking eye contact can convey messages other than those of dishonesty and/or anxiety. Thus, at the beginning of an encounter, a customer may simply avert eye contact with a provider until a minimum level of rapport has been established. If that level is reached, and exceeded, then stronger eye contact will follow.[31] A customer may break eye contact with a provider — by looking up, down, or to one side — in order to more fully evaluate what has been said by the provider.[32] A customer may break eye contact when a provider has broached a delicate or uncomfortable topic — a sure-fire hint to the provider to change the topic.[33] Eye movements may have still other meanings, as will be discussed in the chapter on neurolinguistic programming (pp. 87–93).

The act of simply looking at someone — giving them our undivided attention — may send a message of politeness, concentration and rapport. Similarly, eye contact is also used to regulate conversations. Speakers tend to periodically break and then re-establish eye contact with listeners. The looking-away behaviour seems to be related to the fact that many people find it easier to interrupt a speaker when eye contact is established; a speaker may thus look away to prevent such interruptions. Many people re-establish a firm gaze (and change the pitch of their voice to an upward or downward inflection) when they are ready to 'yield' to the listener, and to reverse roles — becoming the listener while the other person speaks. Listeners tend to look at speakers in a more uninterrupted fashion.[34]

Our eyes also send messages in other ways. For example, when we are interested in something or someone, the pupils of our eyes dilate, or grow larger. Similarly, when we dislike something or someone, the pupils of our eyes constrict, or grow smaller. When we are fearful, interested, or merely in the process of greeting someone, the pupils dilate, the eyelids open further, and the eyebrows are raised (the 'eyebrow flash'). Chinese gem traders in earlier times would often watch the pupils of the eyes of their customers to see how much they really liked a particular gem (and therefore how much they might be willing to pay for it).[35] This non-verbal message might of course be quite different from verbal messages ('No, I don't like it ....' 'Oh, it's all right, I suppose ...'). For this reason, Arab commercial and political negotiators sometimes will wear sunglasses, even when indoors, to conceal messages about real motives and wants.[36] Pupil dilation, together with raised eyebrows, are messages sent out by inexperienced poker players when they are dealt a good hand — messages rapidly decoded by more experienced players.

When we are interacting with someone else, and their eyes glaze over, go out of focus or roll, we can be fairly sure that the message being sent is not a positive one.

VOICE

Sometimes, as the old song has it, 'It ain't what you say but the way that you say it'. Thus, a crucial part of non-verbal communication is the way in which verbal communication takes place. The words we utter can be dramatically transformed by our patterns of inflection, loudness, emphasis, accent, and other factors. All of these non-verbal aspects of speech are vital for understanding others when we can see others completely — for example, in a face-to-face encounter between customer and provider. They become even more important, however, in situations where we cannot see others — for example, on the telephone. We will consider these in chapter 8, 'Communicating with customers on the telephone' (p. 120).

SMELL

Smell as a form of non-verbal communication? Absolutely. Smell is a critical part of the communication that takes place at the interpersonal level of provider and customer, and it is also a critical part of the communication that emanates from the environment, or 'servicescape', in which interpersonal communication takes place (p. 31).

Because providers have to work in close physical proximity to customers, they have to pay attention to basic matters of grooming and hygiene. Most people prefer to deal with people who have clean hair, fresh breath, fresh clothes, non-existent body odour and/or a pleasant perfume or deodorant.[37] In Western societies, smell is virtually a taboo topic, because it is bound up with norms of cleanliness, health and attractiveness. Others may thus be loath to let us know if we violate those norms ('even your best friends won't tell you'), and it is often difficult to get feedback on our own body state. It may be best, therefore, to presume the worst about your body state, and take corrective action. It should be noted that not all cultures share such norms. In some cultures, perfumes and deodorants are frowned upon, because they mask the natural odours of the body (seen as sending messages about moods and states of mind). In other cultures, also, people may prefer to smell the breath of the person they are talking to, for similar reasons.[38]

GESTURE

Gestures are closely linked to posture and touching behaviour. Gestures are movements made with arms, hands, shoulders and legs.

The most basic group of gestures are those of hand-to-head. People usually place a hand or hands on differing parts of the head when there is some stress involved in a situation. As infants we relieved stress by sucking on a real or artificial nipple and, after weaning, on a thumb or finger. As adults, we continue this type of behaviour, calming ourselves with oral gratification in a number of ways — biting nails, biting on knuckles, chewing on pens and pencils, chewing on arms of glasses, chewing gum, smoking, drinking, talking, and so on.[39] As infants, we were soothed by adults stroking our hair, or perhaps we stroked our mothers' long hair, and we as adults recapture this by a variety of hair-manipulation gestures, such as twisting, patting and stroking. Both males and females tend to show that they are evaluating something by stroking the chin (perhaps a downwards displacement from the mouth, with such stress-lowering behaviour enhancing concentration), while males with beards and/or moustaches may use stroking or patting of facial hair when evaluating something or someone.[40]

People sometimes stroke or scratch parts of the face, particularly the nose, when they are lying, or at least are uncomfortable with what they are saying.

This and other possible indicators of lying or deception are shown in figure 3.3. Such signals may prove useful in attempting to decode the communication of others, particularly when we bear in mind that many people can control facial expressions quite well (and 'lie straight-faced.')

- Pinocchio syndrome (itchy nose)
- hand covers mouth
- restricted use of gestures
- avoidance of eye contact
- decrease in smiling
- manipulation of clothing (buttoning up coat or blouse, tugging at fabric, tugging at collar)
- brushing off clothes, picking at lint
- sudden shift in posture — leaning back in chair
- sudden crossing and uncrossing of legs
- erection of 'signal blunters' to hide behind — holding purse, briefcase, folder in lap

Figure 3.3: Possible deception signals

(Source: adapted from Waltman and Golen [1993] and Ekman [1993].)

The more stressed we feel, the closer our gestures are to our bodies. Hand-to-body touching observed in doctor–patient situations is related to anxiety (although hand-to-hand touching may be more about concentration on what is being said than about anxiety).[41] Staying 'close to home' with gestures can also be seen with the barrier cross, a gesture often seen by service providers. When we walk into an area — a shop, a hall, a street, even the next room in our house — many people will move a hand across their body in some way — by scratching the face, by touching a handbag, by touching a cuff-link or watch. This appears to be a protective gesture, with deep biological roots.[42] The more stressed people feel, the more they will perform this 'stress-salute' gesture. People will also perform this gesture if they feel stressed by the presence of someone or the approach of someone.

In contrast to these types of gestures, when people feel confident, for example, in selling situations, they will use strong gestures, away from the body.[43] Gestures of despair and/or 'go away and don't bother me' are those of hand-wringing, the palms displayed ('these hands are empty') and the shrug.[44]

Gestures employed by service providers when interacting with customers sometimes have less dramatic meanings, of course. Commonly used gestures are those used to explain and describe products and processes — for example, pointing, estimating size with hands and arms, mimicking mechanical actions, hand to chest when relating personal experiences.

POSTURE

Posture also reveals much about our inner state of mind. Generally speaking, the more confident we feel, the more we stand up straight; the less confident we feel, the more we will slump over. This slumped posture may be a case of 'fetal closure' — wanting to 'roll up into a ball', as we did when we were fetuses. As with some gestural behaviour, therefore, it is a striving for a more basic feeling of security. Body-lowering of various kinds — bowing, curtsying, squatting — is also a way of showing deference to others, and is part of ritual in some cultures.[45]

Customers who sit forward in their chairs may be signalling that they are positive about what they are hearing, while those who sit back may indicate neutrality, negativity or perhaps deception.[46]

It appears that people who like each other tend to echo or mirror each other's posture (and gesture, and voice mannerisms).[47] This 'postural echo' is a useful way of creating rapport with others (see pp. 89–91), but care should be taken in trying to create it deliberately, as the exercise may come across as a clumsy and manipulative piece of mimicry.

ORIENTATION

Orientation refers to the angle at which a person interacts with another person. Some non-verbal analysts argue that, if we like another person and are genuinely interested in them, we face them directly, with the planes of our bodies parallel. In contrast, if we dislike another person, we tend to shift the plane of our body away from the plane of theirs.[48] Thus, if a person is talking to you, but their body is angled away from you, it might be inferred that the person was not as interested in you and your situation as their words might imply.

Face-to-face orientation is not always ideal, however. Some analysts of customer–provider and negotiation situations suggest that such an orientation may send out a message that 'we are on different sides' rather than a message of 'we are really both on the same side, working towards a mutually beneficial, win–win solution'. A way in which to overcome such dynamics would be to reposition ourselves so that we are seated or standing side-by-side with others.[49]

TOUCHING

Touch is almost certainly a basic human need (see p. 43), but then it all depends what you mean by touch. Touch can be usefully classified into five levels:
1. functional/professional
2. social/polite
3. friendship–warmth
4. love–intimacy
5. sexual arousal.[50]

We have already noted the concept of self-touching as a gesture (pp. 24–25). When touching occurs in customer–provider encounters, it mainly occurs in level 1 and level 2 touching. Professional touchers include doctors, nurses, physiotherapists, masseurs, manicurists, hairdressers, dentists, priests, and perhaps politicians. While there are strong taboos on various types of touching in different cultures, it may be that some people unconsciously or consciously perceive that they are deprived of touch at levels 2, 3, 4 and 5, and thus may seek out the professional touch they get in level 1 interactions.[51] Professionals should not feel too uneasy about this, as they are almost certainly performing a vital social-therapeutic role with some customers; there's a lot of loneliness out there. Thus, for example, therapeutic touch from nurses in nursing homes has been associated with decreases in pain, increases in haemoglobin, decreases in sensory deprivation, increases in reality orientation and 'almost instantaneous calm' in aged persons.[52]

When taboos on touching are strong in some cultures — for example, male-male touching in Australia, America, England and other 'low context' cultures (p. 35), then some may seek touch via violence, sporting rituals or being immersed in crowds.[53]

Level 2 touch can be used to build trust between providers and customers, and may even lead to providers being able to more easily persuade customers, although providers will have to exercise discretion and sensitivity in doing this.[54]

One of the most common forms of professional touching is that of the handshake. Charles Darwin speculated that the handshake is in fact a 'relic gesture', an echo of a time when two men meeting for the first time would grasp each other's right forearm to prevent swords being drawn.[55] The ritual is thus bound up with male dominance and, when offered, may indicate that the initiator of the gesture is on home territory.[56] The emergence of a large-scale presence of women in the workplace has complicated this situation somewhat, so that males and females are sometimes uncomfortable with this ritual. The discomfort is mainly based on confusion as to who should initiate the handshake. The solution is for women to initiate, get the ritual over with, and get down to business.[57] Both sexes should be wary of a 'limp fish' handshake (which may imply ineffectuality) and a 'bone-crusher' handshake (which may imply immaturity).[58]

CLOTHING AND ADORNMENT

Clothing is self-evident, but adornment may not be so obvious. Adornment comprises a variety of social inventions designed to modify appearance, such as make up, hairstyling, jewellery, tattoos, ear-piercing, shaving/not shaving, and a suntan. Clothing and adornment send non-verbal messages by performing one or several of the following functions, examples of which are shown in table 3.1.
1. protection of the wearer
2. protection of the environment from the wearer
3. definition of sex roles
4. definition of social roles.[59]

Table 3.1: Clothing and adornment phenomena

Type of clothing and adornment	Examples
1. Protection of the wearer	• Welder's gloves, apron and goggles • Mechanic's overalls • Underwear
2. Protection of the environment from the wearer	• Clean room uniforms in computer chip manufacture • Surgeon's gown and gloves • Cellophane gloves, hair covering and apron worn by delicatessen assistant
3. Definition of sex roles	• Trousers, dresses, culottes, kaftans, kilts, business suits (for men and women), veils, underwear
4. Definition of social roles	• Uniforms • Blue-collar versus white-collar items • Expensive versus cheap items • Leisure versus work items • Tattoos • Ear-piercing/ear studs for males • Rank insignia (military stripes, decorations, epaulettes, braid)

Service providers need to ensure that clothing and adornment are appropriate for the work environment. Some organisations insist that employees wear a uniform, while in other organisations, uniforms are seen as being 'too military'.[60] In those organisations that require uniforms to be worn, such clothing can give providers a sense of identification, which may lead to a more positive emotional display in comparison with non-uniform wearing staff.[61] Then again, uniforms often convey powerful status and sex-role messages: generally, it is females and lower-status males who are required to wear uniforms. As such, uniforms may signal enforced conformity in less powerful people. Of course, more powerful people may also be wearing a 'uniform', if we define a uniform as a required type of clothing: powerful dynamics of conformity ensure that executives dress and adorn themselves in narrowly prescribed ways, just as surely as uniformed providers or members of a street gang are also conforming to powerful norms (the violation of which will attract various forms of disapproval). Fashionable suits and nose-rings, neckties and reversed baseball caps, can thus be seen as parts of a uniform. Indeed, all fashion can be seen as the ongoing creation and destruction of uniforms for all of us.

All of this is well known by service providers who sell clothes and adornment. They are not just selling things and processes, but social class, sexual attraction (or repulsion), and body image.[62] Indeed, all providers sell more than just things and processes: they sell images, identities, values, hopes, and solutions to fear and insecurity. Clothing and adornment just happen to be one of the most basic and tangible expressions of this phenomenon.

PERSONAL SPACE/TERRITORIALITY

Human beings, like animals, have an invisible 'bubble' of personal space or territory. Within this bubble, we feel secure, but we may not feel secure if others invade our personal space, by standing too close to us and possibly also touching us. Figure 3.4 shows such a bubble. Note that there are four zones:

1. The intimate: within this zone, we will be comfortable with people we like and know extremely well — for example, lovers and relatives.
2. The personal: within this zone, we will be comfortable with people we know quite well — for example, friends and close colleagues.
3. The social-consultative: within this zone, we will be comfortable with people we know fairly well — for example, work colleagues in a meeting.
4. The public: within this zone, we will be comfortable with people we know only slightly or not at all — for example, people in public places.

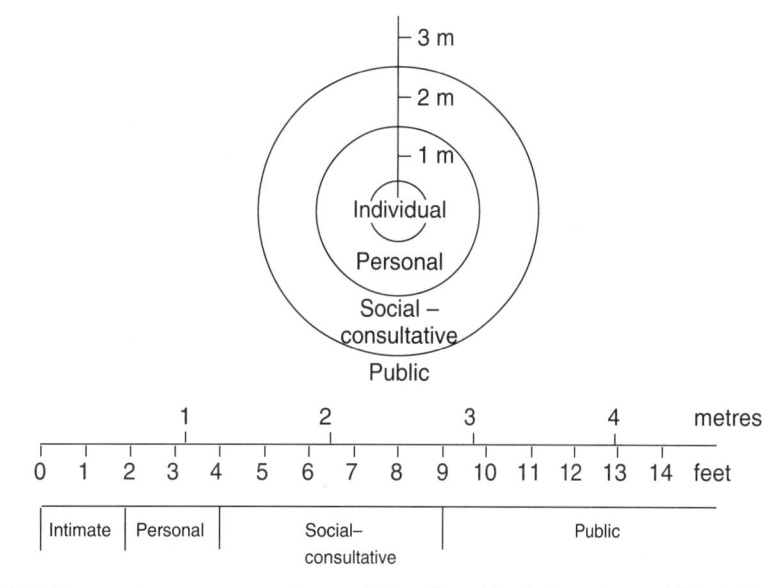

Figure 3.4: Personal space zones for a middle-class North American of North European heritage

(Source: adapted from Hall [1966].)

Note, however, that this personal space bubble relates to a middle-class North American of North European heritage. Personal space varies considerably between cultures and classes, and even sexes. It appears to be the case, for example, that:
- Southern European people have smaller personal space bubbles than Northern European people.
- People with greater prestige and power in organisations demand more space.
- Many males demand more personal space than females.
- People from rural areas have greater personal space needs than people from urban areas.[63]

Personal space, not unsurprisingly, is related to touching behaviour. People with smaller space needs seem to be more prone to use touch as a normal mode of communication, with the opposite case holding true for people with large space needs. Having said this, it is often true that high power/high prestige people — who are rarely closely approached or touched by subordinates — often will assert their power by invading the personal space of subordinates and by touching them.[64]

Personal space can be marked out by garments left on chairs, cups left on tables, photographs and personal items left on desks, bumper stickers on cars ('Not so close — I hardly know you'), 'Private' signs on doors, and floor space in work areas. When the personal space or territory of an animal is violated by another animal, a fight usually ensues to make the space violator back off. Violence may result from space violations in human encounters, but we are more likely to express anxiety and erect barriers in more subtle ways — face scratching, breaking of eye contact, making the face immobile, turning away, surrounding ourselves with objects, and so on. This happens when we are crowded in busy stores, elevators, public transport, sporting events and similar public situations.

Service providers can apply this knowledge about personal space and territory to advantage. It is effective and sensitive to practise the space and touching codes of the culture of the customer being dealt with. This is easier said than done, but observation, inquiry and further research will show just how these codes differ for customers from, say, Northern European, Southern European, Arabic and Japanese backgrounds.

If a salesperson is trying to communicate with someone from a rural background, or someone who holds a senior executive post, it may help to give such people a fair amount of space.[65] Security guards trying to control a potentially violent situation should respect the space needs of the people they are dealing with, giving such people the option of inviting guards onto their territory.[66] Store designers need to be aware of the way store layout (see p. 32) can increase crowding effects, with negative impacts upon buying behaviour[67] (but see also remarks about the stimulus of being in crowded public places, p. 32). Managers of service operations should be aware of the pros and cons of having customers queue for service (see p. 34).

ENVIRONMENT

The environment in which providers interact with customers has been called the *servicescape*.[68] The servicescape is made up of the totality of colours, textures, smells, sounds, temperature, lighting, rooms, floor area, buildings, structures, furniture, decorations, signage, equipment and vehicles that both customer and provider encounter.

What are your initial impressions when you enter a servicescape? If you were asked to describe those impressions, you would probably use a variety of words, similar to some of those which appear in the following list.

Some adjectives that describe environments

cool	glamorous	vibrant	run-down
warm	down-market	manic	impersonal
small	up-market	threatening	caring
cramped	sleazy	comfortable	stagnant
big	loved	traditional	frantic
cavernous	unloved	modern	boring
cosy	parochial	kitsch	exciting
hostile	cosmopolitan	stylish	sterile
fragrant	claustrophobic	real	natural
stinking	agoraphobic	unreal	artificial
plastic	professional	gritty	soft
crass	amateurish	smooth	hard
elegant	disorienting	arrogant	crowded
alienating	chaotic	humble	empty
luxurious	antiseptic	smoky	depressing
impoverished	noisy	dirty	uplifting
overpowering	quiet	tidy	
disappointing	deathly quiet	messy	
showy	tranquil	new	
homely	unsettling	old	

Let's consider some of the aspects of the servicescape, beginning with colour. It is still early days in research into colour's impact upon customer behaviour, but a number of trends seem to be emerging. Of the colours which decorate shop entrances, warm colours, such as red and yellow, appear to be more effective than cool colours, such as blue and green, in attracting customers to enter. However, cooler colours may be more effective in areas where customers need to deliberate over purchases.[69] This would seem to confirm the folk wisdom that warm colours are exciting and emotional, while cool colours are more conducive to thought. Other intriguing correlations between colour and behaviour are emerging. It appears that customers who favour red are more fashion-conscious than those who favour grey, and those customers favouring brown or green tend to dislike using credit.[70]

Colour can be used with light and music to create specific effects. Bright colours, bright lights and upbeat music can create an atmosphere that many people find pleasant to be in, but this type of stimulus manipulation will not be appropriate for a quiet restaurant or for a store where the environment is fundamentally unattractive.[71] Background music, 'elevator music' or Muzak can be used for different purposes: in some environments, it can stimulate customer buying, while in one instance — a 7-11 convenience store — it has been played to subtly discourage a young crowd just 'hanging around'.[72]

We saw earlier how smell can be a powerful communicator (for good or evil) at the interpersonal level (p. 24). The same holds true at the environmental level. Consider the impressions the following smells will evoke in you:

- fresh bread being cooked in a street or in a shopping mall
- anaesthetic in a dentist's waiting room
- the upholstery of a new car
- perfumes and toiletries in shops or on scratch-and-sniff pads and magazine pages
- flowers in a florist's shop
- rotten fruit in a fruit and vegetable shop.

All of these smells may evoke powerful messages. Service providers can manipulate the barrage of smells that greet customers so that the effect is attractive rather than repellent.

Signage is an extremely important form of communication in the servicescape. Legible, accurate, stylish signs — 'You are here' signs, brand names, pedestrian and vehicular traffic signs — are vital ways of making the environment understandable and user-friendly.[73] Automated directories — for example, computers with touch screens — can also help to give customers directions. (Alternatively, some retail centres have chosen to downplay automated systems and instead use human 'greeters' and shopper guides).[74]

When we considered personal space and territoriality (pp. 29–30), mention was made of how crowding can be unpleasant, and thus act as a deterrent to customers even showing up in the servicescape. To counteract such effects, managers and planners often pay close attention to layout factors such as aisle widths in shops and malls and entrances and exits — crowd control, in other words.

It's not always as simple as that, however. Many people go shopping because of the stimulus of the environment and the stimulus of other people — 'It's all happening at the mall'.[75] When people take on the role of customers, in other words, they are not simply satisfying functional needs (buying a dress, consulting a doctor, comparing prices on refrigerators) but are satisfying emotional needs — the need to be with people, to watch other people, to be paid attention to, to see exciting things, to find out what's happening in the world. Indeed, the growing tendency to automate shopping processes, and the rise of 'teleshopping' (shopping from home via computer/television hybrid appliances) may be bad news for all of us in general and lonely people in particular, who use servicescapes to satisfy their needs to be with others.[76]

The madding crowd may be too madding of course: some have suggested that shopping has become less pleasurable and too time-consuming, this being partly due to environments such as large malls, which are increasingly alienating and difficult to negotiate; this in turn may lead to growth in direct selling and mail order transactions.[77]

Can manipulating all of these factors in the servicescape lead to customers buying more? It all depends. Most of these factors are 'emotional' factors in shopping, as distinct from 'cognitive' factors such as price, parking availability and so on. It may be that cognitive factors are more important for determining customers' planned purchases, while emotional factors are more important in persuading customers to spend beyond their original expectations.[78]

Nevertheless, environmental factors should not be underplayed. Carl Sewell, a US car dealer, argues that customers judge providers on the basis of the total environment in the servicescape, starting with the rest rooms:

> Nobody ever bought a car from us just because we had clean rest rooms. But it's like the old Tom Peters' line about finding coffee stains on the pull-down tray when you're on an aeroplane. If that's how they take care of the inside of the plane, you may get to wondering how much maintenance the engines get.
>
> Why would you ever want to give someone a reason — even a subconscious reason — to question doing business with you? ...
>
> Selling should be theatre. We want people to see our product in an environment that makes them say, 'Wow.' The furniture, fixtures, lights — every detail — should contribute to make their visit to our store dramatic, entertaining, fun ...
>
> ... You are the message. With everything we do, we're sending a message, to both our customers and our employees, about what kind of place we're running and what we think is important. So the details count, whether it's the clothes we wear, or the language we use, or the kind of writing paper we choose.[79]

TIME AND CULTURAL CONTEXT

Time is a vital component for people acting in their roles as customers and providers, and indeed in all the roles we play throughout life.[80] There is never enough time, and customers feel that there is less time than ever. To a considerable extent, they are right: contrary to the expectations of futurists writing in the 1960s and 1970s, working hours have gone up and leisure hours have gone down in the 1980s and 1990s.[81] This means that customers want quick service, and want to minimise waiting time. Customers are thus in a hurry — a luxury not always available to providers.[82]

The main mechanism used by providers for rationing service is the queue. In analysing the behaviour of people in queues, Maister has proposed eight 'principles of waiting', which he believes can be used by service organisations to influence customers' satisfaction with waiting times.[83]

Eight propositions about waiting time

1. Unoccupied time feels longer than occupied time.
2. Preprocess waits feel longer than in-process waits.
3. Anxiety makes waits seem longer.
4. Uncertain waits are longer than known, finite waits.
5. Unexplained waits are longer than explained waits.
6. Unfair waits are longer than equitable waits.
7. The more valuable the service, the longer the customer will wait.
8. Solo waits feel longer than group waits.

(Source: adapted from Maister [1985].)

Maister's propositions show us that the perception of time can be as subjective as it can be objective. What can service providers do to ensure that the subjective and objective experience of waiting in lines can be minimised? Solutions developed by various organisations are shown in table 3.2.

Table 3.2: Ways of minimising objective and subjective waiting times

Provide distractions	• piped-in music • piano players • colouring books for children • television, informational videotapes • electronic noticeboards (news headlines, horoscopes) • samples (fresh bread for customers waiting in a take-away chicken place)
Provide monitoring information	• the theatre manager walking up and down lines, telling patrons that they will get seats • Word Perfect's 'hold jockey' — a disc jockey playing music on the customer software support lines, who announces estimated delays before callers receive service
Staff according to peak times	• service staff's breaks rostered around peak times (especially lunch hour)
Thank the customer for waiting	• 'A wait acknowledged is a wait forgiven' (Stephen Broydrick)
Use one line, not multiple lines	• avoids slow lines; gives customer sensation of movement, and thus progress
Use a numbering system	• customers' sense of justice is satisfied, and they can leave queue area temporarily to do other things
Get customers out of line	• advance reservations (mail or telephone), automation (automatic teller machines, cheque-cashing machines)
Let customers know whether they need to be in line, or whether they are in the right line	• signage (in multiple languages), live announcements over public address system (preferably combined with music)
Give priority to walk-up customers over those telephoning	• frustrating to those telephoning, but walk-up customers have made the effort to come in
Make non-front-line staff invisible — conceal or move	• it is frustrating for customers when they see staff seated and not serving
Modify customer arrival behaviour	• off-peak times can be publicised; incentives can be given for customers who use off-peak times
Ensure recorded messages and music do not irritate	• nasal announcements, mispronunciations, no variety, Greensleeves, tuba music

(Source: adapted from Broydrick [1994], Maister [1985], Katz, Larson and Larson [1991].)

Time-urgency, however, is not a universal perception. Other cultures do not experience time in the same way — indeed, queues do not exist in some cultures. A useful model for understanding non-verbal differences between cultures is that developed by Hall (see table 3.3).[84] He argues that cultures can be understood in terms of their 'context'. High-context cultures tend to be more group-oriented, tend to have high sensory involvement in terms of touch and personal space, tend to communicate in subtle, unwritten ways, and tend to have a 'polychronic' sense of time. Multiple things can happen at once, and punctuality and time-urgency are not always understood. Low-context cultures have values and behaviours which are quite opposite to these.

Table 3.3: High-context and low-context cultural characteristics

	High context	**Low context**
Orientation	Group	Individual
Sensory involvement	High: low personal space needs, high contact touch behaviour	Low: high personal space needs, low contact touch behaviour
Messages	Implicit: embedded in social context: ritual, personal relationships, personal word as guarantee	Explicit: words carry most information (emphasis on legal paperwork, etc.)
Time sense/ chronicity	Polychronic: multiple times. Time is circular. Events proceed at their own pace. Multiple events occur simultaneously, e.g., different people in room all on different business	Monochronic: one time only. Time is linear. Events happen sequentially. Punctuality, scheduling, planning very important

(Source: adapted from Hall [1976].)

Hall argues that cultures can be classified on a low-context/high-context continuum:

> (The German-Swiss) are low-context, falling somewhere near the bottom of the scale. Next, the Germans, then the Scandinavians, as we move up. These cultures are all lower in context than the US. Above the Americans come the French, the English, the Italians, the Spanish, the Greeks, and the Arabs. In other words, as you move from Northern to Southern Europe, you will find that people move towards more involvement with each other...
>
> In some cultures, messages are explicit; the words carry most of the information. In other cultures, such as China or Japan or the Arab cultures, less information is contained in the verbal part of the message, since more is in the context. That's why American businessmen often complain that their Japanese counterparts never get to the point. The Japanese wouldn't dream of spelling the whole thing out ... in general, high-context people can get by with less of the legal paperwork than is deemed essential in America. A man's word is his bond and you need not spell out the details to make him behave...[85]

Hall's model can be quite useful for providers in understanding the behaviour of customers from different cultural backgrounds, who may have quite different values and behaviour in relation to things such as punctuality, touching, personal space, individual versus group decision-making, family influences, and negotiation of agreements.

In this chapter, we have seen how various aspects of non-verbal communication can give us insights into the customer–provider encounter. Non-verbal behaviour, as we shall see, is important in understanding some of the models of communication we shall now consider — in particular, those of transactional analysis, assertiveness, and neurolinguistic programming.

ACTIVITIES

1. How might providers detect stress in customers? What can providers do about such stress?
2. Is it ever possible to tell if a person is deceiving us? How can we know?
3. How do powerful (and not-so-powerful) people express themselves non-verbally?
4. How do men and women differ in their non-verbal behaviour?
5. Interview four service providers who are required to wear a uniform. Determine their feelings — positive and negative — about uniforms.
6. Evaluate four different servicescapes. For each of them come up with ten adjectives and describe them in detail.
7. Compare the way three organisations organise queuing behaviour.

TALKING POINTS

YOU DON'T SAY? More of what people say about customers and providers

People don't want to communicate with an 'organisation' or a computer. They want to talk to a real, live, responsive, responsible person who will listen and help them get satisfaction.

Theo Michelson
State Farm Insurance

The war of business has shifted onto a new battleground. In the 1960s, marketing was the watchword for achieving competitive advantage. In the 1970s, manufacturing became the hot topic, and in the 1980s, quality. Now competition has arrived at the fourth battlefield — customer service.

William H. Davidow and Bro Uttal

Formal social training tends to work only when the customer service job is highly standardised. Teaching fast-food clerks to make eye contact with customers, smile at three designated times during each transaction, and helpfully suggest a dessert can produce an impression of better service only if both the customer and the clerk clearly understand the outline and limits of the fast-food transaction, the script, if you will. Teaching employees to behave that way in a fancy restaurant, where the transaction is richer and the script fuzzier, is sure to produce a negative impression. Who wants plastic responses from a waiter who's supposed to earn his big tip? Even in banks, where teller transactions might seem standardised, the script can be fuzzy enough that formal social training backfires. The mechanical smile and the automatic 'Have a nice day' are irritating when they come from somebody who is supposed to recognise the customer's unique financial needs.

William H. Davidow and Bro Uttal

'The First Law of Service' (is) expressed by the formula: Satisfaction = perception − expectation.

If you expect a certain level of service and perceive the service received to be higher, you will be a satisfied customer. If you perceive the same level as before but expected a higher level, you will be disappointed and therefore a dissatisfied customer. The point is that both what is perceived and what is expected are psychological phenomena — they are not reality ... (thus some restaurants deliberately over-estimate waiting times for tables, and patrons are therefore quite pleased when they are seated earlier than they had expected ...) When I have discussed this (phenomenon) with a variety of serving personnel, they always affirm its wisdom. As one waiter pointed out to me: 'If they sit down in a good mood, it's easy to keep them happy. If they sit down disgruntled, it's almost impossible to turn them around. They're looking to find fault, to criticise'.

David H. Maister

Many products are now so complicated that they are undifferentiated regarding quality. Consumers cannot decide that the quality of one service is better than that of another until they encounter problems. Then this product becomes differentiated from other products on the basis of service. Industries in which this situation now exists include consumer electronic products, banking, insurance, air travel, major appliances, and automobiles.

John A. Goodman and Ronald W. Stampfl

We try to do personality screening as much as we can, to find the personalities which will fit into the company culture of putting the passenger first, being patient, not being authoritarian, not being bossy ... we've never had an incentive pay system (to make the cabin crew more customer-oriented). American Airlines once had a system where they tried to measure the people-to-people performance of their crew by a very elaborate system where observers were sitting in the cabin and noting how many positive contacts they were making and finishing, and so on. It didn't work. It goes with the perversion of all kinds of such mechanical systems: (because) you can't order people to be friendly with passengers, you then take out one element that means that. You can observe that somebody goes to another person, talks to him and smiles ... When you introduce such a system, you might have quite a positive effect at the beginning, but people are no fools. They understand what you're up to, and they play the system then, instead of playing the quality you want.

Bernard Oettli
Swissair

Real estate training back at that time ... didn't really tell you how to serve a customer, how to understand the trauma of moving across the country — they're not just out there to buy a house, they're changing their life. So Century 21® started developing training programs to take a real estate salesperson away from selling physical property, to better understand the motivation, better understand the trauma that's inherent in any move ... So Century 21®, in their training programs, addressed how to understand the emotional side of a real estate transaction and then how to serve the client's needs.

Bruce Oseland
Century 21® Real Estate Corporation

4 TRANSACTIONAL ANALYSIS
THE GAMES CUSTOMERS (AND PROVIDERS) PLAY

When a customer buys a good or service, that constitutes an economic transaction. But before the economic transaction comes a behavioural transaction. Transactional analysis is a system of communication that gives us an insight into such behavioural transactions.

TRANSACTIONAL ANALYSIS: THE BACKGROUND

Transactional analysis (TA) was developed by American psychiatrist Eric Berne in the 1950s–60s. The TA model of behaviour and communication was very much in fashion in the 1960s–70s, and underwent something of a decline in popularity in the 1980s. Currently, it seems to be undergoing a revival of interest.[86]

Berne's most famous book on the topic is *Games People Play: The Psychology of Human Relationships*, which first appeared in 1964. More than thirty years later, the book is still selling, and the concept of people playing psychological games has passed into everyday folklore. Such games, as we shall see, can be quite unpleasant, but they do give insights into the darker side of human nature, and a systematic analysis of such games leads us to understand what we can do to prevent or minimise their occurrence.

Berne based much of his system upon the theories of Sigmund Freud, the late nineteenth-century/early-twentieth-century Austrian psychoanalyst. Freud argued that the human mind can be understood as having three components: the *ego*, the *superego* and the *id*.[87] Freud saw these components as being broken up as follows: the id is comprised of the two basic instincts of sex, or pleasure-seeking, and aggression; the ego is our rational self; while the superego comprises our conscience. We are born with the id, and only develop the ego and superego as we develop as children. The ego is the conscious self, while the id and the superego are part of our unconscious mind.

In the Freudian system, the battle between the primal drives of the id and the repressive control of the superego can cause problems for our rational selves, and to the extent that we are not in control of these areas of our mind, much of our motivations are unconscious — in other words, we do not always understand why we do things.

Freud also advanced the notion of *ego defence mechanisms*, or behaviour patterns which protect the ego from potentially hurtful realities. Such mechanisms include *repression*, *denial*, *rationalisation*, *fantasy* and *identification*.[88]

EGO STATES

Freudian psychoanalysis has received much criticism over the years; nevertheless it can still be a powerful tool for understanding human behaviour and communication. The Freudian system has a number of shortcomings, however, which prevent it from becoming an accessible and practical model of human communication. These shortcomings are:

1. It has a specific technical jargon, which makes it difficult for the average person to understand.
2. It is firmly based in the realm of mental illness, which means that it does not always seem to have relevance for 'normal' people like you and me (who are just a little bit crazy rather than seriously so!).
3. It presents a fairly static view of the ways in which people interact with each other in the real world.

Eric Berne developed a number of innovations that went a long way towards overcoming these shortcomings. Firstly, he re-named Freud's superego, ego and id with the more colloquial names of Parent, Adult and Child, referring to these parts of our personalities as ego states (figure 4.1).[89] Indeed, much of TA depends upon colloquial, whimsical language.

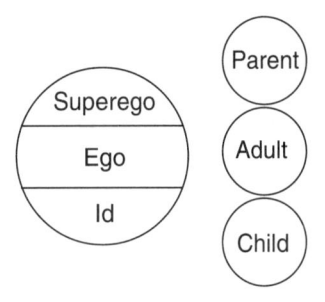

Figure 4.1: Freud and Berne's models of personality compared

In later work, Berne and others subdivided the Parent ego state into the Critical Parent and the Nurturing Parent, and the Child ego state into the Natural Child and the Adaptive Child. All of these states have distinct sets of verbal and non-verbal behaviours (table 4.1.). All these 'personalities' are present within all of us, and may manifest themselves in different situations.

Note that biological or chronological children, parents and adults should not be confused with the Child, Parent and Adult ego states. As we shall see, it's quite possible, for example, for chronological children to operate from Adult or Parent ego states. We'll discriminate chronological states from ego states by giving initial upper-case letters to ego states (Parent, Adult, Child) and initial lower-case letters to chronological states (parent, adult, child). Let's briefly consider the nature of these ego states.

The Child ego state

The Child ego state develops in the very first months of human life. The Natural Child embodies spontaneity, enthusiasm and a sense of playfulness. If the chronological child is given a tough time by its parents or responsible adults, it may learn to be not so spontaneous, to be guarded, and perhaps angry. These behaviours are those of the Adapted Child ego state.

Table 4.1: Behavioural clues indicating which psychological state is at work

Divisions or basic norms	Nurturing Parent	Critical Parent	Adult	Natural Child	Adaptive Child
Voice tones	Solicitous, comforting, caring, soothing.	Condescending, criticising, putting down or accusing, taut, insistent, tongue-clicking, sighing.	Matter-of-fact, even, calm.	Rising, high-pitched, usually noisy.	Whining, shrieking with rage, begging, contrite, supplicating.
Vocabulary clues	What's wrong? Are you OK? Can I help? Don't worry. Everything will be OK.	Shocking. Nonsense. Lazy. Poor thing. Everyone knows that. You should never. The only way. I can't understand why in the world you would ever. It is extremely important. Do it. You never.	How? What? Where? Who? What's the probability? Is it possible? Is it probable? In what way? I speak only for myself and not others.	I'm mad at you. Hey, great. I wish. I dunno. Gee. Crazy. Rats. Wow.	It always happens to me. I guess I'm just unlucky. I never seem to win at anything. That's not fair. Everybody else does it. Come on, let's. I won't.
Physical postures	Open arms protecting from a fall or hurt, pat on back, arm around shoulder.	Stroking chin, puffed up, super correct, very proper. Superior attitudes: talking behind hand, throwing hands in the air.	Relaxed, attentive, eye contact, listening with openness, squared-up posture. Adult listening is identified with continual movement of face, eyes and body.	Playful, excited, running, dancing, jumping up and down, head cocked.	Withdrawn and retreating, beat down, overburdened, self-conscious, teasing, agitated, tantrum behaviour.
Facial expressions	Concerned, supportive, encouraging, warm, happy.	Frowns, worried or disapproving looks, taut lips, jutting chin, stern gaze.	Alert eyes, paying close attention.	Excitement, surprise, eyes, shining, body tense, mouth open.	Downcast eyes, quivering lip or chin, tic, pouting, whining, moist eyes, red face.
Gestures	Reaching for, hugging, holding, protecting and shielding from harm.	Pointing index finger or pencil, tapping foot, arms folded across chest, hands on hips, striking table with fist, shaking fist.	Leaning forward in chair, eye-to-eye contact, listening with openness.	Laughter, limbs moving freely, playful.	Wringing hands, withdrawing into corner, raising hand for permission, stooped shoulders, hung head.
General	Support and concern.	Closure to new data, automatic judgements based on archaic material.	Data gathering, sensitivity, openness and thinking.	Aroused feelings suggesting that the child has been hooked.	Complaining and expectation-meeting, or withdrawing and expectation-avoiding.

(Source: Bennett [1987: 26–27]. Reproduced with permission of the author.)

The Parent ego state

The Parent ego state begins to develop next in the chronological child. Chronological or biological parents can be nurturing or punishing, or both nurturing and punishing. Depending upon what the chronological child's experiences are, the Nurturing Parent and/or Critical Parent ego state will grow, and influence character and communication style — for example, with younger siblings and playmates.

The Adult ego state

The Adult ego state or rational self begins to develop as the chronological child reaches 10 or so months. At this stage, the child begins to test the environment ('What will happen if I do this?') and thus learns to predict what the environment will do.

Operating from different ego states

Depending upon the experiences we are exposed to in our childhood, and depending upon our reactions to those experiences, we develop a range of ego states that determines our character or personality, and also our style of communication. Some ego states are more dominant in some individuals than others, while individuals may shift about from ego state to ego state, depending upon the situation and the people with whom they are interacting. The Natural Child, Adult and Nurturing Parent ego states are considered by most people to be more attractive and positive than the Critical Parent and Adapted Child ego states, and indeed, as we shall soon see, the major part of human conflict and bad communication seems to emanate from those latter two ego states.

We tend to operate from one ego state according to the situation. Thus, the spontaneity of the Natural Child might be appropriate for a social occasion, but not necessarily for a workplace situation. This is not necessarily true, however: perhaps some spontaneity, humour, lateral thinking and creativity is precisely what some too-rational, too-serious workplaces require. The Adult ego state is excellent for rational problem-solving, but may be quite inappropriate in a social situation, such as an office party.

Can you pick which ego state a person might be operating from? Check your skills by completing table 4.2.

Table 4.2: Ego states of customers and providers

Situation	Verbal communication	Non-verbal communication	Ego state?
Provider to customer	Doctor will see you as soon as he is free.	Seated at desk, no eye contact, stern tone, pursed lips, frown.	
Customer to provider	I wonder how loud this CD system can play?	Seated in showroom car, raised eyebrows, sparkling eyes, tilted head, mischievous grin.	
Provider to customer	Will this sum assured be automatically adjusted for inflation between yearly premium payments?	Sitting at table, pencil in one hand, other hand on chin, direct gaze.	
Provider to customer	If you just step this way, Mrs Johnson, I'll get someone who can help you.	Standing, gesturing, palm out, with one hand, gently touching with other, smile, warm eye contact.	
Customer to provider	I just can't understand these forms. Why can't you design them better?	Standing at counter, wrinkled brow, clenched teeth, one hand crumpling edge of form, other hand scratching head, stroking hair, high-pitched voice.	
Provider to provider	No thanks, I don't like dancing, but I would like to talk to you about the problems we're having with that voice-mail system.	Standing at office party, erect posture, serious demeanour.	

STROKES: WHAT YOU STROKE IS WHAT YOU GET

Berne and other TA practitioners argue that we all have basic human needs. These can be meaningfully classified as:
1. stimulus-hunger
2. recognition-hunger
3. structure-hunger.

Let's look at the first two needs now, deferring consideration of structure-hunger until later (see Filling in the time between birth and death: time-structuring, p. 59).

Stimulus-hunger relates most directly to the need to be physically touched. Early research on infants reared in institutions showed that when they were given minimal physical handling, they were slower to develop and became more prone to disease.[90]

Such physical stroking, or the lack of it, is similar to simple recognition of others. We all suffer from, or enjoy, *recognition-hunger*, according to TA specialists. This seems to make sense: solitary confinement and sensory deprivation are regarded as means of torture in most societies.

Consider the following scenario.

> A small child is trying to catch her mother's attention. The child tries smiling, singing, giggling, calling out — all in the hope of getting a smile, or some kind words. The mother, however, is preoccupied on this occasion. Slowly, the child's behaviour changes. She begins to become louder, and becomes more destructive with her toys. She becomes angry towards the world in general and her mother in particular. She drops things, moves clumsily, and creates an intolerable din. The mother reacts, first by frowning, then by telling the child to stop, and finally, by smacking the child and sending her to her room.

TA practitioners describe any type of recognition, verbal or non-verbal, as strokes. These can be physical, entailing actual touching, or non-physical. A positive stroke is something we will like. It might be:
- a smile
- a caress
- a note of thanks
- a pay rise
- applause
- a compliment from a respected peer or superior.

Within the colloquial world of TA, a positive stroke is also known as a *warm fuzzy*. In other words, if someone gives you a positive stroke, it's as if they have given you an object or animal that is warm and fuzzy — that is, pleasant to hold.

A negative stroke is something we will not like. It might be:
- a frown
- a smack
- a note saying: 'Do this again, please — and quickly!'
- a pay cut
- booing
- criticism from a respected peer or elder.

A negative stroke is also known as a *cold prickly* — it's as if someone has given you an object or animal to hold that is cold and prickly.

Most of us prefer warm fuzzies to cold pricklies, but — TA practitioners suggest — if we can't get warm fuzzies, we will accept cold pricklies, rather than face the third option — no strokes at all, or being ignored. Thus, in our noisy child scenario, the child has, in TA terms, realised that she will not get any warm fuzzies on this occasion, and has, in effect, demanded — and received — a cold prickly. She may feel miserable as a result, *but she has not been ignored*.

People can stroke other people, and people can also stroke themselves. Some of these strokes are fairly healthy (such as esteem-building thoughts: 'I did that well. I'm improving'). Some of these strokes are not so healthy, such as compulsive eating, smoking, drinking and shopping.[91] Providers continually encounter customers who are not necessarily in dire need of a garment, a computer, a medical consultation or a haircut, but who are in need of some type of socioemotional stroke.

Strokes and organisations

The concept of strokes can also help us to understand just what goes on in organisations. It has been observed that in small organisations, there are plenty of strokes given, many of them positive. People know what they are doing, and can see direct payoffs for their performance. As organisations become bigger, however, the connection between an employee's work output and the final product or service often becomes tenuous. Also, bureaucratic ways of doing things usually become more dominant. In the bigger organisation, therefore, strokes, particularly positive ones, may not be so readily forthcoming. It may be, therefore, that in some organisations, people perform badly, or less than optimally, if only to get strokes — negative strokes of course, but better than none. Such organisations may suffer often from crises, in need of dramatic solutions. Such solutions, of course, are a good deal more exciting than the boredom of routine. If attention is paid to crises, dramatic solutions and low performance, there will be more crises, dramatic solutions and low performance.[92]

Of course, in order to accept such a model of human behaviour, we need to believe in unconscious or only partly-conscious motivation. Not all people will accept such a model, and therefore will probably have a hard time accepting systems such as transactional analysis. Nevertheless, many people are willing to concede that such patterns of motivation and communication do exist, and thus can see TA as a useful tool in understanding children who misbehave, ineffective organisations and the rest of human nature — including customers and providers.

Conditional, unconditional and mixed strokes

Strokes can also be conditional, unconditional or mixed. An unconditional stroke relates to the way a person is by virtue of their nature or physical characteristics: it is a stroke for being. A conditional stroke is contingent upon a person's behaviour in a particular situation: it is a stroke for doing.[93] A mixed stroke sends two contradictory signals, one positive, one negative — and most people receiving such a stroke usually (correctly) attach greater importance to the negative stroke. Some examples of these strokes are given in table 4.3.

Table 4.3: Types of strokes

Stroke	Type	Verbal expression	Non-verbal expression
Warm fuzzy	Positive conditional	Your deliveries to us this week have definitely improved.	Smile, thumbs up
		I prefer you when you're sober.	Sad smile, caress
	Positive unconditional	I love you.	Adoring gaze
		You Swedish women are beautiful, that's for sure.	Smile, tilted head
Cold prickly	Negative conditional	Can't you wear something more presentable?	Half-smile, hand scratching head, raised eyebrows
		This report is not one of your best.	Tapping fingers, intermittent eye contact
	Negative unconditional	I hate you.	Tears, distorted expression, bunched fists
		That's so typical of an Aries!	Shaking of head, tsk-tsk-tsk
Mixed	Contradictory	This work is pretty good — for a woman.	Downward pitch on second part of sentence
		This dress is — nice.	Sighing, shaking of head, frowning

If you think you're pretty good at identifying this stroking stuff, consider table 4.4. This is similar to table 4.3, but a little more complex. Note that provision is made for strokes directed towards other people, but also for strokes directed towards the self (note that self-strokes are often thought rather than spoken).

Think of a service delivery situation you are familiar with. This could be anything — a medical consultation, servicing a car, making a withdrawal from a bank account, an unsolicited (and unappreciated) phone call from a telemarketer — anything you like.

Make two copies of table 4.4. Complete one copy so that it shows strokes being given by the *customer*. Complete the second copy so that it shows strokes being given by the *provider*.

Table 4.4: Strokes in a customer/provider encounter

SITUATION:				
STROKE GIVEN BY: CUSTOMER/PROVIDER (DELETE ONE)				
Stroke	**Type**	**Given to**	**Verbal expression**	**Non-verbal expression**
Warm fuzzy	Positive conditional	Self		
		Other		
	Positive unconditional	Self		
		Other		
Cold prickly	Negative conditional	Self		
		Other		
	Negative unconditional	Self		
		Other		
Mixed	Contradictory	Self		
		Other		

TRANSACTIONS: COMPLEMENTARY, CROSSED AND ULTERIOR STROKES

Strokes constitute the messages that people send to other people in one-way communication. An exchange of strokes is known as a transaction (hence, transactional analysis), and forms the basis of all two-way communication. There are three types of transaction: complementary, crossed and ulterior.

Complementary transactions

A complementary transaction occurs when two people match communication styles (see figure 4.2). One person sends out a *stimulus* from one ego state to an ego state of another person. This stimulus is matched with a *response* from the other person. Communication here is complementary. This type of communication can continue virtually indefinitely — until at least one person switches ego states. Complementary transactions let us readily see one of the basic tenets of TA: most human communication occurs not in isolated stimulus–response dialogues, but in chains of dialogues. The response in the first part of the chain is thus, from another viewpoint, the stimulus for the second part of the chain, and so on.

A:

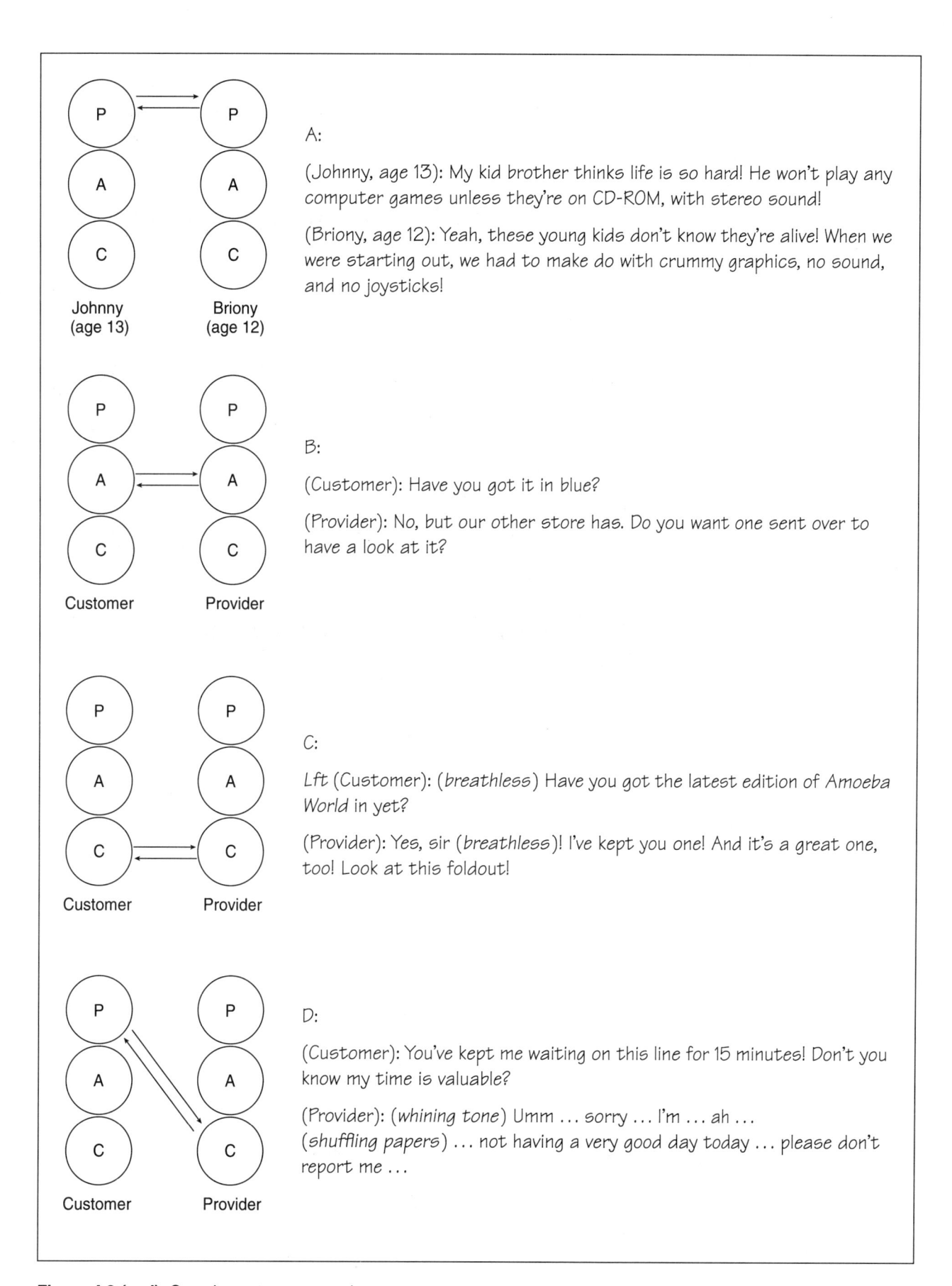

(Johnny, age 13): My kid brother thinks life is so hard! He won't play any computer games unless they're on CD-ROM, with stereo sound!

(Briony, age 12): Yeah, these young kids don't know they're alive! When we were starting out, we had to make do with crummy graphics, no sound, and no joysticks!

Johnny (age 13) Briony (age 12)

B:

(Customer): Have you got it in blue?

(Provider): No, but our other store has. Do you want one sent over to have a look at it?

C:

Lft (Customer): (breathless) Have you got the latest edition of Amoeba World in yet?

(Provider): Yes, sir (breathless)! I've kept you one! And it's a great one, too! Look at this foldout!

D:

(Customer): You've kept me waiting on this line for 15 minutes! Don't you know my time is valuable?

(Provider): (whining tone) Umm ... sorry ... I'm ... ah ...
(shuffling papers) ... not having a very good day today ... please don't report me ...

Figure 4.2 (a–d): Complementary transactions

Crossed transactions

Crossed transactions occur when a person sends out a stimulus to a particular ego state of another person, but is not greeted with a complementary or expected response. Instead, the other person sends an unexpected, often aggressive, response. Crossed transactions are the source of much conflict and misunderstanding in the world.

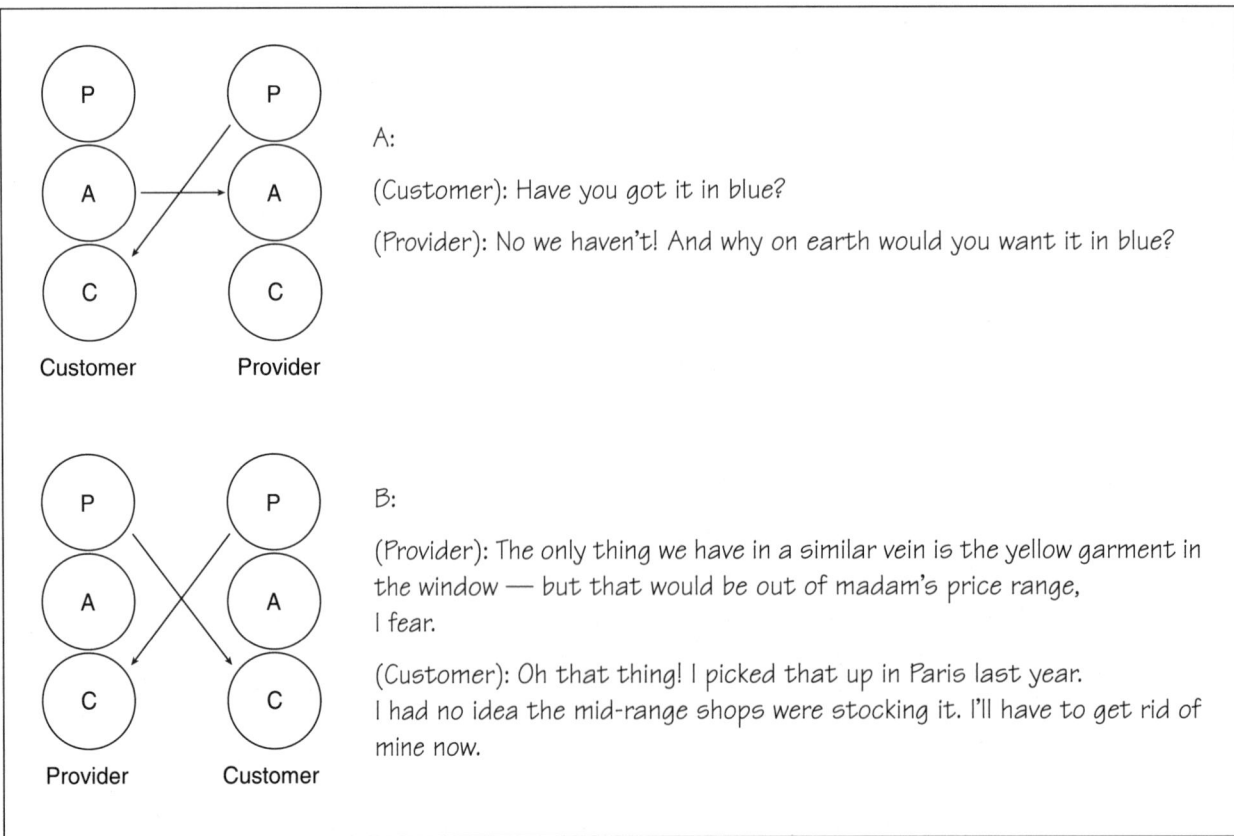

A:

(Customer): Have you got it in blue?

(Provider): No we haven't! And why on earth would you want it in blue?

B:

(Provider): The only thing we have in a similar vein is the yellow garment in the window — but that would be out of madam's price range, I fear.

(Customer): Oh that thing! I picked that up in Paris last year. I had no idea the mid-range shops were stocking it. I'll have to get rid of mine now.

Figure 4.3 (a–b): Crossed transactions

Ulterior transactions

Ulterior transactions occur when we say one thing and mean another. This happens when we communicate with others at two levels simultaneously: the surface or social level, and the deeper or psychological level. The dynamics of such transactions are shown in figure 4.4. Note that the social stimulus and response are different from the psychological stimulus and response.

A:

Social level

(Provider): The only thing we have in a similar vein is this lovely yellow garment in the window — but it's a bit pricey, unfortunately.

(Customer): Yes, you're right. I can't afford it. It would be irresponsible to blow my budget on this garment.

Psychological level

(Provider): Wouldn't you love to have this? Don't worry about the money.

(Customer): Yeah you're right. I love that colour. Who cares about money?

B:

Social level

(Customer): Can you help me with this?

(Provider): Certainly, sir. That's my job.

Psychological level

(Customer): I'm attracted to you.

(Provider): I feel the same way.

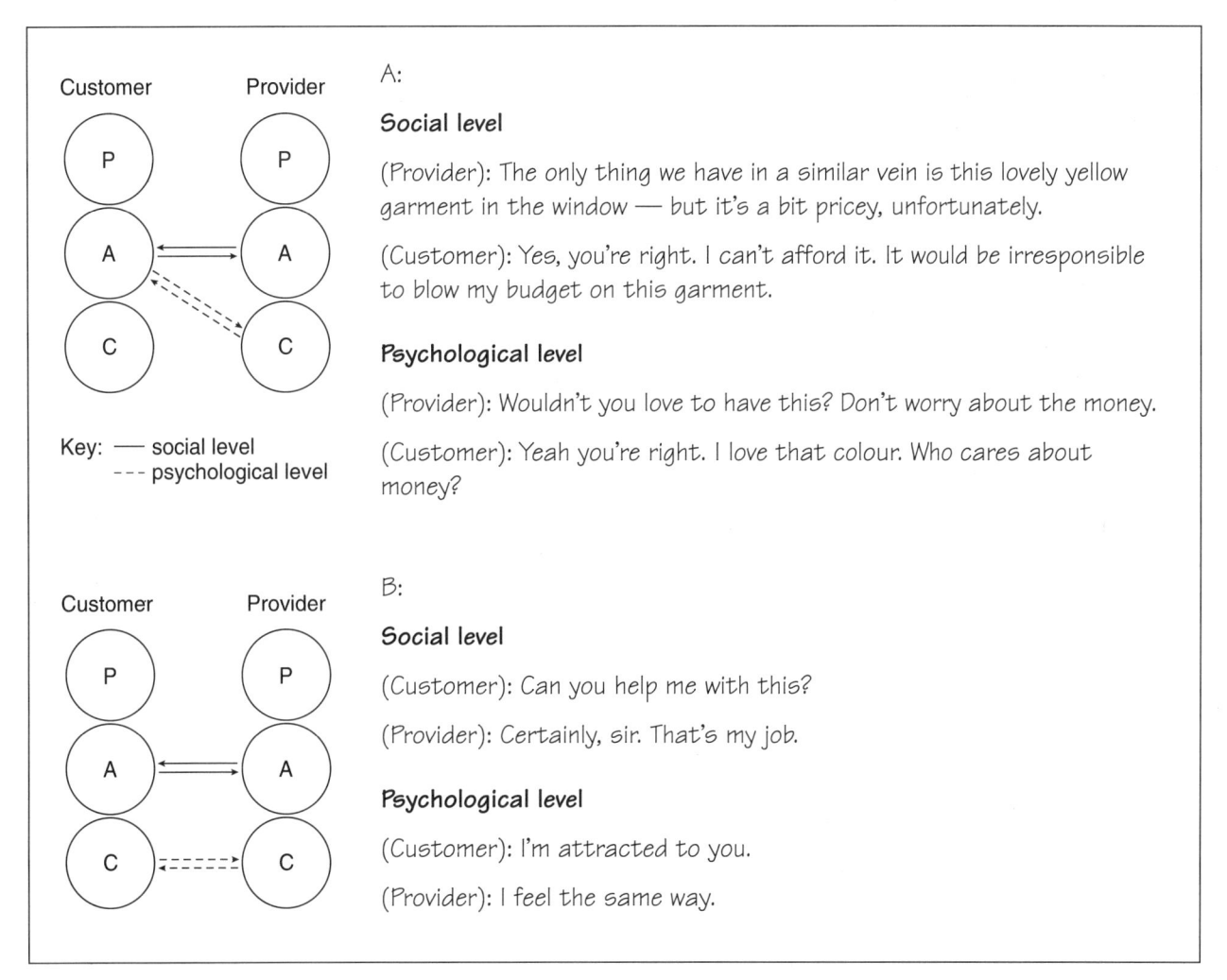

Figure 4.4 (a–b): Ulterior transactions

Transaction 4.4(a) can go one of two ways. The provider is using her Adult ego to specifically manipulate the Child ego state of the customer. If the customer were to respond from the Adult ego state, she would agree with the surface or social message from the provider — 'It does cost too much, and therefore I can't afford it'. If the customer responds from the Child ego state, then she will buy the garment. Here, the Child ego state is the source of several messages — 'I love colourful things, I don't care about rational things like budgeting, and also, who are you to push me around?'

Transaction 4.4(b) shows that there is a hidden agenda or hidden meaning in this conversation. The overt or social meaning is conveyed by verbal communication, while the hidden or psychological meaning is conveyed by non-verbal communication — voice tone, eye contact, smiling, head-tilting, body orientation, and so on. Such verbal/non-verbal incongruence is a usual sign that an ulterior transaction is going on.

MAY I SEE YOUR LICENCE, PLEASE?

TA and what happens when police officers encounter drivers

Using transactional analysis terminology and diagrams, Peoples (1977) gives advice to police officers and administrators on handling some tricky transactions. Similar behavioural dynamics occur, of course, across a wide range of customer-provider encounters.

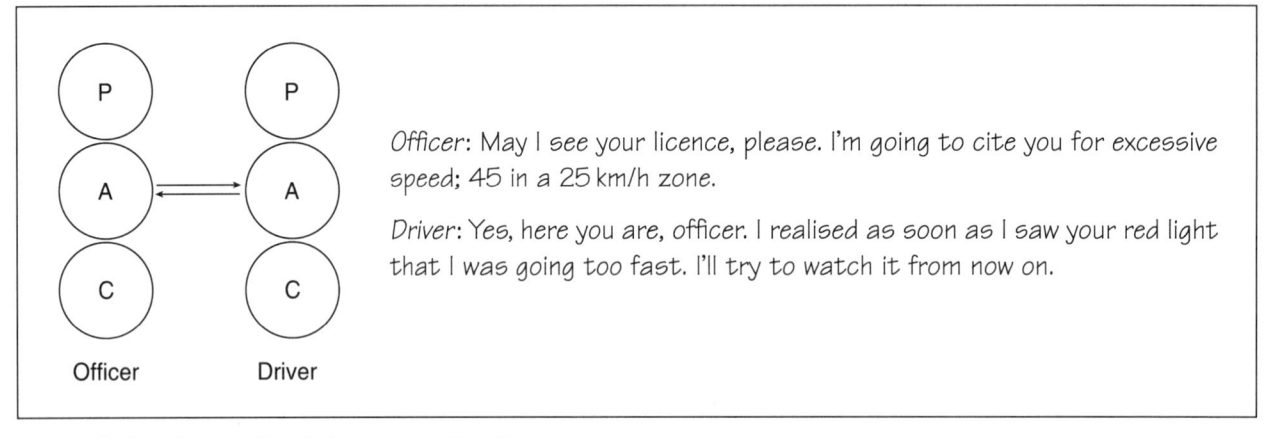

Officer: May I see your licence, please. I'm going to cite you for excessive speed; 45 in a 25 km/h zone.

Driver: Yes, here you are, officer. I realised as soon as I saw your red light that I was going too fast. I'll try to watch it from now on.

Figure 4.5(a): Police officer/driver transaction No. 1

Assuming a straight tone from each participant, the transaction contained objective and factual (Adult) data. This is the ideal traffic transaction, and perhaps this type rarely occurs. Nevertheless, variations of this can be encountered in traffic stops.

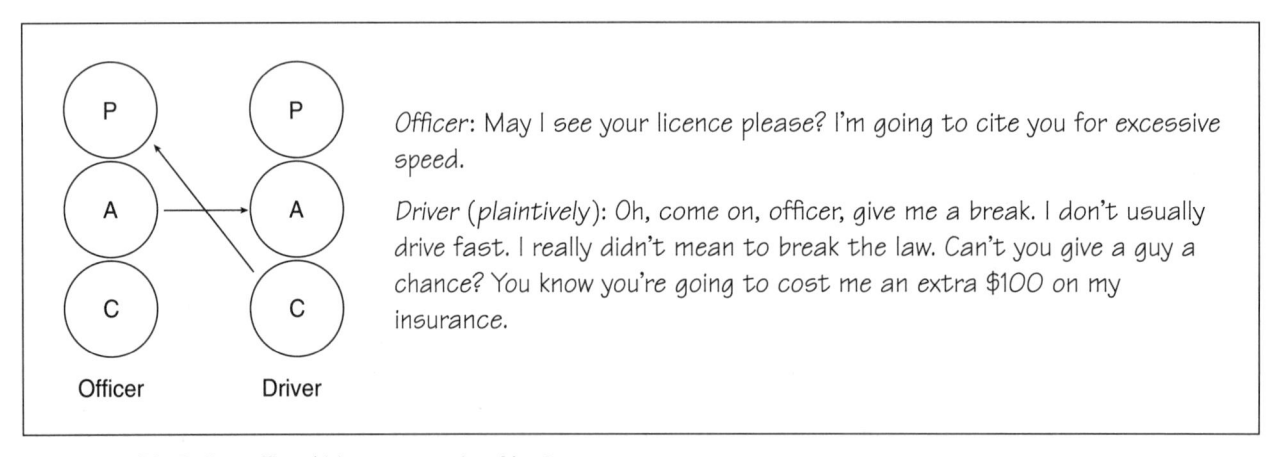

Officer: May I see your licence please? I'm going to cite you for excessive speed.

Driver (plaintively): Oh, come on, officer, give me a break. I don't usually drive fast. I really didn't mean to break the law. Can't you give a guy a chance? You know you're going to cost me an extra $100 on my insurance.

Figure 4.5(b): Police officer/driver transaction No. 2

Implied by the driver is 'I know I am a bad boy and you caught me, but give me another chance Daddy'. The Child is humble and contrite, hoping to 'hook' nurturing feelings from the officer's Parent. Frequently this type of response is known as a game labelled 'Kick Me'. Even though it comes from the humble Child, hostility and resentment are evident, and the driver is attempting to blame the officer for the extra insurance costs.

Officer: May I see your licence, please?

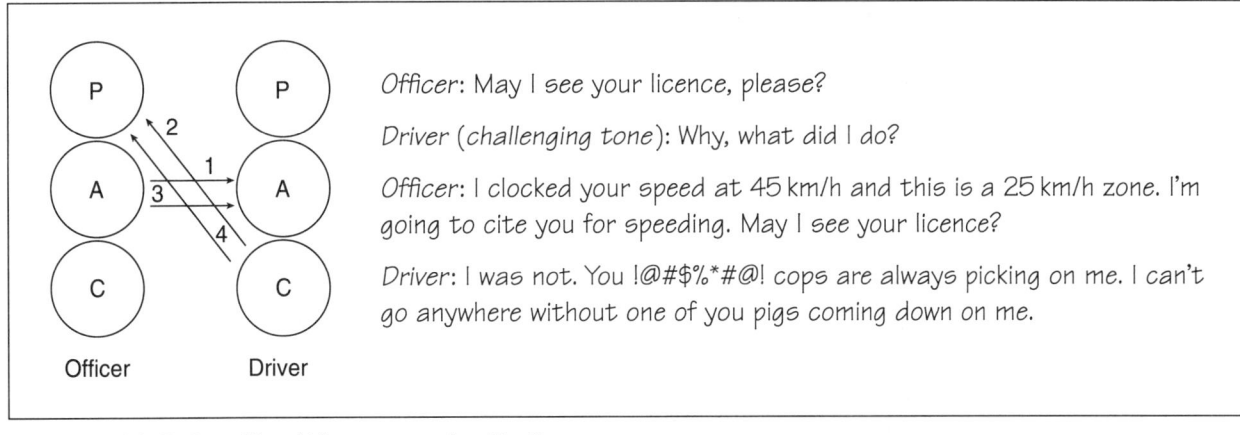

Driver (challenging tone): Why, what did I do?

Officer: I clocked your speed at 45 km/h and this is a 25 km/h zone. I'm going to cite you for speeding. May I see your licence?

Driver: I was not. You !@#$%*#@! cops are always picking on me. I can't go anywhere without one of you pigs coming down on me.

Figure 4.5(c): Police officer/driver transaction No. 3

Hostility and rebellion against authority are the driver's Child responses, with implied resentment about being picked on. This is a predetermined response. The driver identified the officer as a Parent punishing him and responds this way because he expects the officer to represent personal authority.

This type of transaction occurs in some form in the real life of every police officer. This is the type that can easily cause problems. If the dialogue continues and the driver increases the barbs his Child throws at the officer's Parent, he may eventually 'hook' the Parent, and the officer will come down on him. Charges of resisting arrest or police brutality could follow. An arrest may occur in this transaction, regardless of how Adult the officer is, but if it becomes a Parent–Child arrest, it will not be very pleasant for either party. The next time that driver is stopped, his Child response will be more firmly set. The next officer will really be in for it, and he may not live to learn why. This is not theoretical speculation; it is fact. Any experienced officer remembers having to follow behind the shift of Big Duke. Duke had the knack of making people resent him and working the beat after Duke was always more difficult.

In other words, Duke walked his beat as a heavy Parent, putting people down and prodding their Child. People do not like to be treated like a Child from the negative Parent. Hostility and resentment are their natural (conditioned) responses.

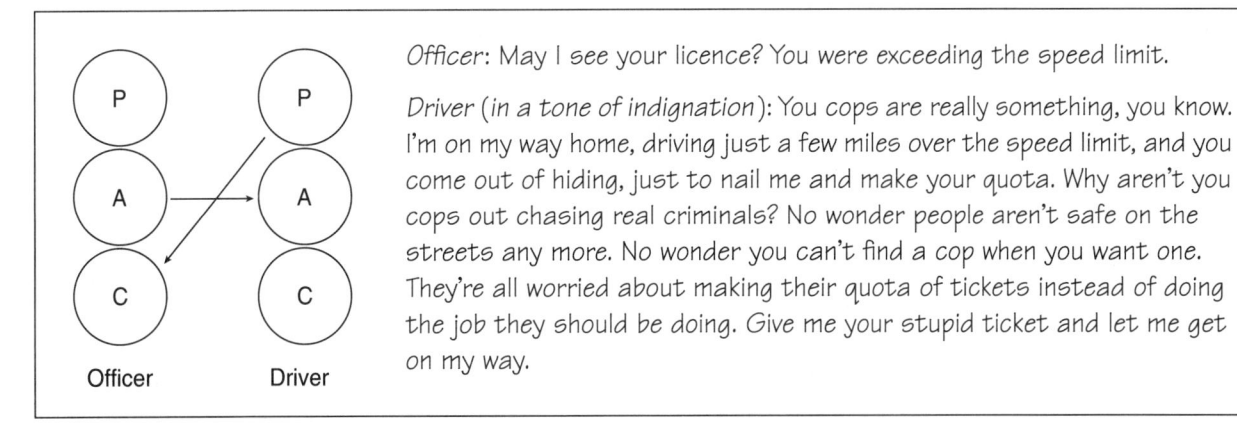

Officer: May I see your licence? You were exceeding the speed limit.

Driver (in a tone of indignation): You cops are really something, you know. I'm on my way home, driving just a few miles over the speed limit, and you come out of hiding, just to nail me and make your quota. Why aren't you cops out chasing real criminals? No wonder people aren't safe on the streets any more. No wonder you can't find a cop when you want one. They're all worried about making their quota of tickets instead of doing the job they should be doing. Give me your stupid ticket and let me get on my way.

Figure 4.5(d): Police officer/driver transaction No. 4

In this instance, the driver feels stupid, foolish, or embarrassed for getting caught. He feels like he got caught with his hand in the cookie jar, but he cannot stand to accept the blame or the responsibility. His defence is to respond from the indignant Parent in an attempt to reverse the situation and put the officer in his place. If he can stimulate either a humble Child response, or a hostile one, from the officer, the transaction will shift from crossed to complementary, and he will have controlled the shift. The humble Child will stroke the Parent, and the hostile Child will feed the Parent indignation. Either way, the driver wins.

If the officer feels offended or indignant, he will respond from his own critical Parent. Once each party is committed to their position, a game of 'put-down' begins; and if each one finally 'hooks' the Child of the other, a good brawl will result.

The professional officer is expected to remain in his Adult in the above situation. That is the only way he can win; that is his only way to achieve effective communication. Merely staying in the Adult will not make all transactions go smoothly. In figure 4.5(d), if the indignant Parent cannot hook the officer's Child, chances are good that he will re-evaluate his position and recognise that to continue ranting will make him look foolish (both to the officer and his own Adult who is beginning to moderate). He will sign the ticket and go quietly. Or, if his Parent commitment is too strong and he feels that he cannot back down, he will continue grumbling, sign the ticket, and threaten with 'your superiors will hear about this'. At this point, no amount of talking will change his position, but that is his problem, not the officer's. In both cases, the officer wins. He has effectively communicated the ticket. And, what is more important to recognise is that when the driver maintains a strong Parent, rarely will he shift to the Child. This means that no matter how much he rants, he will not rebel; he will not let the transaction become a resist charge or arrest situation. The officer wins again.

(Source: 'May I see your licence, please?' from Peoples [1977: 210–213]. Reproduced with permission.)

Police officers do not always operate from the 'neutral' Adult ego state, of course: they're human like everyone else, and can operate from less effective ego states and roles.[94]

THE GAMES PEOPLE PLAY

A psychological game can best be defined as an ongoing series of complementary ulterior transactions progressing to a well-defined, predictable outcome.[95] Transactional analysis theorists argue the following:

1. Game-playing is often the real reason for much human conflict and misunderstanding.
2. People can 'win' such games in peculiar ways — by inflicting anger, frustration, even physical damage, upon others or upon themselves.
3. We sometimes consciously choose to play games, and we are sometimes driven by unconscious motivations to play games.
4. Such games might extend over seconds, minutes, hours, days, weeks, years or decades.
5. It takes two (sometimes more) 'players' to play a game.
6. A game begins, and continues, when one player can induce a reaction from a complementary ego state of another player (also known as 'hooking' — for example, the Child ego state of one player 'hooks' the Parent ego state of another).

These games have general relevance to life in general, and often have specific relevance to the customer–provider encounter. Keep in mind, of course, that all games in such specific encounters are not played solely by the customer.

How do we know whether other people (and indeed ourselves) are playing games? Generally speaking, most human activity that is not concerned with playing psychological games is fairly healthy and oriented towards solving human problems (see time structuring, p. 59). Thus people in non-game situations may use some of the words and behaviours given in the following examples, but the dynamics and the payoffs will be much healthier and positive. Let's now have a look at some of these games in detail, and then go on to consider how games can be avoided, or at least minimised.

Why Don't You — Yes, But . . .

Social level

Customer: This still doesn't work.

Provider: Why don't you try it like this?

Psychological level

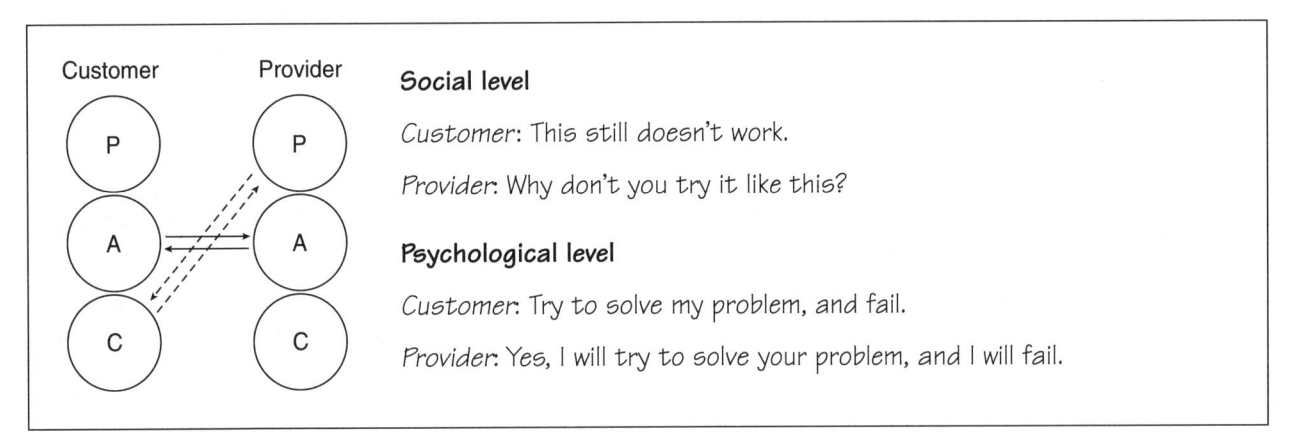

Customer: Try to solve my problem, and fail.

Provider: Yes, I will try to solve your problem, and I will fail.

Figure 4.6(a): 'Why Don't You — Yes, But . . .' model

1. Customer: This still doesn't work.

2. Provider: Why don't you try it like this?

3. Customer: Yes, but I've tried that, and it still didn't work.

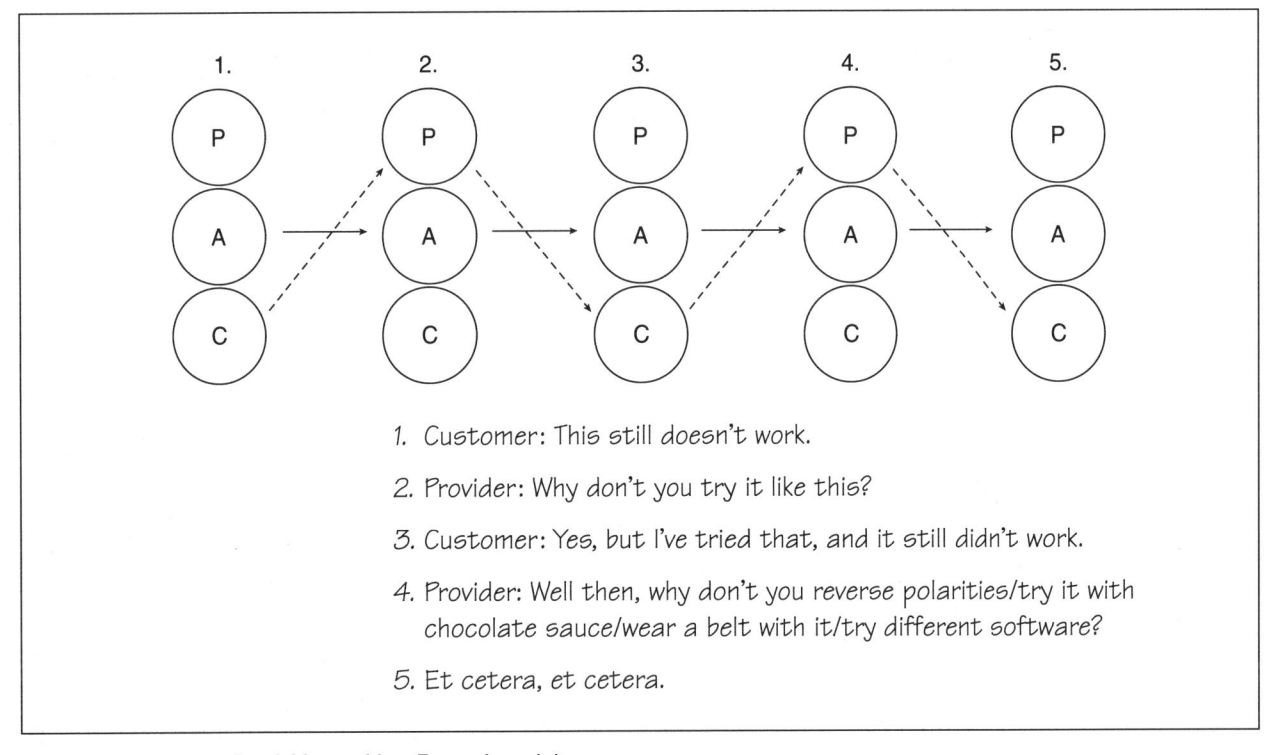

4. Provider: Well then, why don't you reverse polarities/try it with chocolate sauce/wear a belt with it/try different software?

5. Et cetera, et cetera.

Figure 4.6(b): 'Why Don't You — Yes, But . . .' model

Why Don't You — Yes, But ... (WDY-YB) occurs when one person asks another for help (figures 4.6(a)-(b)). At the social level, it is an Adult-Adult transaction: a neutral, factual request, which is met with a neutral, factual response. At the psychological level, however, it is a Parent-Child transaction: the requester does not really want a solution to a problem, but wishes to achieve other, more hidden objectives. These objectives are:

1. to show that authority figures (parent figures) are fools
2. to attract attention and sympathy
3. to legitimise inaction about a life problem (if they can't fix it, what do you expect me to do about it?).

If the other person continues to play (for example, the other person may be playing the complementary game of I'm Only Trying to Help You — see below), then quite a few rounds of suggestions ('Why don't you ...?') and refusals ('Yes, but I've tried that, and it didn't work') might occur. The game ends when the other person gives up in mute frustration, or else becomes angry. At this point, the WDY-YB player 'wins' the game, by achieving the hidden objectives.

I'm Only Trying To Help You

I'm Only Trying To Help You (IOTTHY) is a game played by people who give others advice which appears to be good advice — but isn't. Eric Berne originally identified this game as being played by some welfare workers and therapists, who (unconsciously) gave bad advice to their clients. When the clients failed, the welfare workers or therapists would give more advice. The IOTTHY player seeks a Parent-Child transaction from a willing co-player. The IOTTHY player is behaving like a Rescuer (see p. 61), but most of us could do without such rescuing. What is the psychological payoff for such a player? The player proves:

1. that other people are fools
2. that people are helpless, and in continual need of a helper
3. that the player is such a helper, and thus will always have something to do, and will always be needed
4. that others will love and respect the player for being so caring.

Obviously, an IOTTHY player and a WDY-YB could get along famously, either in a marriage, or in a work relationship, or in a customer-provider relationship. Remember, it takes two to play a game.

Gee, You're Wonderful Professor

GYWP is another Parent-Child game. The GYWP operates from the Adapted Child ego state, and flatters a gullible person operating from the Parent ego state. The GYWP player forms an attachment with a willing co-player (student-academic, apprentice-master, fan-artist, amateur-professional, patient-physician, subordinate-supervisor, provider-client, etc.), telling the co-player that he/she is wonderful, talented, and so on. Once the player has achieved his or her objective (picked the brains of the co-player, 'proved' that the co-player is not so special after all), he or she moves on to another co-player. GYWP is thus similar to WDY-YB, in that the player wins by showing that all parent-figures are fools after all.

Kick Me

Social level

Provider: Hi! Here's my submission. Sorry it's late. I know my competitors got theirs in on time, but could you just squeeze me in and accept this?

Customer: (frowning, shaking head, rolling eyes) Sorry, I can't do that.

Psychological level

Provider): Aren't I pathetic? I deserve to be punished. Kick me.

Customer: Yes, you are pathetic. Here's your kick.

Figure 4.7: 'Kick Me' model

Remember that a game is an ongoing series of complementary ulterior transactions progressing to a well-defined, predictable outcome. Thus, anyone can make a mistake and hand something in late, but if it happens more than once or twice, then perhaps a game is being played. The Kick Me player plays from the Adapted Child position of willing to accept (and indeed, seek out) negative strokes if no positive strokes are available. The co-player here is willing to administer the kick, operating from the Critical Parent ego state (note the non-verbal behaviour). The usual refrain of the Kick Me player is 'Why does this always happen to me?' (see the Victim role, p. 61).

Schlemiel

This is a game similar to that of Kick Me. The Schlemiel player is clumsy, disorganised, sloppy, and messy. If we learn behaviour when we are young, perhaps that is how the Schlemiel got strokes as a child. While the Kick Me player is seeking punishment, however, the Schlemiel player is seeking forgiveness, and thus will need to be a good deal more cute and endearing than the Kick Me player.

Now I've Got You, you Son of a Bitch

Social level

Customer — Adult: Look, you've overcharged me.

Provider — Adult: Now that you draw it to my attention, I guess I have.

Psychological level

Customer — Critical Parent: I've been watching you, hoping you'd make a slip.

Adapted Child: You've caught me this time.

Customer — Critical Parent: Yes, and I'm going to let you feel the full force of my fury.

Provider: Why does this always happen to me?

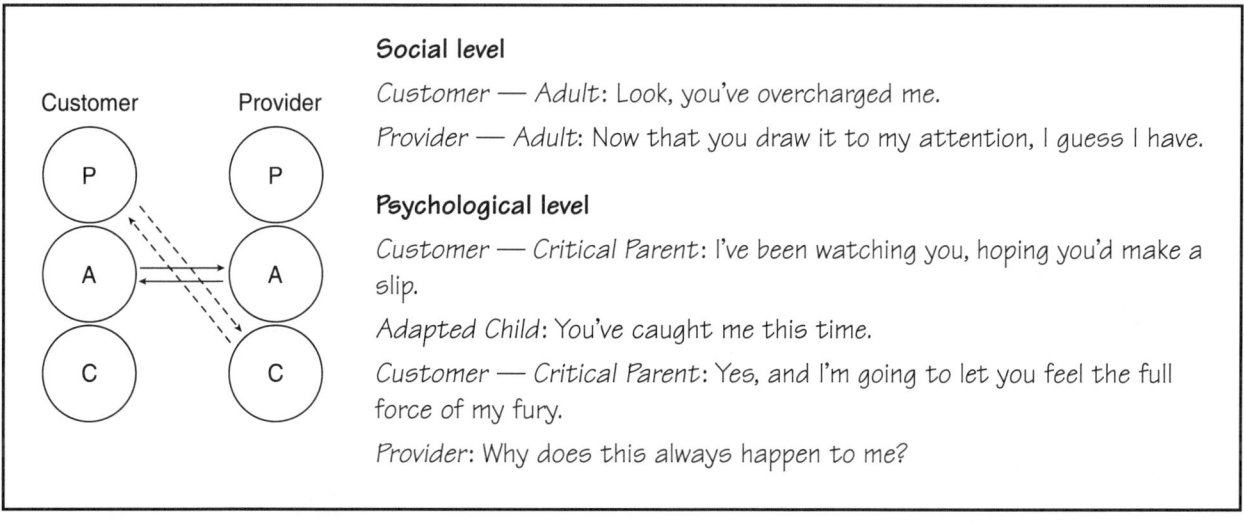

Figure 4.8: 'Now I've Got You, you Son of a Bitch' model

This game (less crudely known as Now I've Got You) is a set-up game. The NIGYSOB player waits for others to make mistakes, then swoops from the Critical Parent ego state. Constructive criticism isn't for this player — it's destruction all the way. Constructive criticism might help other people change, and the NIGYSOB player doesn't want change or real problem-solving. The player keeps other people off-balance, insecure and frightened, thus reconfirming his or her own reputation and competence. This reconfirmation makes him or her more secure — a very important thing, as the NIGYSOB player is usually motivated by deep insecurity (I've got to get them before they get me). NIGYSOB is complementary to games like Kick Me and Schlemiel.[96]

Blemish

Blemish has much in common with NIGYSOB, WDY–YB and also GYWP. As with these games, '... it is played from the depressive Child position "I am no good", which is protectively transformed into the Parental position "They are no good". The player's transactional problem, then, is to prove the latter thesis'.[97]

In brief, the Blemish player seeks out a blemish or weakness in a person or good or service, and is not happy until such a fault is found. In fact, perfection would make the Blemish player unhappy. Thus a good way of detecting whether a game is being played is to confront the suspected player with some type of perfection: if the person is genuinely pleased and satisfied, then no game is present; if the person only sullenly accepts the perfection, or even continues to try and find some imperfection, then a game is being played. Providers should understand that if they are transacting with a customer who is playing Blemish, then the conversation is not a rational, problem-solving one. The best counter-strategy is to try and hook the Adult of the player — for example by placing the onus on her or him to specify what standards he or she is seeking and why.

Harried

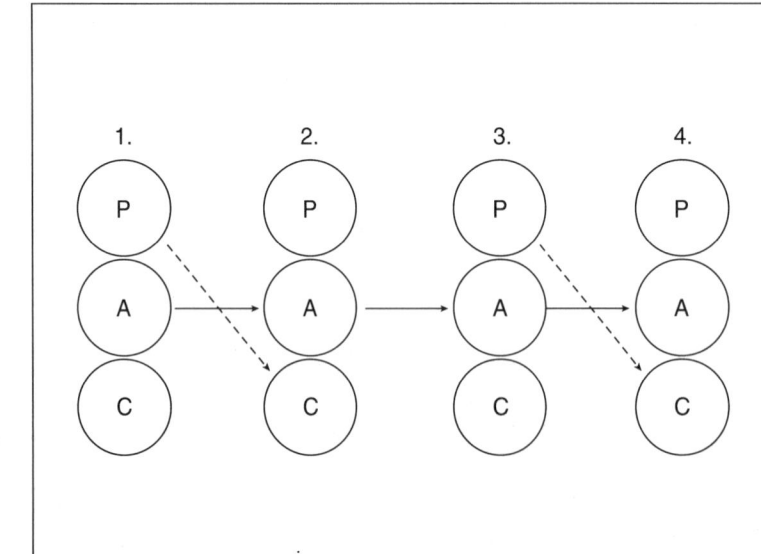

1. Provider: I'm just ringing to tell you that my team and I have been working all night on that proposal. As soon as it's finished, we'll courier it over. I'll do the presentation myself.

2. Customer: There's no panic. The deadline's been extended. Relax.

3. Provider: Oh no. We'll keep going. Someone's got to set an example by submitting on the date as per the guidelines.

4. Wow, you're really dedicated, aren't you?

Figure 4.9: 'Harried' model

The Harried player wants the world to know that he/she is indispensable. A really serious Harried player in figure 4.9 would have sent the rest of the team home just to ensure that the job got done properly. Harried players tend to take on too much — work, social obligations, family commitments — and eventually crash. They are among the great non-delegators, and seekers of role-overload. The player plays from the Parent position, apparently nurturing but actually critical. There may, however, be more than a whiff of the Adapted Child about the behaviour, as the Child tries to live up to remembered or imagined injunctions or messages from parents about striving for perfection, being strong, and so on.

Debtor

Social level

Provider: Have you noticed this bill is overdue?

Customer: Is it really? Gosh.

Psychological level

Provider: Try and get away with it.

Customer: Try and collect.

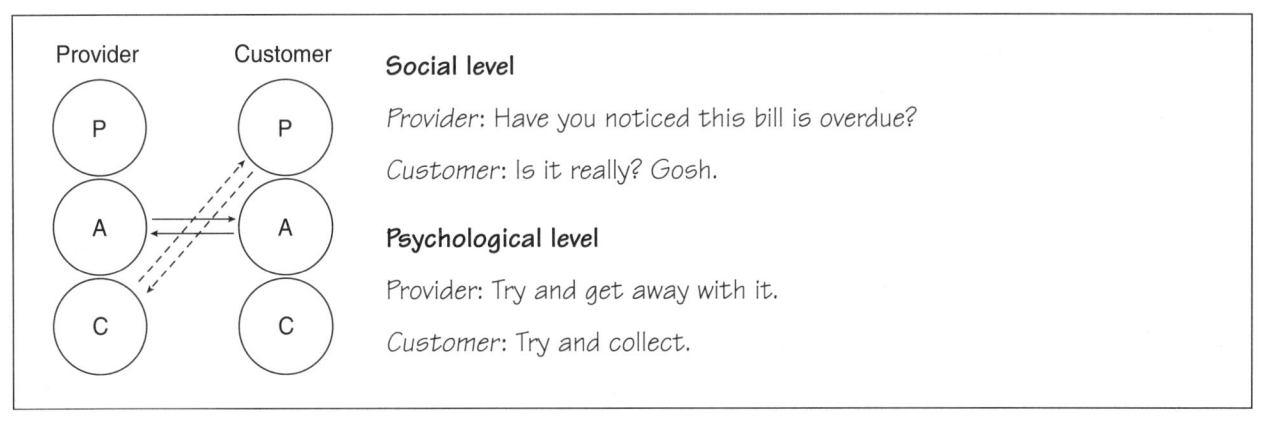

Figure 4.10: 'Debtor' model

We live in a consumer society, and there is always marketing pressure upon people to consume more. People who play Debtor, however, are spoiling for a fight. If they do not pay their bills, and their creditors give up after several attempts to obtain payment, then the Debtor player wins. If a creditor insists on payment, then the Debtor player will aggressively criticise the creditor, blaming them in effect for his or her inability to function as an Adult person. The player will try and derive much sympathy from friends, using words such as 'look what they're doing to us now' (see Pastimes, p. 60). Should the Debtor encounter a creditor playing the aggressive game of Creditor (Try and Get Away with It), then both sides will have an enjoyable time, switching into related Persecutor games like NIGYSOB and Victim games like Kick Me. (For a more adult way of settling debts, see p. 65).

Courtroom

Most games are two-handed affairs, but some involve three or more people. Courtroom is a three-hander. Children will try and get a parent to arbitrate in a dispute (She did this to me! No, he did this to me first!). Stroking theory tells us that with children, such behaviour is often more about attention-seeking than the factual rights and wrongs of a dispute. Courtroom is played in many settings, two of which would be customers with shop assistants and quarrelling family members and police officers called in to settle the 'domestic'. The shop assistant or the police officer has to be careful not to do what is asked of him or her: namely, take sides. As soon as the third party takes the side of one person, then the other person will attack the third party. The best solution is simply to stay in Adult mode, using active listening techniques (see p. 103), but downplaying the use of rational questioning.[98]

Sweetheart

Sweetheart occurs when two people are quarrelling in public. This game also involves a third party. One player will insult or demean the other, but smiling all the while, finishing sentences with words such as: 'Isn't that right, *sweetheart?*' The verbal inflection will be heavily ironic, of course, thus alerting us again to the fact that we must always watch for consistencies or inconsistencies between verbal and non-verbal communication. The other player may burst into tears, become silently depressed, or retaliate with similar insults, perhaps finishing up with words such as 'Absolutely, *darling!*' Customers may play this tableau out before providers. There is less need to get involved here than there is in Courtroom, but if you have to get involved to some extent, stay in the Adult mode, and don't take sides.

Let's You And Him Fight

This is another three-hander, and is a set-up game, like NIGYSOB. The player creates conflict between two other people by various means, such as indicating romantic interest to both, thus turning them into duelling rivals, or else by telling A that B said this, and telling B that A said this, and then standing back and watching the fireworks. Customers may try this on providers: 'Oh, but the man over there said …'/'Look, the person I spoke to last week told me just the opposite …' If the customer is, or is pretending to be, extremely upset, there is the possibility that the emotion will become contagious, and one provider will seek another one in an aggressive and/or distressed manner. Stay calm, stay in Adult mode. The grievance may be a perfectly legitimate one rather than a LYAHF move, but the solution is the same: avoid a witch-hunt, don't blame (even if your colleague is wrong), coolly check the facts, apologise if necessary, take responsibility for the problem, and work actively by yourself or with others to produce a solution. LYAHF players, like Blemish players (and indeed all game players) aren't particularly interested in logical solutions, but once the solution has been produced, and you have communicated it with empathy, then it becomes their problem, not the provider's.

Cops and Robbers

The professional criminal operates in the Adult mode, never moving on a job until the fix is in, avoiding violence and fanfare, and willing to accept punishment the system metes out: 'If you do the crime, you do the time'. The amateur criminal, however, often operates from the Adapted Child ego state: he/she is spoiling for a fight, and when the job goes wrong — as of course it must — and the criminal is arrested, he/she can wallow in victim-talk such as 'Why does this always happen to me?' Less demonstrative criminals may also share this need to be punished. Shopstealers playing Shops and Robbers may try and seek out complementary players, such as store security police partial to a bit of NIGYSOB.

Rapo

Eric Berne originally described this game as a sexual teasing game played primarily by women against men.[99] This is sexist, and it is also too narrow an interpretation of an interesting pattern of human behaviour. Rapo basically consists of enticing someone into a situation, and then when that person has been enticed, and has made commitments (protestations of love, promises to spend), the player humiliates the other person by claiming that is not what he/she meant at all. The game has much in common with WDY-YB and GYWP ('See? All grown-ups are stupid after all!') and NIGYSOB.

Uproar Uproar is played by two people who are spoiling for a fight. In many games, people are spoiling for a fight, although with Uproar — at least as it is played in personal situations — the motivation is to ensure that intimacy, sexual or otherwise, does not occur (see time structuring below). Not for such people the peace slogan of the 1960s, 'Make love, not war' — they would rather do the opposite. In other words, it's easier to argue than it is to communicate and solve problems (although the argument may be seen to be a solution of sorts if it deflects attention away from other matters). Uproar also occurs in a variety of professional settings where people are spoiling for a fight. At the social level, a civilised difference of opinion is taking place, but at the psychological level, a game is being played — it's a case of let's you and *me* fight.

Happy To Help Most games, obviously, are nasty. Are there any good games? If we mean 'good' in the sense of 'lacking an ulterior motive', then the answer is no. If we mean 'good' in the sense that something positive is produced, then the answer is yes — but there's not many of them. HTH is one such game. In it, the player helps people — with money, encouragement, connections — whatever. The motivation is often that of guilt — the player feels guilty for past misdemeanours, real or imaginary, and is trying to atone for or expiate that guilt by doing good works.

TIME-STRUCTURING: FILLING IN TIME BETWEEN BIRTH AND DEATH

If games are so stupid and destructive, why then do they take up so much human energy? TA practitioners argue that games are only one way in which we structure our lives — filling in the time between birth and death — and that there are (at least) five others. The six approaches to time-structuring are withdrawal, rituals, pastimes, activities, games and intimacy. The proportions of time we allocate to each of these time-structuring approaches is consciously or unconsciously chosen by ourselves.

Withdrawal Withdrawal simply means choosing not to receive any strokes from others. We do this by tuning out of a conversation, or conflict, or meeting, or just the hubbub of life itself, and dwelling within our own thoughts and feelings.

Rituals Rituals are stereotyped complementary transactions that are comfortable and reassuring. These can encompass the experience of going to church, to that of receiving an award in public, to the simple verbal exchanges between friends, relatives and colleagues: 'Good morning.' 'Hi, how are you?'

Pastimes Pastimes are also complementary transactions that are more informal and more extensive than rituals — for example the 12-year-old and 13-year-old discussing the woes of the world (p. 47) playing the pastime of Ain't It Awful. This is low-level whingeing/griping/moaning/gossiping-type communication, which is not at all oriented towards problem-solving. Indeed, if an individual suggested some action as being an appropriate response to whining or gossip, she or he would soon find out (via subtle and not-so-subtle rejection signals) that that was not what the pastimers had in mind at all.

Activities Activities are real problem-solving in the real world. This is the world of work, hobbies, sports, duties and chores. These are usually healthy, but they can be unhealthy if, in fact, a game of Harried is being played by a workaholic — a person who cannot let go and have fun, or a person who is fleeing intimacy with others.

Games Well, we know about games now. They are an ongoing series of complementary ulterior transactions which can lead to a well-defined, predictable outcome — and they are not very nice (see p. 48). We play games primarily to avoid boredom, problem-solving and intimacy.

Intimacy Intimacy is primarily honest, and therefore game-free, communication. This can mean sexual intimacy, but it can also mean simply displaying affection by hugging, reassuring someone, sharing a laugh, working at peak performance within a team where all members respect and trust each other, or even having an emotional showdown which clears the air.

Samples of the ways in which these six forms of time-structuring can be experienced within the various ego states are shown in table 4.5.

Table 4.5: Time-structuring in various ego states

	Controlling Parent	Nurturing Parent	Adult	Free Child	Adapted Child
Withdrawal	Silent self-criticism	Silent self-comfort	Thinking about what cities are along the route from London to Singapore	Singing to oneself	Frightening fantasies
Ritual	Taking the children to church	Tucking the children into bed each night	Watching the evening news	Nightly tickle match or pillow fight before retiring	Obligatory yearly church service
Pastime	'Ain't it Awful' (about kids, inflation, etc.)	'Ain't it Wonderful'	Exchanging non-essential information 'Did you read where …')	Telling and knowing jokes for fun	'If It Weren't For Her …'
Activity	Supervising others' work; disciplining employees	Making beds, bathing the children	Figuring a budget	Playing football	Doing chores
Rackets/ Games	'Now I Got You, You Son of a Bitch', 'Blemish', 'Rapo', etc.	'I'm Only Trying To Help You', 'Happy To Help'	—	—	'Poor Me', 'Kick Me', 'Stupid', etc.
Intimacy	—	—	—	Sharing love, joy or pleasure	—

(Source: *TA: The Total Handbook of Transactional Analysis* by S. Woollams and M. Brown [1979:90]. Adapted with permission of the publisher Prentice-Hall, Eaglewood Cliffs, New Jersey.)

TA practitioners suggest that the more awareness we have about these different types of time-structuring, the more chance we will have of gaining a healthier mix of structure in our lives — for example, by playing fewer games and enjoying more intimacy.

To maximise that self-awareness, we need to briefly consider two other TA concepts: roles and life positions.

ROLES: THE DRAMA TRIANGLE

Much game-playing behaviour can be understood by the roles people play. Three roles are important here: those of Victim, Persecutor and Rescuer. These roles are linked and interchangeable, and form the three points of the drama triangle (figure 4.11).

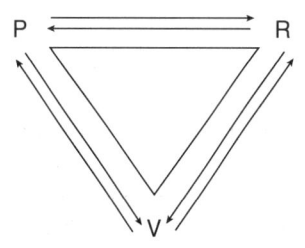

Figure 4.11: The drama triangle

People playing games tend to do so when they are adopting one of the roles of Rescuer, Victim or Persecutor. When we are in different roles, we play different games, as table 4.6 shows.

Table 4.6: Games according to drama triangle roles

Persecutor	Rescuer	Victim
Why don't you … yes, but Blemish Now I've got you, you son of a bitch Rapo Courtroom Gee, you're wonderful, professor Let's you and him fight	I'm only trying to help you Happy to help	Harried Kick me Schlemiel Debtor Cops and robbers

(Source: adapted from Eunson [1987:153].)

It is common for people to switch roles. Consider, for example, the manner in which three members of a family switch roles shown in table 4.7. When only two people are playing, as in table 4.8, the role-switching may not proceed as smoothly, or may be restricted to two roles only — for example, Persecutor and Victim. The interaction in table 4.8 is between a doctor and a patient, but just as easily could have been between a supplier and a customer, a supervisor and subordinate, a parent and a child, or virtually any other combination of two people you could imagine.

Table 4.7: A drama triangle

Person	Role	Role expression
Daughter	Persecutor of father	Why won't you let me go to the concert? Don't tell me you can't afford it again! God, it's so embarrassing, living with Mr Cheap!
Father	Victim	Gee, I'm sorry honey, but I *am* broke. I just don't seem to be able to give you things that your girlfriends get.
Mother	Rescues father, persecutes daughter	How dare you speak to your father like that! We've broken our backs for you! The only reason I'm working is to pay for *your* education, and for the house extensions so that *you* won't feel cramped! Get to your room, madam!
Daughter	In room, as Victim	It's just not fair! They send me to a posh school, but won't let me socialise with my friends. Everyone at school laughs at me 'cause I just stay at home! Why does this always happen to me?
Father	Rescues daughter	Now don't tell your mother, but here's $20. Let's call it an advance on your pocket money. It's only money, after all.
Father	Returning to mother as Persecutor	Mary, I think you came down on that girl too hard. She just wants to have fun, and she's only young once.
Mother	Victim	Well, I can't do anything right, can I? I was only trying to help you. I suppose I'm just a failure as a mother and a wife.
Daughter	Reappearing — rescues mother, persecutes father	Hey Dad, give it a rest — Mum's just a lot more tired than you are, that's all.

(Source: adapted from Jongeward and James [1978], Eunson [1987:152]. Reproduced with permission.)

Table 4.8: Another drama triangle

Person	Role	Role expression
Doctor	Rescuer	How did the new therapy work out?
Patient	Victim, then switches to Persecutor	(*Slumped posture, shakes head*) It's no good … it's just like the rest … I'm never going to get betterr … (*tilts head, narrows eyes*) Why can't you cure me? I'm sure other doctors would give me a better deal than this … (*looks down*) I don't know why I stay …
Doctor	Victim, then low-key Persecutor	Sorry … I was only trying to help … (*strokes brow, shakes head*) … maybe I can't help you … maybe I can't help anyone … maybe I should get out of this game … I will say this for my other patients, though — at least *they're* not ungrateful for what I try to do for them …
Patient	Rescuer, then Victim	(*Embarrassed*) Sorry … I didn't mean what I said … your advice has been OK, really … it's been quite good, actually … it's me who's mucked things up … I'm amazed you even waste your time on a loser like me …
Doctor	Rescuer	Don't be like that — you've got a lot to offer the world. Now there's a new treatment I'd like you to try …

ACTIVITY

THE DRAMA TRIANGLE

Create a script for a drama triangle using a copy of this grid. Think of any situation — for example, a provider/customer one.

Person	Role	Role expression

LIFE POSITIONS

Transactional analysis practitioners believe that our basic life positions determine how we structure our time and play roles. Such life positions, they argue, are determined quite early in life — in most cases, in the first three years of life.

The life positions indicate how we feel about ourselves and others (figure 4.12). If we have had various bad experiences in our early life, then we may learn to *discount*, or exaggerate or devalue, the worth of ourselves or others (see p. 65).

If we are self-confident and secure, and get along with others quite well, our life position is 'I'm OK/You're OK'. This is the healthiest position of all, indicating a positive, problem-solving and loving attitude.

If we feel that everyone else in our world is smarter/bigger/better/faster than we are, then the 'I'm Not OK/You're OK' position is adopted. People operating from this position tend to play Victim games like Schlemiel and Kick Me.

If we feel that we are smarter/bigger/better/faster than everyone else, then the 'I'm OK/You're Not OK' position is adopted. People operating from this position tend to play Rescuer and Persecutor games, although they may also play Victim games such as Harried.

If we dislike ourselves, and also dislike everyone else, then the 'I'm Not OK/You're Not OK' position is adopted. This is the futility position, and might well lead to serious behavioural problems.

I'm Not OK/You're OK	I'm OK/You're OK
I'm Not OK/You're Not OK	I'm OK/You're Not OK

Figure 4.12: Life positions

TA: THE PRACTICAL PAYOFFS FOR COMMUNICATING WITH CUSTOMERS

What practical strategies for communicating with customers can we derive from transactional analysis? The key strategies are:
- Give and accept positive strokes rather than negative strokes.
- Work with your Natural Child, Adult and Nurturing Parent; give up or minimise using your Adapted Child and Critical Parent.
- Stop playing games. Don't be hooked by others into playing the complementary hand. Give an unexpected response. Operate primarily from your Adult, and try and hook the Adult of the game player.
- Invest more time in intimacy, activities and fun.
- Stop playing Rescuer — helping those who don't need help.
- Stop playing Persecutor — criticising those who don't need it.
- Stop playing Victim — acting helpless or dependent when you are quite capable of standing on your own two feet.
- Don't put yourself down — accept that you are OK.
- Don't put others down — accept that they are OK.

TALKING POINTS ✳ **USING TA TO ENSURE THE CUSTOMER PAYS**

Transactional analysis can be useful in communicating with customers who don't want to pay their bills (table 4.9). This grid shows how, when customers are contacted via the telephone, they may resist requests for payment by various types of discounting (see p. 64). Such discounting can usually be met by operating from the Adult ego state, and trying to hook the Adult ego state of the customer.

Table 4.9: Discounting techniques used by customers

Level of discount	Objective	Sample of customer statements	Sample of collector responses
Denies the problem	• To realise there is a problem. • To realise responsibility. • To resolve the delinquency. • To realise time is a factor. • To move to a lower level of discount.	• It's not my bill. • Getting divorced/ separated. • Insurance will pay. • Wrong amount. • I have no bill. • Will pay only direct to store. • They haven't billed me. • Tax refund expected. • Credit card stolen. • Can't squeeze blood out of a turnip. • How did you get my number? • Don't harass me. • I'm black. • Go to hell.	• Our records show your payment history to be . . . • The contract you signed for payment is . . . • You are responsible for your obligations . . . • Bringing your records up-to-date, the amount is . . . • Since time is a factor and it is to your advantage to . . . • We intend to take action. • You can bring your account current by . . . • I prefer to talk about your account. • You're obviously upset.
Denies the significance of the problem	• To realise the significance. • To realise the consequences. • To take some goal-directed action.	• I have more important matters. • What if I don't pay? • I may go through bankruptcy. • I need more time. • I have paid regularly. • Why can't I make payments? • Sue me. • As long as I pay something. • I'll pay when I feel like it. • Don't talk to me as if I were a deadbeat.	• By not bringing your account current you are . . . • When you stop to think about it, the consequences are . . . • I want you to think about the drastic measures you're taking. • Time is important to us and you. Paying regularly has not brought your account current. • The agreement is to pay 'x' $ each billing cycle. • We want you to bring your account current, which is 'x' $. • What do you intend to do? • This call is to arrive at an acceptable solution.

(*Continued*)

Level of discount	Objective	Sample of customer statements	Sample of collector responses
Denies the solvability of the problem	• To realise the problem can be solved. • To understand that it must be solved by the person. • To take positive goal-directed action. • To understand the organisation will support reasonable action.	• I can't pay. • I'm out of work. • I have no cash. • I'm on welfare. • I have many bills. • I want a settlement. • I'll do the best I can.	• If you had the money, would you bring your account current? • Are you looking for work now? • What is your best guess about when you will be working again? • How are you managing to get along now? • So you do have some means of getting by. • Is there some way we can work out bringing your account current? • 'x'$ by ... will do it. • With a cheque for 'x' $, I can then adjust a payment schedule to fit your means.
Denies own/other's capacity to solve the problem	• Arrive at an understanding that the person can do something. • Reach an awareness that resources are available. • Realise that the person can think the problem through.	• I want to think it over. • I am disabled. • Why do you have my account?	• It's important that you act now since your account is 'x' days delinquent. • We need you to bring your account current by ... • The amount you have paid did not bring your account current. • You acted in good faith for 'x' payments, and I'm sure we can work out an agreement. • I have your account because you are 'x' days delinquent.
No denials. Problem-solving	• Get commitment to act. • Set an achievable goal by the person. • Outline immediate next steps. • Jointly define payment agreement. • Reach agreement on an on-going contract.	• I will pay by ... • Cheque going out ... • I already paid.	• Can you get a payment in by ... • When can I expect your cheque to bring your account current? • What are you able to pay now? • What can you pay next month? • Will you call me if your situation changes?

Source: Donatelli [1976]. Reproduced with permission from the *Transactional Analysis Journal*, Vol. 6, No. 2, 1986:192–94, 'TA and collection of delinquent accounts'. © International Transactional Analysis Association. All rights reserved.).

TA: THE OVERVIEW

We've covered a lot of ground in looking at transactional analysis — in fact, we have spent more time on this model of behaviour than we will spend on the various other models of communication which you will find in other chapters in *Communicating with Customers*.[100]

What do you think of TA? Some people find it to be a very powerful and effective model of communication. It has been used extensively in organisations, most notably in customer relations training.[101] Others find it slick, gimmicky and shallow.[102] Still others think that it had some relevance some years ago, but now is rather passé or out of fashion. Even if you are unenthusiastic about this model, it's likely that you gained at least some insights into human communication from it. If you think TA is OK, then that's fine — you now have a potent tool to help you in the task of communicating with customers.

ACTIVITIES

1. Select a chapter from a novel, or a scene from a play, film or television program. Analyse the communication patterns depicted in terms of complementary, crossed or ulterior transactions. Use diagrams to complete this analysis.
2. Write a role-play in which a customer and a provider communicate primarily via ulterior transactions. Pay particular emphasis to the idea of contradictory verbal and non-verbal communication. Ensure that there are at least seven ulterior transactions, and create diagrams of such transactions. Have two people perform the role-play. If possible, videotape it, and play it back, analysing the verbal and non-verbal communication.
3. Brainstorm by yourself or with others and come up with at least two TA games not described here. Analyse the games via diagram analysis.
4. Consider the following letter. Try and ascertain what ego state the writer was operating from, and re-write the letter twice, once each from two other ego states.

CLONE POWER

Site 39, Rintrah Industrial Park, Claymore 23121 Freedonia

Telephone (61.5) 233.4352 • Facsimile (61.5) 233.4378

18 May, 1995
Mr Tom Stearns,
44 Ash Street,
East Coker 23421

Dear Mr Stearns:

Clone Power 786/KL Model

Thank you for your fax of 16 May.

I will not accept responsibility for any operating difficulties you are having with this computer. The fault lies in the way you have installed it, and are operating (or are attempting to operate it).

(Continued)

You should look at your manual, where on p. 12 it shows quite clearly that the alternative yellow power cord B3/201 should be used where electrical current may not always be reliable. You will find the B3/301 in the Peripheral Modules Kit, wrapped in yellow plastic.

Any software problems you are having may relate to the pre-installed operating system, or to software you might have bought. Instructions for the operating system are in the blue manual, which customers must read upon installing our systems. If you have installed faulty software, then we cannot be held responsible for that. Failure to observe common-sense procedures by customers may void any guarantees Clone Power offers.

Please investigate these basic procedures before contacting our offices again.

Thank you for being a Clone Power Customer,

Anthony Venger

Anthony Venger.

TALKING POINTS

COMMUNICATING WITH CUSTOMERS: A SURVIVAL KIT

QUALITY SERVICE TECHNIQUES

Four methods for defusing a difficult situation

- SMILE: give the customer a warm, sincere hello with a smile.
- ANTICIPATE: the customer's complaint and head it off with a sincere, concerned comment (take the offensive with kindness).
- APOLOGISE AND ASSUME RESPONSIBILITY: take the blame for the customer's situation and empathise with them for their problem on behalf of your organisation.
- ACTION: solve the problems promptly.

Six keys to cooling down an irate customer

- LISTEN: carefully and with interest.
- EMPATHISE: put yourself in the customer's place. Use warm fuzzies that are: genuine, specific, timely, and sincere.
- ASK QUESTIONS: in a mature, non-threatening way, that requires the customer to think about his/her answers.
- REPEAT: back to the customer your understanding of their problem, then suggest one or more alternatives to answer their concerns.
- APOLOGISE: without blaming.
- SOLVE the problem: identify solutions to satisfy the customer's needs or find someone who can.

COMMUNICATION TECHNIQUES

Positive strokes

Communicating in a positive manner through warm fuzzies that are:
- Genuine (real)
- Specific (definite, precise)
- Timely (give immediate feedback)
- Sincere (without deceit or pretence).

Negative strokes

Communicating in a negative manner through cold pricklies (any negative word or action).

Additional categories of negative strokes are:
- Zero (absence of any communication technique)
- Crooked (positive communication followed by a negative remark)
- Plastic (comments given as a ritual)
- Hostile (aggressive, threatening communication style).

Quality service

Providing excellence in customer service through six methods of human interaction:
- Feeling good about yourself
- Practising habits of courtesy
- Speaking (verbal and non-verbal communication)
- Listening (anticipating, reading between the lines, asking questions, getting involved, caring about your customers and their needs)
- Performing (providing quality work that is prompt and accurate)
- Learning (job growth through knowing more about your customer, company and products).

(Source: Tschohl and Franzmeier [1991]. Reproduced with permission of the Service Quality Institute and John Tschohl.)

5

ASSERTIVELY COMMUNICATING WITH CUSTOMERS

In *Communicating with Customers*, we consider a number of models of communication. Irrespective of the eternal and universal validity of these models, their immediate practical value is that they let us see — in specific, analytical ways — a basic truth: different people behave in different ways. If we can come to understand this truth, we can develop practical and effective ways of responding to and influencing the behaviour of people on both sides of the service encounter.

A model of communication that has proven to have considerable value in communicating with customers is that of assertiveness or assertion. Practitioners of assertiveness training, or AT*, suggest that most human behaviour can be categorised into four basic patterns or styles — aggression, passivity, manipulativeness and assertion. We will shortly examine the verbal and non-verbal behaviour of these four styles.

The first three styles, or types, of communication are fairly self-evident, but what specifically do we mean by assertion, or assertiveness? By the end of this chapter you should have a comprehensive view of what assertiveness means, but a useful interim definition would be **getting what you want from others without infringing upon others' rights**.

ASSESSING YOUR ASSERTIVENESS

Do you think that you are an assertive person? Do you usually get what you want from others, without infringing on their rights? A useful way of beginning to approach the question of what we mean by assertive or unassertive behaviour is to consider table 5.1 (p. 71). Horizontally, we see various people you might interact with in your personal and professional life. Vertically, we see various assertive behaviours or communication strategies. A discussion of these behaviours follows (pp. 72–74).

By completing this table, you will come up with a reasonably accurate picture of your assertive or non-assertive behaviour. Complete the table by asking yourself the following questions:

Do I (*row heading*) to/from/of/with (*column heading*) when it is appropriate?

For example:

Do I (*refuse requests*) from (*authority figures*, e.g., bosses, professors, doctors) when it is appropriate?

---

* Not, of course, to be confused with transactional analysis, or TA — although you may see a number of similarities between the two approaches.

Scoring the assertiveness self-assessment table

Complete the table by using these numerical ratings:

Usually   3
Sometimes   2
Rarely   1

After completing the table*, total your scores and rate yourself thus:

180-240: Quite assertive
120-179: Fairly assertive
 60-119: Fairly unassertive
  0-59: Not very assertive

Table 5.1: Assertiveness matrix

Behaviours	Friends of the same sex	Friends of the opposite sex	Intimate relatives, e.g., spouse, boyfriend, girlfriend	Parents-in-law, and other family members	Children	Authority figures, e.g., bosses, professors, doctors	Business contacts, e.g., salespersons, waiters	Co-workers, colleagues, and sub-ordinates	TOTAL SCORE
Give compliments									
Receive compliments									
Make requests, e.g., ask for favours, help									
Express liking, love, and affection									
Initiate and maintain conversation									
Stand up for your legitimate rights									
Refuse requests									
Express personal opinions, including disagreement									
Express justified annoyance and displeasure									
Express justified anger									
								GRAND TOTAL SCORE	

(Source: adapted with permission from Galassi and Galassi [1977: 9].)

---

* Galassi and Galassi (1977) suggest that it is usually inappropriate to express liking, love and affection to authority figures and business contacts. If you agree, simply leave those particular cells blank or colour them in. Make the appropriate adjustments in scores as well: reduce the range figures by 3 or 6, e.g., if you feel that it is inappropriate to express such feelings to both authority figures and business contacts, then 'quite assertive' behaviour would fall in the range 174-234, and so on.

ASSERTIVE AND NON-ASSERTIVE BEHAVIOURS

Giving and receiving compliments

What do compliments have to do with assertive behaviour? Assertiveness is concerned with the full range of human communication, not just those parts concerned with conflict. Sometimes, some people have difficulty expressing any type of feeling, positive or negative; at other times, some people are more comfortable with expressing positive feelings, but not negative ones; while at still other times, some people are capable of expressing negative feelings, but not positive ones. You're a complete person, so you should be able to give expression to a complete range of feelings.

Many people are uncomfortable giving compliments to others, as they fear that the person they are complimenting may imagine that manipulation and/or dishonesty lie behind the compliment. This fear, while understandable, is unfortunate, and leads to impoverished human communication. To use transactional-analysis terminology, such fears mean that there will be a plentiful lack of positive strokes about, and that can't be a good thing.

Similarly, when others pay us compliments, we either fear a manipulative intent behind such a compliment, or else we go through a false modesty charade — 'it was nothing' 'I was lucky, that's all'. We also fear that if we acknowledge the compliment, others will think that we are vain and egotistical.

It is often the case that people who pay (non-manipulative) compliments to others do so because they feel sufficiently secure and non-threatened in their personal and professional lives — they operate from a position of strength, in other words — and thus know that their words will not be misconstrued as sycophancy or crawling. The same people feel sufficiently unthreatened to receive compliments graciously, knowing that their acceptance is not code for comically pompous self-regard. Secure and competent people are often quietly self-confident and generous people, self-confidence being another word for assertiveness. If you can pay and receive compliments without an emotional sideshow of dissembling, therefore, you're well on the way to being assertive.

Making requests — asking for favours, help

Often we do not make direct requests of others because we fear that such requests will be seen as signs of weakness. If we do make requests, we may take indirect means, such as:
- beating around the bush, and then eventually requesting, using a series of qualifying phrases ('if you don't mind', 'if it's not too much trouble', 'I would be most awfully appreciative if . . .') (passive style)
- blustering on, making statements that sound more like threats than requests ('See here, do you think you could get around to . . .') (aggressive style)
- beating around the bush, then slyly slipping in what we really want ('Oh by the way . . .' 'Oh, just one more trifling thing . . .') (manipulative style).

These approaches are not only verging on dishonesty, but they also waste a lot of time. Employing such indirect approaches, or simply not even employing direct approaches, means that we simply are not as effective as we could be: making requests is simply the first step in getting what you want, and in an increasingly interdependent world, everyone needs something from others. Providers know all too well that customers often have difficulty with this simple communication strategy. Life's too short, otherwise: ask for what you want if you really want it.

Expressing liking, love, affection

We now move into more intense levels of feeling, and perhaps even greater degrees of avoidance and being threatened. If you have these feelings — liking, love, affection — and you've got the chance to express them, then express them. Without becoming unduly morbid, it's useful here to consider death, in the sense that it is a extreme defining point of human experience. When someone — a friend, relative, lover or colleague — dies (particularly in unexpected circumstances), it is quite common to hear people say such things as: 'I didn't even get a chance to tell her I loved her'. 'I never got the chance to tell him how much I respected and liked him.'

Hindsight is 20–20. If you can think of no other reason for expressing liking, love or affection, then use the morbid argument — I'd better do it before it's too late. There are other reasons, of course, not the least of which is the fact that expressing such feelings is probably the strongest positive stroke you can give others — and who knows, if you model a particular behaviour or strategy, others might reciprocate. Much assertive behaviour is about taking risks in the messy, semi-uncontrollable realm of emotion, and this is the most intense area of (positive) feeling we are considering — no risk, no reward.

Initiating and maintaining conversation

You've either got the 'gift of the gab', or you haven't, right? Wrong. Most human behaviour appears to be learnt rather than genetically transmitted from generation to generation, and that which can be learnt can be improved upon. Social skills, such as initiating and maintaining conversations, comprise an important part of assertiveness: if we can control or at least influence the flow of words at relatively low levels of emotional intensity, then we stand a better chance of using words (means) to achieve our objectives (ends) at higher levels of emotional intensity. We will soon see (p. 79) how specific verbal skills such as free information give the assertive person the tools to transform the most unpromising interactions into problem-solving dialogues.

Standing up for your legitimate rights

We will later consider (p. 82) the various rights of the provider and customer. For now, it is enough to say that your rights are under threat or are destroyed when your sense of fairness is threatened or ignored. Knowing that someone else does not respect your rights is one thing; doing something about that person's behaviour is quite another. We are not quite talking about 'better to die on your feet than live on your knees', but we are talking about similar ways of thinking and acting: if you have to fight, then it's better that the other side fights fair, and perhaps you have to show them what that means.

Refusing requests

'No' is such a little word, yet most of us have a lot of difficulty in saying it. When others make unreasonable requests of us, it should be simple to use this little word, but often it isn't. Smith (1975) suggests that we are often manipulated into granting requests because of self-talk (see p. 78), which is a type of internal dialogue that plays within our minds. Manipulative requests can be anything from a boss asking you to work overtime when you don't want to, to someone trying to bluff or ingratiate you into a sexual encounter. The usual self-talk in such situations is 'When I say "no" I feel guilty, but if I say "yes", I'll hate myself'. To be able to say 'no' in a firm, polite, but effective manner is an extraordinarily helpful skill, which seems to desert us at many times. We usually respond in counter-productive ways — for example:

- 'No! How many times have I told you . . .' 'How dare you . . .' (aggressive)
- 'Oh all right, if that's what you want . . .' (passive)
- 'Look, I'd love to help you out, but I've made arrangements to sit with my sick elephant tonight . . .' (manipulative)

Expressing personal opinions, including disagreement

There is a difference between having opinions and being opinionated, but many of us have difficulty in seeing that difference. It has to be possible for you to speak out, however, to speak your mind — otherwise others will think your silence means consent. As with expressing liking, love and affection, use reverse hindsight to motivate you. Don't be the person who says: 'What I should have said was . . .' 'I was going to say that . . .'.

Expressing justified annoyance, displeasure and anger

We are now in the territory of more intense negative feelings; as with positive feelings, it is vital that we feel comfortable, or at least not too uncomfortable, in expressing such feelings. If we bottle up, or suppress, strong feelings, then our ill-feelings towards others may turn inward — dislike and hate of others may become self-dislike, self-hate. With such bottled-up feelings, particularly negative ones, there is a real danger that when we finally can't stand it any more and do blurt out our feelings, we might do so in an out-of-control manner. At the very least, you will not achieve your objective; at the most, you may say and do things you will regret. To be in control of a situation, you have to be in control of yourself.

FOUR STYLES OF BEHAVIOUR

We should now have a clearer idea of what assertive and non-assertive behaviour is. It's useful to classify behaviour into four types — aggressive, passive, manipulative and assertive. We have already touched upon a few aspects of the verbal behaviour of these four types. Let's now consider the full range of verbal and non-verbal behaviour of aggressive, passive, manipulative and assertive people (table 5.2).

Most of us have one dominant style of behaviour, but we sometimes use other styles, or mixtures of styles, in different circumstances. A person may be aggressive towards some people in one situation, passive towards others in a second situation, manipulative towards still others in a third situation, and assertive towards yet other people in a fourth situation. One of the most common transitions between styles is that of the transition from passivity to aggression. A person who is bullied in one set of circumstances may be a bully herself in another situation: the frustrations and humiliations endured in the first situation may fester and explode in the second situation, with no guarantee that the person will be in control of her emotions at that point.

Assertiveness is usually the most effective and honest style of behaviour and communication. The other three styles tend to be less effective because they tend to call forth reactions of anger, confusion, frustration and dislike from other people.

Table 5.2: Four styles of behaviour

	Aggressive	Passive	Manipulative	Assertive
General behaviour	• I win–you lose approach — often very insecure • abuses rights of others • wishes to dominate, humiliate • believes in own perfection, indispensability, superiority to others • doesn't trust, delegate • often over-reacts — then feels guilty • self-righteous, patronising • punitive, critical • sees others as objects to be used • makes enemies — creates own enemies (overt, covert opposition) • verbal and non-verbal behaviour usually congruent	• I lose–you win approach • ignores own rights • abdicates authority; gives decisions to others in order to avoid responsibility (then resents others making decisions) • helplessness — feels a victim of life's cruel game • broods, stews on others' aggression • complains, doesn't act • most stressed by confrontation • avoids conflict at all costs • has difficulty in accepting positive feedback • 'shyness' • verbal and non-verbal behaviour often not congruent	• I'll let you think you've won approach • undermines rights of others • wants power without responsibility • over-politicised — always tries to get own way through connections, name-dropping, mutual back-scratching, secret networks, hustling, wheeler-dealing • backstabbing, bitchiness, character assassination, rumour mongering, innuendoes • seduction, manipulation • flattering while undermining • sabotage — procrastination, habitual lateness, 'forgetting' • feigned innocence • feigned stupidity — slow learner • coyness, archness • intellectualisation — disclaims emotional involvement • sees others as objects to be used • verbal and non-verbal behaviour often not congruent	• I win–you win approach • respects rights of others, but not at expense of own rights • takes appropriate action towards getting what is wanted, without denying the rights of others • negotiates, evaluates • trusts, delegates • deals with power and politics openly • proactive — is solution-oriented • consistent • acknowledges and respects others' feelings, including fear, anger • takes risks with expressing feelings — models behaviour for others • claims right to make mistakes • claims right to be non-assertive • feels good about self now and later • non-verbal and verbal behaviour congruent

(*Continued*)

	Aggressive	Passive	Manipulative	Assertive
Verbal cues	• talks loud, fast • abuse, obscenities • interrupts others, completes sentences for them • tsk, tsk, tsk • lot of 'I' statements • 'You must/should/ought …' • 'You always/never …' • explains badly: either impatiently, aggressively ('surely you've got it now!') or condescendingly, patronisingly, as if speaking to a child or intellectually handicapped person (learner's inevitable failure confirms her belief that 'kindness' doesn't work) • opinions expressed as facts: requests expressed as instructions or threats	• stumbles over words — 'um … ah…' • uses continuers — 'sort of … like … you know … and that … and them …' • mumbles — needs to repeat words • overpolite • 'Why does this always happen to me?' • few 'I' statements • avoids saying 'no' • breathy, child-like voice (you mustn't attack me, I'm too weak) • 'I should have …' • 'If only …' • 'This is probably stupid, but …' • upwardly inflects often (seeking approval) • monotone (resignation, depression) • whingeing, whining • silence • trails off sentences — expects to be interrupted • sighs	• sarcasm • undue emphasis on words — 'Who, *me*? Oh *no! Never!*' • hostile kidding • silent treatment • 'I'll wrap him/her around my little finger …'	• 'I choose to …' • 'Let's look at what alternatives we have …' • when, where, who, what, how • no 'shoulds', 'oughts' • 'Tell me something good' — accentuates the positive • 'Tell me the good news and the bad news' • says no when it can't be done — doesn't feel guilty • distinction drawn between fact and opinion • constructive criticism, without blame or assumptions • appropriately firm, warm tone • expressive, emphasising key words
Eyes	• glaring — tries to stare down • rolls eyes in disgust • looks down nose • breaks eye contact to interrupt, freeze out	• evasive eye contact; often downcast • rapid blinking • tears	• rolling eyes • over-elaborate winking • raised eyebrows — wide-eyed puzzlement, wounded innocence when accused • not establishing eye contact when trying to get something from someone • all-too-deliberate eye contact (linked with touching at key points in conversation) • tears	• direct — not staring

	Aggressive	Passive	Manipulative	Assertive
Facial expression	• eyebrows raised in mock amazement, disbelief • frown • bared teeth • clenched teeth • jutting jaw • flared nostrils	• eyebrows raised — questioning, pleading • weak smile; smiling at everyone, even when angry — propitiation • blank expression — mask of pain • super-mobile expression (cf children, slaves, social inferiors) • nods continually • sullen sulk • rapid biting, wetting of lips • rapid swallowing, blushing	• pursing of lips • fawning expression • facetious expression • conspiratorial expression	• attentive • congruent with what is being expressed
Posture	• rigid • relaxed while others are tense • walks fast • arms crossed — unapproachable • invades others' personal space	• slumped over — fetal slouch, infantile rocking • rigid	• huddling conspiratorially • body oriented away from 'uninteresting', 'uninfluential' people — even when speaking to them	• relaxed • open
Gestures	• hands on hips • clenched fist • pounds fist into palm • points finger • shakes head as if other person isn't to be believed • snorts, exhales loudly and martyr-like • whistles in mock wonder • impatient tapping of feet, drumming of fingers • steepling • hands behind head • feet on desk	• wrings hands • covers mouth with hands — oral insecurity • self-touching • toes clenched, fingers clenched • feet turned inward • arms crossed — protective • shuffles feet • fidgets with object • sighs often	• melodramatically sighing with exasperation • yawning • drumming fingers, tapping toes — impatience • hand in front of mouth when talking • steepling • over-deliberate touching of others when trying to obtain something	• open hand movements (showing honesty; inviting others to speak) • establishes appropriate body contact with others

(Source: adapted from Alberti and Emmons [1978]; Beck and Beck [1989]; Bloom, Coburn and Pearlman [1975]; Burley-Allen [1983]; Gillen [1990]; Kelley [1979]; McNeilage and Adams [1982]; Phelps and Austin [1988].)

SELF-TALK

The ways in which we think have a strong bearing on the ways in which we behave. Our thoughts can be described as *self-talk*, or the conversation we have with ourselves. Just as conversation or dialogue can lead to particular conclusions, self-talk can predispose us to behave in particular ways. We are not always aware of our self-talk, however, and we are also not always aware that if a negative pattern of self-talk is allowed to develop unchecked, it can lead us to indulge in word-games and faulty logic, and thus behave in ineffective (and unpleasant) ways.[103]

There are specific patterns of self-talk for each of the four communication styles we have been considering. Some examples of such patterns are given in table 5.3.

Table 5.3: Patterns of self-talk

	Customer	**Provider**
Aggressive	I'm as mad as hell … what a dump this place is … and where's the staff? You can never find one when you want one … here's one of the little punks … lady, I'm about to wreck your day! … hah! Look at her cringe … she didn't like that! Well, there's more where that came from!	Oh God, here comes another one … I'm sick of having to pander to dimwits like these! I wonder what this towering intellect wants … oh, it's a return is it? I wonder if you read the instructions, pal? If you can read, that is … let me read something to you, pal — the riot act! Cop this! … I love to watch 'em squirm …
Passive	Oooh … I hate places like this … I can't stand the noise … and the people … they all look much more confident than me … those dresses don't look too bad, I suppose … I suppose they won't have my size … oh, they do … this is a bit too glamorous for poor old me … oh no! It's a salesgirl! Oh, I never know what to say! … put it back and get out, quick! …	Hope no-one wants anything today … I feel a bit sick as it is … oh no! It's one of them! A customer! And it's a return! He's going to blame me, I know it! Oh god, where's Jane, or the supervisor? Why does this always happen to me? I've got to get another job, a less stressful one …
Manipulative	Aah, now this is more me … fits, too … hmmm … I do look good in this … Wonder if I can get a discount on this … maybe if I tell them Uncle Jack works here … where's my chalk? There … dear me, this garment seems to be marked … tsk, tsk, tsk … they'll have to mark it down now … oh, it's a salesman … salesboy, more like it … go away, salesboy, I'll only talk to your boss …	Oh no, another peasant … flash 'em the big smile … lady, if you think you'll get into that, your ego is bigger than your waist … chat 'em up, tell 'em it looks great … a sucker born every minute … hey, that's the mayor's wife over there … hope she remembers me … quick, where's Jane? Fob this one off onto her … my commission will be bigger with the big spenders …
Assertive	Right, let's get this straightened out. The guarantee on this is still valid, and I know that they'll acknowledge that … I feel fine, relaxed but ready for confrontation if it comes … I know what I'm talking about, and I know my rights … I can solve this quickly, and get what I want …	Hello, what's this? Someone with a return? Well, if it's faulty, it's no wonder he looks unhappy — he has a right to be … I know I can straighten this out quickly … he's angry, but I won't take it personally … Smile, deflect the anger and solve the problem … I know I can do this well … I feel fine, relaxed but ready for confrontation if it comes …

What pattern most closely resembles your self-talk? If your self-talk most closely resembles the assertive pattern, then that's great — you're probably a fairly effective person in your personal and professional life.

If your self-talk most closely resembles one of the other three patterns, then that's not so great — your effectiveness may be limited because other people react negatively to your aggressive, passive or manipulative behaviour.

To hear self-talk accurately, you have to learn to listen to yourself. Listen carefully to the way you think, and then ask yourself whether the flow or sequence of your self-talk will lead you to behave effectively or ineffectively. You have the ability to edit your self-talk as you go, to shift your behaviour away from an unassertive style to that of an assertive one.

BEING ASSERTIVE: SOME VERBAL SKILLS

We now have a fairly clear idea of what assertive and non-assertive behaviour is. Knowing about assertiveness and being assertive, however, may well be two different things. To be assertive, we need to have practical skills that will build our confidence and enable us to communicate more directly and effectively. Such skills do exist, and some of them are listed in table 5.4.

Table 5.4: Verbal skills in assertive behaviour

Verbal skill	Description	Rationale
Broken Record	The skill of calmly repeating what you want, over and over again, just like a broken record.	If you know that you can depend upon Broken Record, you do not have to psych yourself up for a dialogue with someone else, and you can also calmly sidestep irrelevant logic and baiting from the other person.
Fogging	The skill of calmly acknowledging that criticism of you may well be justified.	Your antagonist, instead of lashing out and hitting something solid, thus lashes out, but finds no resistance, as if he/she was trying to punch fog. Fogging helps separate personalities from problems.
Free Information	The skill of giving and recognising basic factual information.	This can help conversation move beyond the basic 'what do you think of the weather' type lines.
Self-disclosure	The skill of revealing positive and negative aspects of yourself to others.	This is the next step on from free information.
Negative Inquiry	The skill of actively seeking constructive criticism from others.	This will provide you with useful information and/or exhaust the manipulative ploys of others.
Positive Inquiry	The skill of actively seeking information from others about what solutions they see to their problems.	This will provide you with useful information and/or exhaust the manipulative ploys of others.
Workable Compromise	The skill of proposing a negotiated solution to a conflict.	Such a solution will satisfy both parties, without sacrificing the self-respect of either party.

(Source: adapted with permission from Eunson [1987].)

Let's now have a look at these skills in action. Consider the following example of a dialogue or an encounter between customers (C) and service providers (SP).

C: Hey! Come here!

SP: Can I help you, Sir?

C: This Super Widget you sold me is a disaster! Look at it!

SP: You may be right. Perhaps some Super Widgets are defective. We can fix the problem quickly. If you have proof of your purchase, I can fix your problem right away. (Fogging, Broken Record)

C: That's not what I've heard. You mongrels give everyone a hard time when in fact you're the ones whose fault it is!

SP: We have a strict no-questions-asked return policy, Sir. I understand how you feel — I get frustrated myself if something I spend my hard-earned cash on goes astray. If you can just give me some proof that you purchased it here, I can fix this immediately. (Free Information, Self-disclosure, Broken Record)

C: Well of course I bought it here! See, there's a pile of them over there. I was here two days ago! Are you calling me a liar?

SP: We simply require some proof of purchase so that we can clean up our paperwork with the manufacturer, Sir. Anything would be acceptable: a cash register receipt or a credit card slip or a warranty slip. If you bought it on our in-house credit card, I could bring it up on the terminal here, or perhaps you can recognise someone who served you — it's not lunch yet, so we're all here. (Free Information, Broken Record, Workable Compromise)

C: Look, I don't know where it is! It could be anywhere! Are you doubting my word?

SP: Not at all, Sir. By the way, this is the K2 model, which has been superseded by the K3. We haven't stocked K2s for at least a year. The K2 might still be under warranty, however, if you could produce the warranty slip. If you would like to look at home, you could take the Super Widget with you, or leave it here, and I'll give you a receipt for it. (Free Information, Broken Record, Workable Compromise)

C: Look, don't worry about the money. It's only peanuts anyway. I'll just take a replacement model — that blue one would be nice.

SP: That is a K3 model, Sir, and this is a K2. There would have to be a charge, which might not be in your interests. Also, we and the manufacturer might not accept it back because of these scratches on this side. You might be better off selling it yourself elsewhere, and putting that money towards a K3. We might be able to take something off the price. (Free Information, Workable Compromise)

C: Those scratches are there because the handles are in the wrong place! It's crummy design! Why should I have to be ripped off because of your crummy design? Tell me that!

SP: Perhaps there is a design fault, Sir. Can you show me how the handles don't work? (Fogging, Negative Inquiry)

C: This is an outrage! You're calling me a liar again! You haven't heard the last of this! I'll take this straight to the top!

SP: That's your perfect right, Sir. Would you like to speak to the manager? You could also, if you like, fill out one of these customer feedback forms. They go straight to the general manager, and our policy is to respond to them within 48 hours. (Free Information, Negative Inquiry)

C: Um well, ah, I don't know whether I want to take it that far ...

SP: Well, those options remain open to you if you wish to exercise them, Sir. The simpler alternative, of course, is to simply produce some proof or purchase, or warranty documentation. If your warranty is still operating, I'm sure we could talk trade-ins — although those scratches are a problem. Do you think it's reasonable that we have to make allowances for the scratches in the trade-in price? (Free Information, Broken Record, Workable Compromise, Positive Inquiry)

C: Ah ... yeah ... look, I'll take it with me for now ... I'll have a look around at home, and ring my credit card company ... I'll be back.

SP: Certainly, Sir. I'll put a hold on the blue K3 for a week. (Free Information)

Using verbal skills such as these can help shift customer–provider encounters from the negative realms of aggression, manipulativeness and passivity to the more positive realm of assertiveness. Assertive communication usually means that both sides of the encounter can preserve their dignity and sense of self-worth, and can get on with the healthy life-activity of solving problems.

RIGHTS OF THE CUSTOMER AND THE PROVIDER

Assertively handling the customer-provider encounter can also mean that the rights of the customer and also those of the provider are respected. 'Rights' are not always ascribed to the roles of customers and providers, but such rights do exist. If such rights are defined, defended and observed, then the service encounter will not only be more just and equitable, but also more effective and efficient. Some of these rights are listed in table 5.5.

Table 5.5: Rights of the customer and provider[104]

Rights of the customer	Rights of the provider
The customer has the right: • to value for money • to full and undivided attention of a service provider • to open channels of communication for feedback, complaints or compliments • to have allowances made for atypical, emotional behaviour caused by stress of actual or potential confrontation • not to be hassled or stampeded, to be given time to think things over, to cool off • to say no • to explanations, apologies • to reparation for loss, inconvenience, and then some • to not have intelligence, taste questioned • to not have time wasted • to be listened to • to solutions, alternatives, choices, options • to expose a problem, and not be treated like a criminal • to have promises kept • not to be abused, grovelled to or conned	The provider has the right: • to have human dignity respected • not to be treated like a commodity or slave • to not have intelligence, taste questioned • to be given the opportunity to apologise and explain • to be given time and opportunity to fix things • to be listened to • not to be blamed for other's mistakes • not to be abused, grovelled to or conned • to say no

Communicating with customers in difficult situations can lead to positive resolutions or outcomes if a provider:
- respects the rights of others, while ensuring that her/his own are not trampled upon
- deploys positive, assertive self-talk
- visualises or imagines positive expectations of a good solution
- behaves assertively.

```
┌─────────────────────────────────────┐  ┌─────────────────────────────────────┐
│ Your rights                         │  │ Their rights                        │
│                                     │  │                                     │
│ To be treated with respect          │  │ To be treated with respect          │
│ Not to be blamed personally         │  │ To get what I pay for and seek      │
│ To be given a chance to rectify     │  │   redress if I do not               │
│   and make-up for mistakes          │  │ To feel that they *deserve* my money│
│ To be listened to                   │  │ To be listened to                   │
│                                     │  │ To receive prompt attention         │
└─────────────────────────────────────┘  └─────────────────────────────────────┘
```

Positive self-talk

Customers have a right to complain and get what they pay for. Handled properly, I can demonstrate how customer orientated we are and ensure that this person becomes a loyal customer.

Positive expectation

A calmed down customer who appreciates the way I've sorted out the problem for them.

Assertive behaviour

A show of concern; a lot of listening; attentive expression; eye contact; confident, calm tone and clear speech when I do talk; asking questions to clarify; giving them options; using appropriate verbal skills.

Outcome (what you want to achieve *and* what you want to avoid).

- A loyal customer, grateful for the care and attention I've shown
- Me feeling good about myself and my job

- The customer becoming angry
- Me too!
- Me feeling bad about myself, my job and customers

Figure 5.1: Communicating assertively with customers: a model

(Source: adapted with permission from Gillen [1990:258].)

ACTIVITIES

1. Drawing upon information contained in your completed version of the assertiveness matrix (p. 71), write a plan describing how you might increase your score.
2. Make several copies of table 5.6 (p. 84) Use it to:
    (a) analyse the verbal skills used in the customer–provider encounter on pp. 80–81
    (b) write your own dialogue for an encounter with a customer. Once you have completed the lines you might use, incorporate them into a full dialogue, using the encounter on pp. 80–81 as a model. The customer may use a number of aggressive and/or manipulative and/or passive ploys.
3. Create your own list of rights for customers and providers.

Table 5.6: Examples of verbal skills in assertive behaviour

Verbal skill	Description	Rationale	Examples
Broken Record	The skill of calmly repeating what you want, over and over again, just like a broken record.	If you know that you can depend upon Broken Record, you do not have to psych yourself up for a dialogue with someone else, and you can also calmly sidestep irrelevant logic and baiting from the other person.	
Fogging	The skill of calmly acknowledging that criticism of you may well be justified.	Your antagonist, instead of lashing out and hitting something solid, thus lashes out, but finds no resistance, as if he/she was trying to punch fog. Fogging helps separate personalities from problems.	
Free Information	The skill of giving and recognising basic factual information.	This can help conversation move beyond the basic 'what do you think of the weather' type lines.	
Self-disclosure	The skill of revealing positive and negative aspects of yourself to others.	This is the next step on from free information.	
Negative Inquiry	The skill of actively seeking constructive criticism from others.	This will provide you with useful information and/or exhaust the manipulative ploys of others.	
Positive Inquiry	The skill of actively seeking information from others about what solutions they see to their problems.	This will provide you with useful information and/or exhaust the manipulative ploys of others.	
Workable Compromise	The skill of proposing a negotiated solution to a conflict.	Such a solution will satisfy both parties, without sacrificing the self-respect of either party.	

TALKING POINTS

YOU DON'T SAY? More of what people say about customers and providers

There is only one valid definition of business purpose: to create a customer. It is the customer who determines what a business is. What the business thinks it produces is not of first importance — especially not to the future of the business and to its success. What the customer thinks he is buying and considers 'value' is decisive — it determines what a business is, what it produces and whether it will prosper.

Peter Drucker

Just because you don't think it's a big deal doesn't mean your customer doesn't think it's a big deal. When your customer *says* it's a big deal, it's a big deal. And when your customer says, 'It's *no* big deal', it's *still* a big deal. Otherwise, why would they bring it up?

Kristin Anderson

Ginger and Pickles were the people who kept the shop. Ginger was a yellow tom-cat, and Pickles was a terrier.

The rabbits were always a little bit afraid of Pickles.

The shop was also patronised by mice — only the mice were rather afraid of Ginger.

Ginger usually requested Pickles to serve them, because he said it made his mouth water.

'I cannot bear,' said he, 'to see them going out the door carrying their little parcels.'

'I have the same feeling about rats,' replied Pickles, 'but it would never do to eat our own customers; they would leave us and go to Tabitha Twitchit's.'

'On the contrary, they would go nowhere,' replied Ginger gloomily.

(Tabitha Twitchit kept the only other shop in the village. She did not give credit.)

Beatrix Potter
The Tale of Ginger and Pickles

When a new person walks through that door, that human is a total stranger in our home. Yes, the salon is our home. We feel comfortable there in the salon because we work there every day. We know where the shampoo area is, where the coffee machine is, and where the bathrooms are. The stranger opens the door, like opening the door to a strange family's home, and sees either a cold, lonely place where faces stare at him waiting for him to explain the reason for his intrusion, or a warm, inviting atmosphere of people who by their attitude invite him to come closer. Every stylist and receptionist in our home is trained to be sensitive to the new client's needs of acceptance and reassurance. We work hard at making our home their home.

Michael R. Edmonton
Alberta hair stylist

Customer satisfaction can only be achieved when you effectively communicate, communicate and communicate with your customer. You can never overdo this aspect of your business. Also, communication is a two-way street — you need to hear as much as you say.

D. J. Zolkiwsky
A.T.& T. Bell Laboratories

But for the time being, says Thomas Kelly, assistant professor at Cornell University's School of Hotel Administration, 'The American service economy is burdened with people who frequently view service as "servile" work. In our culture, (service) jobs are not considered a worthwhile occupation. When workers view giving service as beneath them, it shows'.

Indeed, 'The customer is always right', the motto of the early American merchant class, is likely to be the punchline in jokes told by service employees today.

The younger generation of individualistic workers would much rather be 'in command' than 'in service'.

Ask a passing waiter for a glass of water, and you're informed that it's not his table. Seek the attention of an idle clerk, and he or she acts as though you're interrupting. Watch the office worker sit within arm's reach of a ringing telephone and ignore it because it's not his or her time to answer.

Do service workers act this way because they are unmotivated? Is business partly responsible for their lack of motivation? There's evidence that the answer to both questions is 'Yes'.

In a cover story on service, *Time* magazine reported: 'Many sales clerks, delivery truck drivers, and other service workers are unmotivated because of the low pay and the lack of career paths in their jobs'. Says journalist David Halberstam, whose best-seller, *The Reckoning*, chronicled the decline of America's auto industry: 'The main questions are, "Does this job lead to anything? Does it have any dignity?" No'.

John Tschohl and Steve Franzmeier

I did not stop at the manager's office. I did not make a scene. But I did solemnly promise myself that under no conditions would I ever return to that store. I have also told every friend I have about my experiences with this store. But note that management knows nothing of what happened. If they are judging their effectiveness as managers on how many customer complaints they get, they are living in a dream world. Most customers are nice customers. They never complain, no matter what kind of service they get. They never kick, nag or criticise in a public place like some people do.

But let me tell you what they will do. They will tell between ten and twenty people of their experience, and management will never suspect a thing. And most important, they will exercise their right to vote; they will never go back. That is why we must never forget that, when you lose a customer because of poor service, chances are you will never know it.

James H. Donnelly Jr

This guide is dedicated to the British Rail Manager who, learning that I had waited fifteen minutes to buy a ticket and had missed my train, remonstrated: 'It doesn't matter if you have to wait half an hour or longer, you can't pay on the train!'

David Clutterbuck and Susan Kernaghan
Making Customers Count: A Guide to Excellence in Customer Care

The view that an industry is a customer-satisfying process, not a goods-producing process, is vital for all business to understand. An industry begins with the customer and his needs, not with a patent, a raw material, or a selling skill.

Theodore Levitt

6

ESTABLISHING RAPPORT WITH CUSTOMERS
NEUROLINGUISTIC PROGRAMMING

NEUROLINGUISTIC PROGRAMMING: MODES OF PERCEPTION

Another model of communication that can help us in dealing with customers is that of neurolinguistic programming, or NLP. NLP practitioners believe that rapport or empathy with others can be considerably assisted by understanding specific differences between individuals, and by using specialised techniques of establishing and maintaining rapport.[105]

REPRESENTATIONAL SYSTEMS

Human beings have five senses (at least), and we use these senses to process information about the world and ourselves — external and internal experience. NLP practitioners argue that we all have specific sensory preferences — that is, we do not use all five senses equally. There are three major types of representational systems. These are:

1. visual
2. auditory
3. kinaesthetic (relating to feeling, taste and smell).

How can we tell which representational system is dominant in any given individual? There are two methods by which we can do this: analysing the individual's vocabulary, and analysing the individual's eye movements.

People use words in specific ways. If the NLP model holds true, any individual will tend to favour words and phrases that reflect a particular representational system (see table 6.1).

Table 6.1: Verbal cues to representational systems

Visual	Auditory	Kinaesthetic
An eyeful	Announce	Active
Angle	Articulate	All washed up
Appear	Audible	Bearable
Beyond a shadow of a doubt	Blabber-mouth	Bind
Bird's eye view	Call	Break
Blind spot	Clash	Cold
Catch a glimpse of	Converse	Come to grips with
Clarity	Crashing	Concrete
Clear	Divulge	Control yourself
Clear as day	Earful	Cool
Clear-cut	Earshot	Cool/calm/collected
Colourful	Express yourself	Cool customer
Enlighten	Give an account of	Emotional
Examine	Give me your ear	Feel
Eyeful	Gossip	Feel it in my bones
Focus	Harmony	Firm
Foresee	Hear	Flow
Fuzzy	Hold your tongue	Freeze
Get a perspective on	Hum	Get a handle on
Glance	Hush	Get in touch with
Glimpse	Idle talk	Get the drift of
Hazy	In a manner of speaking	Grasp
Hindsight	Interview	Grip
Horse of a different colour	Keynote speaker	Hand-in-hand
Horizon	Listen	Hang in there!
Idea	Loud	Hassle
Illusion	Loud and clear	Heated argument
Image	Mumbo jumbo	Hold it!
Imagine	Music to my ears	Hot-head
Inspect	Noise	Hunch
In view of	On the same wavelength	Hurt
Look	Outspoken	Intuition
Look back on it and laugh	Pay attention to	Lukewarm
Looks like	Power of speech	Motion
Make a scene	Proclaim	Nail
Mental picture	Pronounce	Not following you
Mind's eye	Purrs like a kitten	Pain-in-the-neck
Naked eye	Quiet	Panicky
Notice	Rap session	Pressure
Observe	Rings a bell	Pull some strings
Paint a picture	Roar	Push
Perspective	Rumour	Rough
Picture	Scream	Scratch the surface
Perception	Shrill	Sensitive
Photographic memory	Silence	Shallow
Pinpoint	Sing	Sharp as a tack
Plainly see	Speechless	Smooth operator
Pretty as a picture	Squeal	Softly
Scene	State your purpose	Solid
See eye to eye	Talk	So-so
Shed some light on	Tattle-tale	Squeeze
Short-sighted	Thunderous	Stiff upper lip
Sight for sore eyes	Told	Stress
Sketchy	Tongue-tied	Stuffed shirt
Survey	To tell the truth	Tension
Take a peek	Turn a deaf ear	Thick-skinned
Tunnel vision	Unheard of	Tied up
Vision	Voiced an opinion	Touch
Watch	Well-informed	Topsy-turvy
Well defined	Word for word	Warm
Witness		Wring

(Source: adapted from Zarro and Blum [1989] and O'Connor and Seymour [1993].)

People can thus be classified into visual, auditory and kinaesthetic types. These types also have specific ways of using their eyes. Why eye movements? Because, say NLP practitioners, different parts of the brain handle different senses, and when we are thinking about or are remembering ('accessing') different types of experiences or data (visual, auditory, kinaesthetic), the eyes move in specific patterns. Thus, when someone is thinking about something visual (or accessing visual data), such as a painting or a face, that person's eyes will move up to the left, up to the right, or remain de-focused. When a person is thinking about something auditory (or accessing auditory data), such as music or speech, then that person's eyes will move to the left or to the right or down and to the left. When a person is thinking about something tactile, olfactory or gustatory (or accessing kinaesthetic data), then that person's eyes will move down and to the right (figure 6.1).[106]

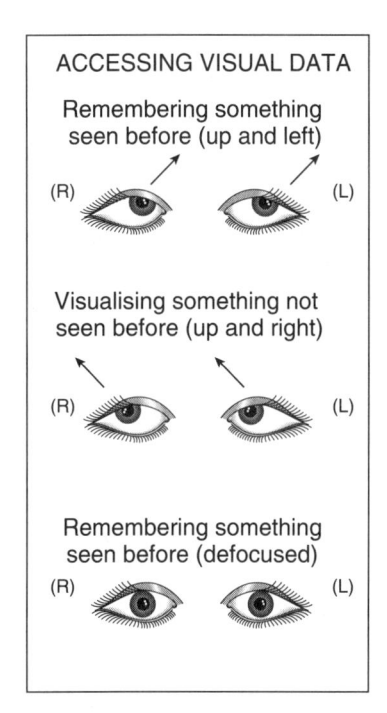

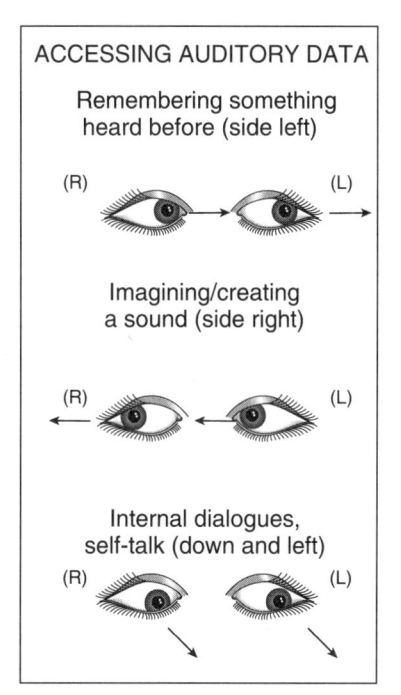

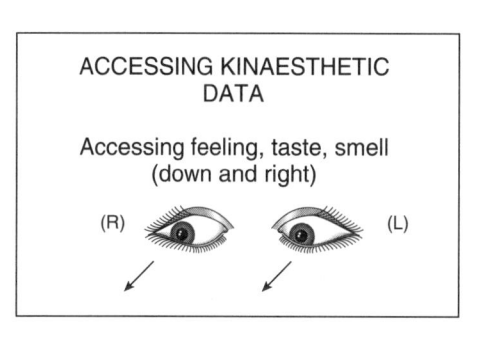

Figure 6.1: Eye cues to internal states in NLP

Establishing rapport: word matching

By listening to the words used by customers, and by watching their eye movements, it may be possible for a provider to determine whether the customer is operating in a visual, auditory or kinaesthetic mode. Rapport or communication can be enhanced if the provider matches the language of the customer. Similarly, lack of rapport might occur if the provider uses language that does not match the representational system of the customer (table 6.2). As one NLP practitioner puts it, 'The meaning of communication is the response you get. If you are not getting the response you want, change what you are doing'.[107]

Establishing rapport through other means

People who have high rapport with each other often have similar voice tone and tempo, breathing, movement or gestural rhythms, and postures. A provider can move towards improved rapport with a customer by trying to match, synchronise or harmonise with these different aspects of a customer's behaviour.

Table 6.2: Communication matches and mismatches

Customer says ...	Provider should give higher priority to saying ...	Provider should give lower priority to saying ...
I don't *see* why I should choose this model over the cheaper one.	• Well, the *design* is more attractive. • The *colours* are more attractive. • You *look* good using it.	• It's extremely *quiet* in operation. • It has a really professional *feel*.
My *gut reaction* is to take it, but perhaps I'd better not.	• Take your time, and *get in touch* with me in a few days. • I understand how you *feel*. • It's bound to have a great *impact* on others.	• You look *pretty as a picture* in it. • If you *listen* to the *opinion* of the experts, I think you'll find they prefer this.
The deal *sounds* OK, I suppose, but I'll need more time.	• I give you my *word*, you won't *hear* of a better deal. • Give me a *call* in a few days' time. We're ready to *listen*.	• I think it's just what you're *looking* for. • I've got a *hunch* that the whole thing will run as *smooth as silk*.

A person's voice can be loud or soft, and deep or high in tone. Tempos can be fast or slow, and there can be considerable variation in pauses. Accent can also be a crucial aspect of the way in which a person speaks. A person's mix of all these factors can be influenced by personality, socioeconomic class, and geography. People are most aware of accent, and least aware of the other factors. It would be inappropriate and counterproductive to imitate another person's accent — such a communication strategy would almost certainly cause confusion and resentment. However, other aspects of voice can be matched. Consider, for example, the case of an encounter between a provider — whose 'natural' vocal style is deep, fairly loud, slow and with few pauses — and a customer, whose 'natural' vocal style is high, fairly soft, fast and with numerous pauses. It is likely that there will be more rapport between the two if the provider moves closer to the style of the customer.

Further subtle signals of rapport can be created by attempting to match the breathing patterns of others. Breathing can be fast or slow, deep or shallow. It can sometimes be difficult to detect a person's breathing pattern because of the obscuring effect of several layers of clothing, but close observation of the person's chest and abdomen, and of shoulders silhouetted against a background, can reveal all.[108]

An individual has a repertoire of gestures, mannerisms and tics — drumming fingers, scratching a chin, smoothing hair, tapping a pen, pushing glasses back on the nose, stroking a chair arm, tapping toes, and so on. It is not necessary to exactly copy these movements in order to build rapport, but similar movements, paced at the same rhythm, may be of assistance.

Postures are larger scale movements than gestures, and thus are easier to observe. Rapport can be established by mirroring another person's posture — erect, slumped, relaxed or tense.

Rapport can thus be established by matching or synchronising words, voice, breathing, gestures and postures. Once a certain level of matching has been reached, it may be possible to reverse roles — to switch from following the behaviour of others to pacing and leading the behaviour of others. Matching or synchrony — or the lack of it — may well be the index of the healthiness or otherwise of relationships between customer and provider, among work colleagues, between lovers, or among family members.

Rapport: the perils of mimicry and manipulation

Matching, however, if clumsily done, will be obvious, and the person being matched will feel that he or she is being mimicked and manipulated. At the technical level, matching can be subtle and undiscovered if done smoothly and gracefully, and if lags are built in: for example, if the person being matched changes posture, then you should wait 20 to 30 seconds before copying that posture.

At the ethical level, the question still remains, however: is this acceptable, non-manipulative behaviour, or is it something else entirely? While some people are critical of NLP on this issue, most NLP practitioners see no problem, believing that the potency of these techniques can be neutralised by circumstances: if customers really don't want to buy, but are conned by providers using NLP, then the customers will have their revenge.[109]

CHUNKING UP, CHUNKING DOWN

'Chunking' is a term derived from computer science, and it simply means to break into bits. To *chunk up* means to move from the specific to the general, or from a part to the whole. To *chunk down* means to move from the specific to the general, or from the whole to a part. Chunking sideways is all about lateral thinking: perhaps what is really wanted is quite different. Service providers can use chunking to create new perspectives on what customers really want, rather than just stick with the customer's initial frame of reference (see figure 6.2).

CUSTOMER (*after spending a long time fingering a price label*): I'd like this model, please.

PROVIDER: Certainly, madam. That's our top model. It vacuums very deeply, and can, in fact, be used to shampoo carpets...

CUSTOMER (*sends non-verbal signals of impatience, polite boredom: open mouth, fidgeting fingers, looking at watch*)

PROVIDER: Can I ask you — what do you need from a vacuum cleaner? (**chunking up**)

CUSTOMER: Well, what I really need is a machine that can mop up water.

PROVIDER: Ah, well, while this machine is top class, and can do that, it might be more than you need, and you might end up unhappy with this price. This model here, for example, doesn't shampoo, but it does collect water — and it's a good deal less. (**chunking down**)

CUSTOMER: Yes... and it doesn't look too bad, does it?

PROVIDER: It's one of our best machines. Pardon me for asking further, but what water-spill problems do you have to deal with?

CUSTOMER: Oh, we have a refrigerator with a defrost that doesn't work very well, and it creates a real mess every few weeks.

PROVIDER: Do you think you might be better off taking the cheaper vacuum cleaner, or even not buying a vacuum cleaner from us at all, but instead putting your hard-earned money to better use by trading in your old fridge on one of these marked-down ones over here? (**chunking sideways**).

CUSTOMER: I... I hadn't thought of that...

Figure 6.2: An example of chunking as used by a provider to a customer

ACTIVITIES

1. Add at least ten other words or phrases to each column of table 6.1.
2. Using table 6.2 as a model, complete this table to indicate matches and mismatches in communication.

Customer says . . .	Provider should give higher priority to saying . . .	Provider should give lower priority to saying . . .

3. You are a salesperson at the local Toyobenz car dealership. Your colleague, Jean Bryan, has taken ill, and won't be back for some time. She has asked you to look after three prospective customers, all of whom have recently expressed interest in the new Dynawhiz electric car. Her notes about the customers are sparse, but this is what they say:

Mr Wellcome: Likes low profile of DW. Says he could just visualise himself driving it home to surprise family, wants more info on colours available.

Ms Ping: Impressed by quietness of DW. Wants someone to tell her more about features.

Dr Rantling: Wants info. re suspension of DW — OK for off-road? Said he'd keep in touch, but hasn't done so.

Send a letter to each of these people. Enclose the standard Dynawhiz brochure, but attach a short (100–200 words) letter to each person. Write each letter so that it reflects the possible representational system of each customer. Invent whatever details you feel are necessary.

4. Create customer/provider dialogues from three different industries which show chunking-type dialogue.

TALKING POINTS

BAD COMMUNICATION AND NON-COMMUNICATION IN THE SERVICE ENCOUNTER IN AUSTRALIA

With that grand finale, I walked out of the hotel. As I rode to the airport, I wondered why the entire ridiculous encounter had to occur in the first place. A simple acknowledgment or apology would have ended the problem on a happy note. I would have felt that I had done the hotel a service by informing them of the mishap, and their acknowledgment would have made me happy, and a win–win situation would have resulted.

But the behaviour of the employee turned the situation into a lose–lose one. Undoubtedly fresh out of an assertiveness training course, the front-desk manager did her best to turn the situation around to where I was explaining my behaviour for a problem the hotel caused. She was determined not to accept personal responsibility for my problem and did her best to absolve the hotel of any responsibility. An employee will always lose such contests of mental gymnastics with a customer. And even if the employee should win, the organisation will always lose.

James H. Donnelly Jr

You don't get a second chance to make a first impression. And it's the customer's perceptions that count.

Howard G. Seebach
DuPont

Ronald Conway (1978, 1994) puts forward some controversial views about communicating with customers.

Curiously enough, work output is not linked with work satisfaction. As far back as the post-World War II years, Katz found that Americans who worked hardest in the Chesapeake and Ohio railroad gangs were rather less personally satisfied than their more casual peers. Likert took the question further by showing that the higher the level of skill, the more productivity and job satisfaction were likely to be 'in phase' with each other. Nevertheless, Argyle tends to find that those who work hardest of all are those who work to forget their troubles, attesting once again to the extent to which modern man can either over-respond or under-respond to his labour tasks for remarkably similar reasons. The central variable seems not the task but the attitude brought to the task by outside factors.

In Australia, the worst under-responders are likely to be not so much among assembly-line process workers — among whom are many industrious labourers from European ethnic groups — but in the lowest echelons of the white-collar sector. Almost every exasperated Australian has had some experience with vagueness, incompetence, inexperience, tardiness or blank unconcern from lower-rung public servants. The same can be said of many so-called 'service' groups such as over-chatty ladies at cash registers or workers in many self-service stores and supermarkets. And the process is not all one-way. This is shown by actual physical attacks on relatively blameless counter staff (with echoes of the 1930s depression) at Commonwealth Employment Service offices by irate job-seekers in July and August of 1977. Even in less-strained situations the lack of courteous communication between vendor and consumer in many low-level transactions in Australia is striking. There is little empathy on either side and the greatest degree of curtness or simple rudeness is practised not between employer and employee but between the employee and those 'territorially alien' people on his own socio-economic level.

Some of the harshest exchanges and sharpest practices are usually between the lower-income worker and his own kind. 'Goodbye, take care' or 'Have a good day' are part of the common pattern of greeting and departure even in the roughest American cities and workplaces. With us, such expressions are often regarded as 'crawling' or perhaps a symptom of dim-wittedness. The failure of gracious or genuinely friendly communication among countless workers of both sexes is daunting. A decline in the command of reasonable English by a media-mesmerised generation is not likely to improve the situation in the near future ... (Conway, 1978: 200–201).

Since I wrote these comments in 1978, the situation worsened until the close of the 1980s when union militancy in 'service' industries was weakened by the effects of recession. This forced employers to adopt tougher standards for communication. But the real problem remains largely untackled, particularly among *male* employees. Here, it can be seen that poor communication skills (accentuated by the permissive, often careless, schooling standards of the '70s and beyond) lay behind the defensive rudeness and seeming lack of empathy between servers and served. Behind a lot of egalitarian bluster lies an inner awareness by some men that they lack the expressive capacities to relate graciously to people, even when there is a felt need to do so. Curtness, in the '90s, can often be a cover-up for a sense of social incapacity, a sense that even many ethnic newcomers have better communication skills than some of the 'old' Australians. A lot of this goes beyond the workplace, where even parents communicate badly with one another (the *over*-articulate wife versus the *under*-articulate husband). This is transmitted freely to offspring. Militant feminism has only compounded the problem by confronting men rather than tactfully helping them in what has become an evident disability (Conway, 1994).

7 LISTENING, QUESTIONING AND COMPLAINTS
USING FEEDBACK TO IMPROVE SERVICE

LISTENING: WHY SHOULD YOU BOTHER?

The more world-weary service provider might say that customers — both internal and external — don't appear to have much to say, so why bother to listen? Appearances are often deceptive, of course, and people are usually saying something of value, even if it is not what they strictly intended to say. Quite apart from the sheer old-fashioned courtesy of paying attention to others, no matter what, there are sound reasons for really listening to what others are saying.

1. **Listening to others lets them solve their own problems.**

There are a number of parallels between the customer/provider encounter and the employee/manager encounter when it comes to listening. (In a sense, in fact, the service provider is a manager of customers.) For example, managers in organisations sometimes think that listening to their subordinates is a waste of time, because 'they only come in here to whinge about their problems'. Nicholas Iuppa suggests that this may be a serious misperception of the way human communication and problem-solving really works, and that in fact 'management by listening' has a lot going for it: on many occasions, if the manager simply listens to someone talking about a problem (perhaps interrupting subtly here and there to nudge the monologue down one track rather than another), then the solution to the problem becomes apparent — a problem well-defined is half-solved, as the maxim goes. The speaker has unconsciously and tacitly delegated the problem to himself or herself, and solved it.[110] The person has realised the truth of the maxim of English novelist E. M. Forster — 'How do I know what I think until I hear what I say?' This revelation is quite likely to occur if you are the first real listener such a person has encountered in a world of non-listeners. Thus service providers and managers may not have to work so hard at providing solutions after all — they just have to be the audience, not the actor.

2. **Listening to customers is a good method of pain-avoidance, and of getting things right the first time.**

Service providers, like all human beings, often ignore information provided, advice, or the model of others' experience:
- 'Our techs say that if you turn it like that, it'll break off.'
- 'Are you sure? Surely this is covered by the three-year guarantee? Our legal people might kick up a fuss about it . . .'
- 'Look, I like this perfume as much as you, and . . . ah . . . the price is good, but . . . um . . . I might be allergic to it . . .'

Human beings often don't listen — and we pay the price with failure and pain. Only in hindsight do we say, 'If only I'd listened'.

Sometimes it's poor time management on our part: we think we don't have time to listen — but as the maxim has it, there's never enough time to do it right, but there's always enough time to do it over. Sometimes it's pride: we don't want to be beholden to others. Sometimes it's the sheer thrill of risk-taking: we want to be in charge, to be the expert, to lead the faint-hearted into new experiences. It's fun and liberating not to listen sometimes, but sometimes it can be quite counterproductive and stupid.

3. **Listening to others is one of the key factors in the way members of an organisation keep in touch with internal and external customers.** Researchers at the University of Minnesota concluded that nearly 60 per cent of misunderstanding in the business world can be traced to poor listening, and only 1 per cent to written communication.[111]

Apple Computers in the US gets its executives out from behind their desks and out of their offices and down onto the toll-free customer service telephones, and gives them a listening certificate for participating in such a program.[112] A Canadian bank instituted a listening program wherein all managers spent time each day calling customers, asking 'How can I help?': the feedback from customers was phenomenal, as was the new business which ensued.[113]

Kenichi Ohmae, a Japanese management consultant, points out that successful Japanese consumer electronics firms like Sony send their product design engineers out on the road for up to six months each year, listening to customers, salespeople and dealers, so that current products might be improved and new ones anticipated. In other words, the focus shifts from inside-out research-driven marketing ('We know what they want') to outside-in customer-driven research and marketing ('Tell us what you want').[114]

A San Francisco hospital was able to reduce its costs, shorten the lengths of patients' stays, reduce patients' returns to hospital, and increase patients' satisfaction simply by instituting a communication program, where listening to the patients' needs was paramount.[115] A Lutheran minister of a Pennsylvania church boosted attendances at his services by 25 per cent by getting out of his church and sitting down at a local coffee shop and listening to the local farmers.[116]

LISTENING: WHAT IS IT?

We all know, of course, what listening is — or do we? Listening may not be the same as hearing. For example, if we define listening as concentrating upon and comprehending aural stimuli, then people with moderate hearing loss are usually better listeners than people with normal hearing.[117] How can this be? Because people with moderate loss of hearing have to try harder when trying to understand sounds — their hearing is more 'focused' than people who take their hearing for granted.

Focusing your ears: the cocktail party effect, and other strange phenomena

Stop what you are doing for the moment, close your eyes, and just listen: what do you hear? Are there any background noises which — now you are concentrating, or shifting your aural focus — are becoming foreground noises, such as:
- an air conditioner
- a car driving by
- a dog barking in the distance
- the sound of breath moving in your nose
- a tap dripping
- trees rustling in the wind
- a radio playing
- a clock ticking?

These noises were thrust into the background because of the process of concentration, and rightfully so: hearing, like all channels of perception we use, can only handle so much information at a given time, and so we make decisions to exclude certain noises or stimuli and to include others.

Are these decisions made consciously or unconsciously? When filtering, or *selective perception*, of stimuli takes place, both conscious and unconscious processes are at work, although it is often difficult to draw a line between these two sets of processes.

For example, imagine you are at a party, surrounded by a hubbub of noise thrown up by multiple conversations taking place around you. You will not be able to discriminate many words from the background noise of these conversations, but if someone utters your name or a word or phrase that — within your value system is negatively or positively emotionally charged for you (for example, obscenities, the name of someone you are fond of) then the chances are you will hear it (the so-called 'cocktail party' effect). Similar processes of selective perception take place when we are perceiving the world via our other senses, such as sight (for example, scanning a list of names and seeing yours 'jump out' at you). Selective perception or attention may not be so much the conscious 'tuning out' of information inconsistent with our value system as the unconscious 'tuning in' of information consistent with our value system.[118]

Proceeding deeper into the unconscious mind, is it possible for us to perceive something, to have our behaviour changed by that perception, but not be aware of the original perception — to not recognise that that perception has taken place? Proponents and opponents of *subliminal perception* claim that this can happen: for example, audio tapes have been made of music with soft voices whispering 'Don't shoplift', for playing over department store Muzak systems, while videotapes with beach scenes and classical music (and aural and visual subliminal messages) are marketed with claims that they can help people lose weight, control smoking, and so on.[119] Do such systems work, and if they do, should they be allowed to work? The answers to both these questions will have to wait, pending more conclusive evidence as to whether subliminal perception really does exist and to what extent it can be manipulated.

'Listen, kid' — childhood conditioning and listening

Much of the way in which we listen — or don't listen — can be tracked down to our childhood experiences.[120] Many parents send out messages, both verbal and non-verbal, that teach children the essence of effective listening. Some parents, however, send out negative messages to their children:

- Children should be seen and not heard.
- Shut up and listen.
- Don't pay attention to him.
- Don't interrupt your elders.
- Don't speak until you're spoken to.
- Listen to your mother and do what you're told!
- Oh, that's nice, Julie ... Oh, John, did you pay the gas bill? Well, why not? Don't you ...
- Not now, darling (*click — remote control*), Daddy's watching TV (*click*) — we'll talk about it later ... (*click ... click*.)
- Really? So, how did the other kids in the class go? (glazed expression, stifled yawn, glancing at watch).

Punishing others for not listening, while themselves modelling bad listening behaviour, is not the best way possible for parents to teach effective listening:

> It is hardly surprising that children learn not to attend or listen, since what they hear when they do is often unpleasant and unrewarding ... Listening may come to be associated with negative feelings of discomfort and resentment. Perhaps it is better not to listen if you are likely to hear only nasty things. Note how acute a child's hearing suddenly seems to be when ice-cream or television is mentioned.[121]

In school as at home, there are not many rewards *for* listening, merely punishments for *not* listening.[122]

The listening phenomenon: how big? how effective?

How large a phenomenon is listening? In the range of communication skills, how large a share of our time does it take? Estimates vary, but some listening researchers estimate that the majority of people spend 60 to 70 per cent of their waking hours communicating, and of that time the proportions of listening, speaking, reading and writing undertaken by most people are writing (9 per cent), reading (16 per cent), talking (30 per cent) and listening (45 per cent) (figure 7.1).[123] Indeed, 'We listen more than we do any other human activity, except breathe'.[124]

These figures can vary considerably from individual to individual, of course. We also probably need to take them with a grain of salt, just as surely as we need to with figures which are used to suggest that non-verbal communication is more than 50 per cent of all communication (see chapter 3, 'Non-verbal communication'). Nevertheless, the figures are useful if they get us to re-think the humble or ignored skill of listening, and give it more weight than we might otherwise do.

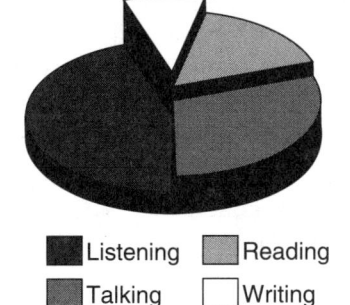

Figure 7.1: Time spent on different communication processes

(Source: adapted from Rosenblatt, Cheatham and Watt [1982: 117].)

- Listening
- Reading
- Talking
- Writing

The listening phenomenon: how fast? how slow?

There is a substantial gap between the rate at which most people talk (125-175 words per minute) and the 'thought rate' or rate at which information is processed in our minds (400-800 words per minute).[125]

The most effective way to exploit this gap is for the listener to analyse what is being said, to anticipate what the speaker might be about to say, and to memorise what is being said by repetition or association with other concepts.

Unfortunately, many people exploit the gap ineffectively, and begin to daydream and wander while the speaker is talking. While a surprising amount of these activities can be undertaken without losing the thread of what is being said, one daydream tends to lead to another, and all too often the listener is no longer paying attention.

At the other extreme, slow speech, or speech with numerous pauses in it, can also be difficult to listen to. Although such slowness or pausing can indicate that the speaker is seriously depressed, it can also mean, simply, that the topic being discussed is a complex one, and in such circumstances it is more acceptable for both speaker and listener to pause and ponder than it might be within a normal social conversation.[126]

LISTENING, GENDER AND POWER

Listening behaviour can vary considerably according to the gender and power of differing individuals, and this can have important — and often negative — impacts on the provider–customer encounter.

As we have seen earlier (p. 23) high-status people tend to interrupt low-status people more than in the reverse situation. This reverse situation also applies to touching and invading personal work space.

This means, in practice, that some managers interrupt employees more than vice-versa, thus modelling bad listening behaviour, which — not surprisingly — is then emulated by employees. As we have seen (p. 7), employee–customer communication is usually a close imitation of manager–employee communication. Bad listening habits can thus spread like a disease throughout service organisations.

Sex roles are also a critical factor in understanding listening behaviour. In one US survey, it was revealed that when two men or two women were talking, the number of interruptions between partners was much the same, but when a man and a woman were talking, the man made about 96 per cent of the interruptions. About one-third of the time, women made 'retrievals', or attempted to pick up the conversation from the point where they were interrupted.[127]

This male non-listening, interrupting behaviour was linked to males simply 'tuning out' early in the conversation: some men, after listening for only a few sentences, switched from listening to the speaker (outward orientation) to 'self-listening' (inward orientation), or concentrating on what could be added to the conversation, and then proceeded to jump into the conversation prematurely, without first trying to draw out the speaker or even take in more information before reaching a conclusion. This may be the result of sex-role conditioning, where males have been trained to add to the conversation and be problem-solvers.[128]

Other research suggests that males are superior to females in comprehension of factual material, whereas females are more sensitive to the non-verbal cues and expression of feelings that accompany the words of speakers.[129] Whether this is true or not remains to be seen, but the implication seems to be clear: many males appear to have a listening problem when interacting with females, and it would not be surprising if this general pattern continued in interactions between male service providers and female customers.

LISTENING AND NON-VERBAL COMMUNICATION

In most encounters with others, we need to 'listen with our eyes' as much as listen with our ears — that is, we need to observe the non-verbal behaviour that accompanies the words we are listening to (see pp. 20–36). We need, for example, to be aware of any contradictions between what a customer is actually saying, and what the customer is 'saying' non-verbally. Such a contradiction implies that we need to use techniques of active listening (see p. 103) and questioning (see p. 105) to draw out the customer, and find out what the things are that she or he *really* needs to talk about with us.

We also have to be aware of the ways in which our own non-verbal communication can help or hinder the process of effective listening. Listening responsiveness is associated with non-verbal behaviours such as:

- nodding the head
- leaning forward
- orientating the body towards speaker
- establishing direct eye contact and giving visual attention (not being distracted by external tasks, events, people or internal thoughts)
- eyebrow raising
- smiling
- mirroring the facial expression of the speaker
- refraining from distracting mannerisms, such as doodling with a pen, fidgeting, playing with a watch
- making appropriate non-word noises or 'friendly grunts' — 'mm-hmm,' 'uh-huh'.[130]

LISTENING: NOT-SO-REMOTE SENSING

We need to be aware of the full picture when a customer is in front of us, or is on the telephone line. Is the customer agitated, or ill at ease? Many customers find the encounter with sales providers a stressful situation, particularly if they envisage some type of conflict. This is usually the case when a customer has a complaint, for example. Customers — like all of us — may have had to 'psych themselves up' to go into battle over a complaint. The ideal model of behaviour we would all like to aspire to in such circumstances is that of the assertive person — cool, nerves under control, focused, and methodical (see pp. 70–84). Many people, however, customers included, are not cool, but are slightly out of control in such circumstances. The sensitive service provider listens and looks, and sees this, and makes allowances for such behaviour. Customers in such circumstances may exaggerate ('I must have rung here twenty times this morning!'), and may lash out at the first person they encounter. The good listener doesn't take everything literally or personally.

Sometimes the defensive behaviour of the customer is all-too-understandable: while it is a comforting truism to say that the customer is always right, in fact the customer is often wrong (about a third of the time, in fact).[131] When we are wrong, and know we are wrong, we don't want to lose face. Once we get things off our chest, we tend to become more reasonable. At this point — if the service provider has been patient, and has listened — the customer may well provide his or her own answer to the problem (see p. 95).

Sometimes customers are like researchers, or field workers, or spies: they bring back bits of information, parts of a jigsaw, and it is up to the provider to know what to do with such fragments of reality. Thus, when a customer presents an opinion, observation, problem or complaint, that opinion, observation, problem or complaint may not be a cause but a symptom — the surface reality, and not the underlying reality. By listening, and by questioning, it is possible to discern the causes, to bring the underlying reality to the surface. Thus it is vital for listeners not to jump in too soon, interrupting, suggesting quick fixes (table 7.1).

Table 7.1: Using effective listening to solve customer problems

Customer input	Apparent reality (symptom)	Quick fix	Underlying reality (cause)	Solution
'This paint doesn't give much coverage.'	Paint is inadequate.	Sell twice as much cheaper paint.	Surface has dark colour paint on it; is inadequately prepared.	Tell customer how to prepare surface.
'I almost drove into that crate near the door. You should watch where you put things.'	Customer is just a whinger, looking for faults.	Ignore — get on with more important work.	Crate is, in fact, expensive shipment of industrial diamonds which staff thought had been stolen.	Drop everything. Grab crate. Thank and reward customer.
'I had some trouble breathing last night.'	Patient is declining in health.	Change medication to a more powerful, riskier drug.	Respirator is faulty.	Attend to respirator. Leave medication unchanged.
'Oh ... yeah ... we can afford those payments ...' [scratches face, wrings hands]	They can afford the refrigerator.	Get them to sign quickly.	They can't afford the refrigerator.	Talk further about other payment options, other models.

Jumping in to implement quick fixes, while well-intentioned, may miss the point entirely. Listening providers are, in fact, gathering feedback, so that the organisation can not just 'shut up the complainers', but can use the new data to change the entire way in which service is provided (see pp. 8-9, 106-107). Quick fixes usually lead to dissatisfied customers, because their real needs have not been satisfied. Only real solutions can lead to satisfied customers, and good listening habits can help to reveal those solutions.

Sometimes customers consciously or unconsciously send verbal signals. Many customer-provider encounters are in fact negotiations, and signalling is a vital part of negotiation.[132] Typical signals (and their meanings) are:

Signal	Meaning
'It's very nice, but we *just* can't afford it.'	Can you bring the price down?
'*As it stands*, that offer is just ridiculous.'	Why don't you change it slightly, and we'll agree.
'I'm not going to sign an agreement *in that form*.'	Show me a more interesting agreement.
'There's no way we can go for that, *given the current state of the economy*.'	We'll buy if you lower the price/defer payments/link them to the consumer price index, etc.

Bad listeners would take such signals literally, and that would be the end of the matter — sooner or later, the customer would walk away, unsatisfied and perhaps no longer a customer. The good listener listens for the non-literal meaning, and is thus more tuned in to what the customer *really* wants.

ACTIVE LISTENING

Active listening means moving beyond passively receiving input from customers and moving towards sympathetic response and reality-checking. Active listening stands half-way between passively receiving input and using questioning techniques (p. 105). Two active listening techniques are *reflecting* and *clarifying*. Sometimes when a customer is upset or is not communicating clearly, it can help to simply reflect, or echo, the feelings and perceptions of the customer:

Customer	Provider
...and then the handle fell off!	I can see that you're upset about the quality of the mower. You feel that the engine housing should have been better secured.
...and so it's my mother that really makes me feel sick!	Hmm...you feel that the medication is not really what you need because it's problems in the family that are really making you upset.

This type of response lets the customer know that you have really listened to what has been said. It should be pointed out that this type of response is not necessarily an expression of agreement with the customer's viewpoint: customers are not always looking for agreement, just as they are not always looking for quick fixes; they just want to know that someone is listening. Solutions can come later.

Clarifying can also be a useful active listening technique. This simply means that you paraphrase or sum up in your own words what you think the customer has said:

- Let me just check and see if I've got this right...
- What I hear you saying is...
- What I think you have just said is...

This is 'playing back' to the customer what the customer has just said. This serves three purposes:

1. It can be a check on reality, to see if that in fact *is* what the customer said.
2. It can give gratification to the customer to hear his/her views expressed in someone else's words.
3. It can slow down the interaction, giving the customer a chance to cool down.

BAD LISTENING HABITS

We now should have a fair idea in what ways listening is very different from hearing. Let's consider how we can recognise good listeners, and not-so-good listeners (table 7.2).

Virtually all listening takes place on a one-to-one, face-to-face basis, as indeed does most communication in general. There are other types of listening, however, and we shall soon see that 'strategic listening' is a vital survival technique for virtually all organisations (p. 106).

Table 7.2: Good and bad listening behaviour

The bad listener ...	The good listener ...
daydreams, wanders, 'internally listens' while speaker is speaking.	exploits gap between speaking rate and thinking rate by analysing, anticipating and memorising.
doesn't look at the person speaking.	keeps eye contact with speaker.
is distracted by work, other people, clocks, televisions, noises.	concentrates on speaker.
keeps body oriented away from speaker.	is oriented towards speaker.
gives no feedback (facial responsiveness, 'friendly grunts').	gives feedback.
keeps objects (pen, equipment) in hand while speaker is talking.	puts things down, has hands free.
ignores speaker's non-verbal communication.	tunes in to speaker's non-verbal communication.
interrupts.	occasionally reflects and clarifies, but allows other person to complete what she/he has to say.
jumps to conclusions — focuses on symptoms and quick fixes.	is patient. Sees complaints as opportunities for problem-solving and learning. Focuses on underlying causes.
is prisoner of gender, power stereotypes (interrupting, quick fixes).	not a prisoner of gender, power stereotypes.
takes criticisms personally.	doesn't take criticisms personally.
takes all customers' words literally.	doesn't take all customers' words literally.
blames the customer. Becomes defensive about the organisation, and is judgemental and punishing when a customer complains.	suspends judgement as to who is to 'blame'. Customers are often wrong, but solutions rather than justice are what is important.
blames the organisation. Colludes with customer.	doesn't blame. Seeks solutions in the future, not revenge for sins in the past.
is thrown by stressed-out behaviour of customer, and becomes stressed-out in turn. Loses control of situation.	realises that customer must have had to 'psych up' to make a complaint, and has respect for their gumption. Makes allowances for customer being slightly out of control.
shoots the messenger. Anyone who criticises the way in which service is delivered, or who passes on customer complaints, is criticised, or made to look like a troublemaker, or an incompetent. This ensures that few criticisms or complaints are ever heard.	encourages constructive criticism, passing on of complaints. Wants to be the first to know, not the last. Listens and learns.
misses signalling behaviour of customers.	picks up on signalling behaviour of customers.
judges others by looks, opinions — prejudices shut down listening.	suspends judgement on others — listens to what is being said, not who is saying it.

QUESTIONING

Questioning techniques complement listening techniques. Questions are tools that allow the provider to probe further to find out just what it is that the customer wants and needs (wants and needs, of course, not necessarily being the same thing). Providers need to be able to creatively use and combine different types of questions (table 7.3). Some types of questions lend themselves to manipulative situations, and ethical providers will not, of course, use questions in such ways.

Table 7.3: Some question types used by providers in encounters with customers

Question type	Examples	Nature	Analysis
Open	• What were your first thoughts when it broke down? • How do you normally buy your stationery supplies?	Begin usually with How, What, When, Where, Who, or Why.	Provide maximum choice to customer. Gets customer talking in initial phases of encounter.
Closed	• Did you turn it off when it first broke down? • Do you normally buy your stationery supplies from Universal?	Begin usually with Can, Did, Do, Have, Is, Will and Would.	Requires simple yes/no response. Useful for establishing facts and gaining commitment, especially in latter phases of encounter.
Alternative	• Would you like to pay cash or charge it? • Would you like it in black or in blue?	A form of closed question.	Can focus customer's mind on a limited menu of choices. Can also be used manipulatively when menu of choices is deliberately restricted (e.g., when other choices are actually available).
Probing	What are you really looking for in a station wagon?	Can be open or closed — usually open.	A direct, up-front way of getting information and opinions. Appreciated by some customers, not appreciated by others.
Leading	So you'd have no problem meeting these levels of mortgage commitments?	Usually a form of closed question.	A closed type of question, but context, wording and inflection often suggest that there is only one answer — 'Yes'. Can be used manipulatively.
Softening up	• Would you say that you tend to wear these more stylish lines? • And do you think this more subtle blue is more flattering to your skin tones?	A form of closed/leading question.	Softening-up questions are usually asked in a sequence, all of which prompt the customer to say 'Yes'. At the end of such a sequence, a closed question is usually put about purchasing. The customer may, by this time, be conditioned to say 'Yes'. Usually used manipulatively.

(*Continued*)

Question type	Examples	Nature	Analysis
Hypothetical	Assuming you were in the market for a house next year, what area and price range might you be looking for?	Can be closed or open.	Useful for opening up discussions, breaking deadlocks, responding to customer signals.
Rhetorical	• You wouldn't buy from Universal, would you? • Surely, after you have considered the options, you'd have to look at this model, right?	Closed.	Closed, but implication is fairly heavy that there is no real choice.
Testing	• Is this OK so far? • Are you getting a clearer picture now of what's available?	Can be open or closed.	Provider can use to check with customer to see if information is getting across. If trust has been established, customer often responds as if all such questions are open ones — i.e., will give an extended response.
Third-party	We supply this model to Universal, and they've been very happy with it, price-wise and reliability-wise. Is this the type of thing you are interested in?	Statement plus question.	Endorsement of service from another customer is linked with inquiry. Persuasion by association.

(Source: adapted from Eunson [1994a], Alessandra, Wexler and Barrera [1987], Collis [1992].)

COMPLAINTS, FEEDBACK AND STRATEGIC LISTENING

As we have seen earlier (p. 8), most customers dissatisfied with the service provision of an organisation don't complain. We have seen that it is much cheaper to keep existing customers satisfied than it is to get new customers. We have also seen that complaints do not necessarily arise as a result of on–off, isolated events — they may well be clues to deeper, underlying problems that an organisation has. If this is the case, then organisations should not be discouraging complaints, or discounting their importance, but, in fact, should be going out of their way to *encourage complaints*. Complaints thus are not so much annoying problems as opportunities for learning. Complaints, like compliments, chance observations, and opinions, are all part of the feedback that organisations get from their customers (figure 7.2). Ineffective organisations will not understand such feedback, or if they do, will not act on that feedback to make changes in the way they do things, in the way they deliver service. Effective organisations will take all forms of feedback, including complaints, and plug them into the planning process, so that service delivery is modified and progressively improved.

How do organisations detect this feedback? They detect it by 'strategic listening'. This means that front-line staff are trained in listening skills, and feed this information back to senior managers. It also means that organisations set up mechanisms such as the following for obtaining customer feedback:[133]

- toll-free telephone hot lines
- electronic computer bulletin boards
- customer advisory panels

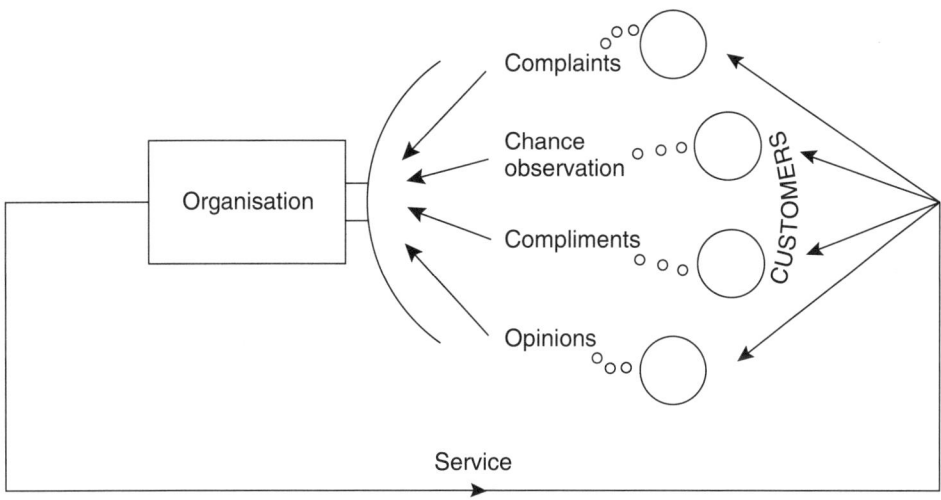

Figure 7.2: The feedback model of service delivery

- focus groups (groups of customers are brought together to discuss products and services while being observed by market researchers)
- mystery shopping services (trained observers pose as customers, and evaluate service provision)
- pre-paid mail-in comment cards systems.

Listening skills, then, are not simply a 'soft' interpersonal set of skills that are 'only' about being courteous and nice to people — a 'nice to have' rather than a 'must have' priority item. Listening skills have a strategic significance for organisations: organisations that don't listen to customers are destined for the scrap-heap, while those that do, are bound to flourish.

ACTIVITIES

1. Stop several times throughout the day, and listen to all the sounds around you. How many of them do you ignore, and why?
2. Carry a portable cassette recorder (with a long-playing tape) with you. Record various segments of your day. When playing back, note any sounds you did not notice at the time of recording.
3. Consider table 7.1. (Using effective listening to solve customer problems, p. 101). Draw up a chart with the same categories (Customer input, Apparent reality (symptom), Quick fix, Underlying reality (cause), Solution), and analyse at least three other situations you have experienced or can imagine.
4. Consider negotiation signals (p. 102). Think of at least three other signals (and meanings) that customers might use in customer/provider interactions.
5. Have another person tell you about a situation she or he feels strongly about. Respond to him or her by using the active listening techniques of reflecting and clarifying.
6. Consider table 7.2 (p. 104). Think of at least two other bad/good pairs of listening behaviours.
7. Devise at least one type of question that *customers* might use. Analyse it (or them) as per table 7.3 (pp. 105–106).
8. Consider table 7.3 (pp. 105–106). Create a role play in which a provider uses at least three different types of questions in interacting with a customer.
9. Interview employees and/or managers from two organisations. Find out what 'strategic listening' programs (if any) their organisations have in place to gather customer feedback. What impact does such feedback have upon service delivery?

TALKING POINTS

CUSTOMER LISTENING IN THE AMP

Strategic listening is fast becoming an accepted concept in modern organisations. Note the value placed upon the concept in this extract from a planning document produced within a large Australian insurance company.

> If we are to become a customer-focused organisation, it is fundamental that we listen to, and understand, our customers. Our customers are both external (agents, policyholders) and internal (staff, peers). This will allow us to be more experimental, learn more, take more chances and be more innovative. By listening to customers and understanding our customer needs, we will know what they expect and therefore we will begin to bridge the gap that often exists in customer service: the gap between what is expected and what is delivered.
>
> Satisfied clients are those who are also likely to keep their policies in force and purchase other products according to their needs.
>
> AMP, as a market leader, has chosen to exceed industry standards. As part of our recognition of the need to gain and retain customer satisfaction, we have developed and promoted 'plain English' guidelines for customer complaints and have set stringent internal rules for adhering to them.
>
> Complaint service is important. However, it must be placed in perspective as a means to improve our service to customers. Much greater emphasis should be placed on a long-term strategy to improve the quality of customer service and reduce the number of complaints. Our ultimate goal should be prevention, that is, elimination of causes of the problems.
>
> To a greater extent, we will actively seek out opinions on our service delivery from all our customers, not just those who come to us. Our objective is to become proactive and maintain a clear understanding with our customers, so that we can deliver the service they are expecting before any problems fester out of control, and customers take their business elsewhere.
>
> One of the methods to achieve this objective is customer surveys, which satisfy the marketing concept of meeting client needs. It is important to maintain a constant customer relationship, by establishing and reviewing needs, and having a 'match' with what the customer expects of us and the service we actually deliver.
>
> Timing of seeking customer response is crucial in obtaining a clear picture of the state of our service delivery. A perfunctory 'How did you find our service?' at the point of policy issue is worthless. Problems often don't arise until after the 'transaction'. Unless we seek customer opinion at this time, we will again lose the opportunity to fix our customer relationship and retain business. This is an essential element of a customer service culture: we can't just go through the motions — we must actually produce a result that is pleasing to the customer. And the only way we can do this is to ensure that all staff — on the front line and elsewhere — are focused towards satisfying the customer and are thus empowered to do so.

(Source: Graeme G. Rogers, Customer Service Division, *Strategic Measurement and Improvements in Customer Service: Australian Mutual Provident Society* [1992]. Reproduced with permission.)

HOW TO HANDLE CUSTOMER COMPLAINTS

- Don't be defensive.
- Be composed at all times.
- Don't take criticisms personally. It's not *you* the customer is angry with; try to be objective and put yourself in their shoes.
- Offer an apology even if the disservice is not your fault. 'I'm terribly sorry you are so upset' does *not* admit blame but does establish some rapport with the customer.
- Show empathy by using such phrases as, 'I can understand how you feel', 'I appreciate what you're saying'.
- Address customers by name.
- All communication should be in the first person. Use: 'I am sorry', not the royal 'We'.
- Don't make excuses or blame others in your organisation. The customer wants a solution to the problem, not an inquisition of your internal operations.
- Give the customer your full attention and establish eye contact. Sympathetic nods help defuse situations and many customers feel they are receiving a fair hearing if they see someone jotting down a few notes.
- Paraphrase their complaint in your own words to determine if you have correctly understood the situation. Play the situation back to them to check for understanding: 'I just want to check that I have understood you correctly'.
- If you don't know the answer to their problem, don't lie. Adopt the old teaching maxim and admit you don't know but make a commitment that you *will* find out and get back to them within a specified time.
- Do call back when you say you will, even if, for some reason, you haven't been able to obtain a satisfactory answer by then.
- Make the customer part of the solution — not part of the problem.
- Tell them what you *can* do ... not what you can't do. For example, rather than say: 'I'm terribly sorry but you must give seven days' notice to transfer money from a term deposit to a cheque account', adopt the following 'can do' approach which says the same thing but in a different way: 'Yes, I can transfer the money from your term deposit to your cheque account, with a slight interest charge of X dollars, since you were unable to provide seven days notice'.
- Find out what it will take to turn their dissatisfaction into satisfaction. Do they want a refund, credit, discount, replacement? Offer a solution and obtain the customer's agreement that this would satisfy the complaint. Ask: 'Will this problem be solved if we ...?'
- If they agree to the solution, act quickly before they change their mind. If they don't like your solution, ask them what they think is a fair outcome.
- Follow up.
- And remember: *You can never win an argument with a customer!*

(Source: from *Good Service is Good Business* by Catherine DeVrye [1994: 47–48]. Prentice-Hall, Sydney. Reproduced with permission of the publisher.)

We have been given two ears and but a single mouth, in order that we may listen more and talk less.

Zeno of Citium

The wise old owl sat in an oak.
The more he saw, the less he spoke.
The less he spoke, the more he heard.
Why can't we be like that old bird?

Nursery rhyme

The reason you don't understand me, Edith, is because I'm talking to you in English, and you're listening in Dingbat.

Archie Bunker

I would walk twenty miles to listen to my worst enemy, if I could learn something.

Leibniz

Speech is a joint game between the talker and the listener against the forces of confusion. Unless both make the effort, interpersonal communication is quite hopeless.

Norbert Weiner

If you're talking, you aren't learning.

Lyndon B. Johnson

Man's inability to communicate is a result of his failure to listen effectively, skilfully, and with understanding to another person.

Carl Rogers

Martyrs do not make good listeners.

Eastwood Atwater

In my work as a psychiatrist, I sense again and again the desperate feelings of people who feel no-one respects what they have to say. Often, people's physical ills are a disguised message, a 'ticket of admission' to see someone who will listen to a complaint. Regrettably, many doctors don't want to be bothered by anything other than a clear physical problem. Yet a sensitive doctor realises some time spent in careful listening will point to a hidden agenda of a patient's concern. And that act of listening can give more relief to a patient than any ten prescriptions of a tranquilliser.

Dr Walt Menninger

If employees feel their supervisor won't listen to them, they will find other employees or the union representative who will; if young people feel their parents won't or don't listen to them, they may find friends, gang members or people whose influence might be detrimental. And if customers feel a supplier really isn't listening, they will find a competitor to the supplier who will. There is no such thing as a vacuum in communication.

Norman Sigband and Arthur Bell

All this has been said before, but since no-one listened, it must be said again.

Andre Gide

There are many who would say that unvarnished listening is the chief distinguisher between leadership success and failure, especially in times such as these when the empowerment of everyone is paramount. Oddly enough, to listen, per se, is the single best 'tool' for empowering large numbers of others.

Tom Peters

In many instances, when we listen empathetically, it is relatively simple to respond to what isn't said within what is. Such a response will assist the communication to continue or it will close the loop. What is he or she really saying with the comment, 'Since I took over the department, production is up over 60 per cent', or 'It's almost too hot to fix dinner tonight', or 'I guess I was lucky winning three sets in a row', or 'What do you think of this necktie?'

Norman Sigband and Arthur Bell

The most prevalent mistake that people make about listening is to regard it as passively receiving rather than as actively participating ... Catching is as much an activity as throwing and requires as much skill, though it is a skill of a different kind. Without the complementary efforts of both players ... the play cannot be completed.

Mortimer Adler

Listening is hard work and requires increased energy. Your heart speeds up, your blood circulates faster, your temperature goes up.

Harold T. Allen

8 COMMUNICATING ON THE TELEPHONE

THE PROS AND CONS OF TELEPHONE COMMUNICATION

So far in this book, we have been primarily looking at the customer–provider encounter as something that happens face to face. Some people in organisations interact with external (and internal) customers mainly on a face-to-face basis, but it's true to say that in many organisations, *most contact — at least with external customers — occurs on the telephone*, and not on a face-to-face basis.

So what, you might say. Surely there is virtually no difference between communicating face to face and communicating on the telephone? Well, actually, there is. In fact, there are numerous differences. The telephone is only the most visible of a range of existing and emerging technologies that help (or hinder) effective communication.[134]

The complete communicator needs to be aware of the strengths and weaknesses of both channels of communication.

For example, face-to-face interaction allows a full range of non-verbal communication to be employed (see table 8.1). Until the videophone becomes a widely used tool, we cannot see people when we are talking to them on the telephone. Thus, we cannot see gestures, postures, facial expressions, clothing and adornment, and so on. This full continuum of information about the other person is available to us when we confront that person. A customer can thus see what providers look like. It is also easier for customers and providers to discuss visual material and objects — forms, letters, machines, and so on.

It is an unfortunate reality of some organisations that customers get stalled, screened away from 'important' people, and generally given the runaround. Sometimes this is done maliciously by providers, and sometimes it done defensively. The system has not provided the front-line providers with answers, and thus they cannot really help the customer — or at least not just yet. From the customer's point of view, the face-to-face encounter has the advantage of preventing — or at least of making less likely — such negative behaviour: 'I'm here, and I want action — now!'

The down-side of face-to-face encounters is that they take effort, time and money — especially so when compared to the telephone. From the provider's viewpoint, face-to-face encounters may be less desirable for the same reason that they are desirable for customers: it is more difficult to stall, screen, and to give the runaround. It is also harder, however, to defer and re-direct, and deferring and re-directing communication is quite reasonable and honourable in some circumstances: information is not immediately to hand, or someone who can help isn't on the premises just at this moment, or is in another location.

Table 8.1: Telephone versus face-to-face communication

	Face to face	**Telephone**
Pro	• full range of non-verbal communication available • easy to discuss visual material and objects • more difficult for others to stall, screen, give runaround	• more convenient • briefer • simpler • cheaper • good for routine repetitive transactions • easier to say 'no' • advantage to caller — easier to get others to say 'yes' • easier to take notes • easier to defer, re-direct • easier to stall, screen, give runaround • allows younger, more inexperienced people to appear more authoritative
Con	• less convenient • less brief • more complex • more expensive • difficult to say 'no' • more difficult to defer, re-direct • more difficult to stall, screen, give runaround	• full range of non-verbal communication not available • more difficult to discuss visual material and objects • advantage to caller — harder to say 'no' • may lead to 'ping-pong' — people only talk to machines

Communicating on the telephone can be more convenient, briefer, simpler and cheaper than communicating face to face. It's not necessary for people to physically travel to a location to get satisfaction or information; they can, as the telephone advertisements have it, 'let their fingers do the walking' (through the telephone directory). This is particularly important for routine, repetitive transactions.

It's often easier to say 'no' on the telephone, because one does not have the other person physically present. On the other hand, if one is the caller, one has the advantage, and may be able to bulldoze the other person into agreements and activities they would never have agreed to if they had had time to think.

It's easier to take notes while on the telephone, primarily because it is not necessary to go through the polite non-verbal behaviour of visually acknowledging the other person. It is easier to stall, screen and give the runaround on the telephone. It is also easier to defer and re-direct: a caller can be placed on hold while documents are found, or confidential conversations are hastily held ('Quick! It's Mrs McGillicuddy on line 2! What's happening with her llamas?'); the inquiry can be effortlessly transferred to someone who knows more about it; and a message can be taken, by a person or by a machine, so that the call can be returned at a later time.

It's also a point to consider that younger and more inexperienced people can sound more authoritative on the telephone than might be the case face to face.[135]

Communicating on the telephone has a down side, however. The full range of non-verbal communication is not available to either party, and thus there is greater potential for misunderstanding. It is also obviously more difficult to discuss visual material and objects (this can be partly offset by using faxes of visual material and photographs of objects). If one is the callee, and not the caller, one can be caught at a disadvantage, and thus might be bulldozed or pressured into saying 'yes' to something that would have received a firm 'no' in a face-to-face situation. Finally, even though telephones and answering machines may make it easier for two people to be less dependent upon physically meeting here and now, such technology can also lead to 'ping-pong' — I leave a message for you when you're not in/you ring back, I'm not in, you leave a message/I ring back again, you're not in again, I leave a message again ... and so on. This, to say the least, can be frustrating. In such a situation, technology does not liberate us, but enslaves us.

THE TELEPHONE: KNOW THE BASICS

The telephone is just a lump of plastic and wires, so there's no need to be threatened by it. If you learn about the technology of the phone, then your communication effectiveness can be increased substantially.

It's remarkable how organisations spend considerable sums of money in installing or upgrading the hardware of telephone systems, but spend virtually no money in training people how to use such systems. This is often true for people working with centralised technology, such as switchboard/PABX operators, and it is almost always true for people working with basic handsets — the majority of people who have telephones on their desks or on their walls. This is sometimes due to managers not allowing time and money for training programs, and it is sometimes due to managers and staff in general believing that such training is quite unnecessary — 'Surely everyone knows how to operate a phone!' Even the most basic phones today, however, can perform some quite fancy tricks, and you should know how to exploit such technology. If there is no training program in your workplace, it will repay your efforts to study the manual, brochure or instruction sheet that arrived with the phone at the time of installation. If such documentation has perished, or has been damaged, get a new set of information from the administrative area that looks after such things, or from the supplier or manufacturer. Set aside time to read the instructions, or if you're just not that disciplined, resolve to read a section each time you get put on hold when on the phone.

You should know, at the very least,
- how to transfer a call
- how to put a caller on hold.

You should also have to hand
- pens that work
- a telephone message pad
- an internal telephone directory.

MORE TECHNOLOGY

If you have an answering machine or a voice-mail system, you should observe some basic principles.

- If you do not have much experience in recording messages, make more than one attempt. Most people seem to need at least 5–10 attempts before they get the sound and message they want.
- Try to sound relaxed and natural. You may find it useful to write out your recorded message, and then read it out while recording.
- Record when there is minimal background noise.
- Leave the jokes to the comedians, or your home machine.
- Try and change the message regularly. For example, record a new message each day, announcing the date and day. This at least gives callers the idea that you listen to your messages, and therefore you will get back to them sooner rather than later.
- Ask callers to leave the information you need, but don't overload them with obligation. Prompt them to leave their name, organisation, contact number, date and time of calling, and the reason for their call. If there is a time limit on your tape, let them know how much time they have.
- If possible, give them the contact number of someone who will actually be present, so that callers will be able to talk to someone about urgent matters. If appropriate, give an after-hours number.
- Messages left on personal telephone answering machines can be very brief (and indeed may even be cryptically short, to preserve privacy). Business messages, however, usually need to be longer, giving maximum information to the caller and, wherever possible, providing courses of action that are alternatives to simply leaving a message. Such messages don't need to be sagas, but they do need to be thorough. The longer the message, of course, the more likely the caller is to disconnect in annoyance, without leaving a message (figure 8.1).

> Hi. This is Leanne Roberts in the marketing department of Juggernaut Manufacturing, on Extension 2951. Today is Tuesday, March 4. I will not be at my desk until after 2 p.m. Central Pacific Time tomorrow, Wednesday, March 5. If you need to speak to someone else urgently, please contact Tim McCaw on 2957. That's 897.2957 if you're ringing from outside Juggernaut. Alternatively, if you want to go back to the switchboard and you have a touchphone, press 2 now. If you'd like to leave me a message, please wait for the beep, and leave it then. There's no hurry — you can talk as long as you like. Please leave your name, date and time of calling, a number where I can reach you and some details of what it's all about. If you need to send me a fax, please send it on 899.2341. That's 899.2341. I look forward to catching up with you. Here comes the beep ...

Figure 8.1: A long but effective recorded business message

ANSWERING THE TELEPHONE

There are two groups of people who answer business phones: specialists, such as switchboard or PABX operators, and the majority of people who use handsets, connected to switchboards. (This distinction is beginning to break down, however: in some phone systems, technology now makes it possible for any handset to become a switchboard.) Sometimes switchboard operators are required to undertake duties in addition to that of answering the switch (acting as a receptionist, doing paperwork, opening and despatching mail). Similar types of communication rules apply to all such users.

If you are occupied on a task, or are eating, drinking, smoking or chewing, and the telephone rings, you need to discontinue the other activities and concentrate upon the upcoming conversation. Similarly, if you are conducting a conversation with someone in your workplace, and your telephone rings, then you need to consider a number of things.

- Which is the more important conversation: the face-to-face one I am having in the present, or the telephone one I may have in the immediate future?
- How can I extend maximum courtesy to the person here with me now and the person trying to get through to me?
- What technology do I have at my disposal (to take a message, to screen the call, to divert the call)?

If you decide to take the call, excuse yourself from the face-to-face conversation, and concentrate upon the upcoming conversation.

Pick up the phone and greet the caller with statements such as those shown in table 8.2.

Table 8.2: Suggested greeting responses

	Switchboard operator	**Handset user**
Courteous opening greeting	Hello/Good morning . . .	Hello/Good morning . . .
Where statement	Juggernaut Manufacturing . . .	Juggernaut Manufacturing, Marketing Department . . .
Who statement	This is Leanne . . .	This is Leanne Roberts on Extension 2951 . . .
Action orientation statement	How may I help you?	How may I help you?

The courteous greeting is a nice touch. Sound as though you mean it (even though you may not feel like it). Try smiling as you say words like these. It helps to brighten up a gloomy world, and if you are dreading the unknown from the outside world, such breezy and brisk professionalism may disarm the most grumpy caller. Check to see that it *is* still morning (or afternoon, or evening): some people are sticklers for precision in these matters. There is an even more basic reason for giving an opening greeting: sometimes — for a variety of reasons — the first part of a greeting statement is lost, or not heard. Better the lost part should be the least important part.

Next comes the *where* statement. You are telling the caller the destination of his/her call. If it's a wrong number, the caller will need to know this right away, so that further time won't be wasted or confusion caused.

Next comes the *who* statement. Don't be anonymous. Take responsibility for the call. For switchboard operators, a first or Christian name may be adequate: it's warm, it gives a personal touch, and that's all the caller needs to know. Handset users should give a full name, and an extension number. Callers have a right to know who they are talking to, and how they can get in touch with the same person at a future time.

Finally comes the *action orientation* statement. 'How may I help you?' shows that you want to help, that you want to solve problems, and that you are prompting the caller to be specific from the outset. At some stage in the call — preferably sooner rather than later — you should try and get the caller's name and details, if these are not offered. In fact, with angry customers, such a simple inquiry may help to cool them down. Using the customer's name at least twice in the conversation can help to establish rapport. Try to establish just what form of name the customer is comfortable with (first name, or title and last name). Remember that older people and people from certain cultures may be uncomfortable with first-name informality.

Know the organisation

Putting people on hold while you find out things or while you are transferring them to other areas requires some measure of technical skill. But you also need to know a good deal about your organisation. For example, some inquiries may require you to make inquiries of your own:
- Who looks after enrolments?
- Who knows about vehicle maintenance?
- This guy on the line says that Laurie in spare parts said that he could pay via credit card. What's Laurie's surname, so I can look him up in the internal directory?

You should have a good working knowledge of who does what in your organisation, and be able to contact them at short notice. Everyone within an organisation is someone else's internal customer (p. 10) at some stage, and it may be necessary to train staff so that everyone knows what everyone else does. The bigger the organisation becomes, the greater is the necessity for such training. Substitutes or backups for such training include organisation charts, staff manuals (preferably with photographs), internal phone directories, induction lessons and tours for new staff, and social gatherings for all staff.

Taking messages

In order for a message to make any sense — to communicate — you need to record a number of things:
- the name of the person. Check spelling, and if necessary, pronunciation.
- the day, date and time they called
- the number they can be contacted on
- their availability for a call-back (for example, 'between 2 and 4 this afternoon'). If the call is from an area within another time zone, find out the differences from local time (phone books should have this information), and note this.
- the name of the organisation or department
- the nature of their query: what is the problem to be solved?

Once you have recorded such information, you should read it back to the person calling, to check to see that you have an accurate account of the situation (see figure 8.2).

> OK, Mr Cariloe, can I just check this with you? You want to speak to Ms Houghton. You've rung today, Friday May 4, at 1:37 Melbourne time. Your name is Mr Jess Cariloe, that's J-E-S-S, surname C-A-R-I-L-O-E, and you are from Clone Power Computers in Singapore. Your direct number in Singapore is 65.390.4122. I'll just put the exit code from Australia in front of that — that's 0011. You want Ms Houghton to ring you back regarding the despatch schedules she faxed to Mr Yee — that's Y-E-E — yesterday. You'll be available between 2 and 4 this afternoon, your time, and all day tomorrow. Singapore time is — let's see — 2 hours behind Australian Eastern Standard Time. Have I got that right? Fine. I'll put that in the middle of her desk.

Figure 8.2: Taking a message effectively

This all takes time of course, but any impatience or frustration experienced by the caller as you read the message back will usually be more than outweighed by the feeling of reassurance that *their message will get through without distortion* — that communication, in fact, will have occurred.

PLACING CALLS

When you are placing a call, you need to be organised. Don't just jump straight into calling, motivated by anxiety, eagerness, or both. You need to:
- know what you want to say — what you want to achieve from this phone call. If necessary, write out a 'script', noting key words and phrases that will help convey your message. If it's an important phone call, role-play these words and phrases with a friend or colleague taking the part of the person you are going to call. Don't end up thinking to yourself: 'What I *should* have said was ...'
- have the right tools at hand: files, relevant paperwork, your diary, active computer screen, pens that work.
- do it.

Leaving messages

You should be equally as methodical when you are leaving a message, either with a person or on a machine. Many people still feel uncomfortable leaving messages on answering machines or voice-mail systems. Try to overcome this uneasiness — the technology is there to work for you, and it's a waste of your time and money to keep ringing back, on the expectation that you will encounter a human being. People are often uneasy about talking to machines, because it's like dropping a message into a black hole: there is no give and take, none of the two-way communication that is the essence of a normal conversation. Practice can overcome this, however: practise leaving messages on a machine you can play back, and critique your own performance. Your first attempts will probably be awful — gabbled, disorganised, not saying everything you wanted to say, forgetting to leave your name and number — but over time your performance will improve. You've got to work twice as hard in leaving a message because you do not have someone on the other end of the line to cue or prompt you to leave maximum information; you have to cue or prompt yourself. There's absolutely nothing wrong, by the way, with writing out your message, in full or in note form, on paper or on a computer screen, and using that as a guide for your message. That way, if your brain freezes when the beep sounds, you have a 'script' to work from.

Your message should include:
- your name. Spell your name if there is even the slightest chance of misunderstanding.
- the day, date and time you are calling
- your organisation or department
- your contact number
- your availability for a call-back ('between 2 and 4 this afternoon'). If you are calling an area within another time zone, mention the differences from local time.
- the nature of your query: what the problem is to be solved.

> Hello, Ms Houghton. This is Jess Cariloe from Clone Power in Singapore. That's Jess, J-E-S-S, Cariloe, C-A-R-I-L-O-E. My direct number here is 390.4122. Singapore's country code is 65, and the exit code from Australia is, I think, 0011. So that's 0011.65.390.4122. You sent a fax to our Mr Yee yesterday, regarding despatch schedules. We've got a problem with two of those dates — the 14th and the 16th of June. They don't tally with our copy of the original agreement. Could you ring me back soon so we can clarify this? It's 11:37 a.m. here — that's two hours earlier than Australian Eastern Standard Time in Melbourne. I'll be at this number between 2 and 4 this afternoon, my time, and I'll be in all day tomorrow — that's 9 a.m. to 5 p.m., my time. I hope to talk to you soon. Bye.

Figure 8.3: Leaving an effective message

WORKING ON THE TELEPHONE: A PERFORMING ART

Whether you are placing calls or receiving calls, it's useful to remember and to practise a few key strategies:

- Use questioning and active listening techniques to get to the heart of what the customer wants (pp. 100–106). Note in particular the technique of repeating in your own words what it is you think the customer wants.
- Wherever possible, create choices and opportunities for the customer — don't restrict these.
- Create decision points in your conversation: this lets customers know that they are in joint control of the conversation, and it triggers solutions to problems.
- Keep in mind the customer's point of view: that's what motivates him or her. The smell of success is WIIFY: What's In It For You?
- If your organisation has made an error, or if the customer is wrong, don't lay blame — that's history, and people only get defensive, and then hostile. Concentrate on solutions, and take responsibility for generating and carrying out those solutions.
- Within limits, match the pace and vocabulary of the customer. Don't mimic, just create some rapport (see pp. 89–90).
- Use the customer's name several times; this also creates rapport.
- Don't get stampeded or panicked — stay calm. Courteously, but assertively, reserve your right to investigate the situation and get back to the customer with a second phone call.
- Know your stuff; be aware of your organisation's policies and procedures, so that you can communicate with confidence.
- Know the mechanics of your instrument — the telephone.
- Know the mechanics of your other instrument — your voice. Be aware of the non-verbal aspects of your voice (see table 8.3). Make sure, at the very least, that your voice doesn't obscure or contradict what it is you are saying with your words (see chapter 3, 'Non-verbal communication'). Even better, work with your voice, get to know it well so that it complements your thoughts and words. Record yourself on a tape recorder, answering machine or voice-mail system: is this really how you want to sound, or do you need to make changes?

Table 8.3: Non-verbal aspects of speech

Non-verbal aspects of speech	Points to consider
Loudness	Too much? Not enough? Just right?
Pitch	Low? High? Just right?
Inflection	Upward? Downward? Appropriate?
Articulation	Mumbling? Over-precise? Just right?
Tone	Monotonous? Too theatrical? Just right?
Nasality	Too much? Not enough? Just right?
Speed	Too fast? Too slow? Just right?
Pronunciation	Accurate? Inaccurate?
Emphasis	Appropriate? Inappropriate?
Accent	Acceptance problems?

THE CHAMBER OF TELEPHONE HORRORS: WHAT *NOT* TO DO ON THE PHONE

We have considered many of the do's of good telephone communication with customers. How about the don'ts? Listed below (table 8.4) are quite a few of such don'ts with some more acceptable approaches. Undoubtedly you can think of quite a few more don'ts yourself.

Table 8.4: Words and behaviours to avoid while on the telephone

Words/behaviour	Possible interpretation	Better approach
(Picks up receiver while conducting a conversation with people at the other end — possibly muffling mouthpiece — eventually answering.)	I am rude and disorganised, and you are less important than the people in here.	(Conclude or defer conversation at home end. Pick up receiver, giving caller total attention.)
(Other people talking loudly in background.)	The culture of this place is that we're all rude and disorganised, and at the moment you're interrupting us.	(Don't allow situation to occur.)
Yeah, hi . . .	I am really sloppy on the phone; can you imagine how I handle your business?/I think that you are a mind-reader and that you know who I am.	Hello, Accounts. This is Mark Rousseau speaking. How can I help you?
Yo . . .	I think this is trendy (but it's just boorish).	Hello . . .
2451.	12! Next question?	Extension 2451, Marketing, Jane Storm speaking. May I help you?
Hello, Marketing . . .	This is not a person but a department speaking/I wish to remain anonymous.	Hello, Marketing, Leanne Roberts speaking. How may I help you?
Leanne speaking . . .	I was only given one name at birth/there are three Leannes on this floor; wouldn't you like to find the right one if you rang back?/I'm trying to remain semi-anonymous.	. . . Leanne Roberts speaking . . .
NSMSU, Leanne Roberts speaking.	Only idiots don't know what NSMSU means. Are you an idiot?	Northern Sector Marketing and Sales Unit, Leanne Roberts speaking.
Oh that's easily fixed. You just superfreneticize the veeblefetzer until the LCDs reach their peak values, and then you . . .	Only idiots don't know these terms. Are you an idiot?	Yes, we can fix that. If you'll just bear with me while I walk you through the procedure . . . If you look near the top left-hand corner, you'll see a red cone-shaped object, about 10 cm long. That's called a veeblefezter. Now . . .

(*Continued*)

Words/behaviour	Possible interpretation	Better approach
Looo … Margen … Lah Ribud megin … Kin hebu …	I am too sloppy to actually speak clearly; can you imagine how I handle your business?	Hello, Marketing, Leanne Roberts speaking. How may I help you?
(Picks up phone while eating, drinking, smoking, chewing.)	I am rude and disorganised, and you are less important than my lunch/drink/cigarette/gum.	(Don't allow this situation to occur.)
Just a minute (puts caller on hold.)	I'm running this show; I'm not interested in your opinion as to whether you want to be put on hold.	I can get that information for you quickly. Would you mind if I put you on hold?
Just a minute (transfers call).	I'm running this show; I'm not interested in your opinion as to whether you want to be transferred to someone else.	Andrew Johnson in our Claims area can help you more than I can. Would you mind if I transferred you to him?
Just a minute (drops receiver).	I am clumsy and inconsiderate/your eardrums need the exercise.	Just a moment/can you hold, please? (Carefully puts receiver down/puts call on hold.)
Just a minute (muffles receiver with hand).	I am not a professional person/I am stupid enough to believe that you can't hear what I'm saying through my hand.	Just a moment/can you hold, please? (Puts call on hold.)
(Continues to shuffle papers, audibly sign papers, while conversing.)	You are not important/you bore me.	(Don't allow this to happen.)
He's with an important client at the moment.	As opposed to you, who are not important.	He's with a client at the moment. Can he ring you back, or can I perhaps help you?
I have no idea when she'll be back.	This place is really disorganised/you are wasting your time talking to such an unimportant/apathetic person as me.	She'll be back later, possibly after two. Can she ring you back, or can I perhaps help you?
I don't know. They never tell me anything.	This place is really disorganised/you are wasting your time talking to such an unimportant/apathetic person as me.	I'm afraid I don't know that. Can I help you with anything else, or can I put you in touch with someone who might know?
I'm sorry, we can't take messages.	We just like frustrating people/we like going out of business/we are a monopoly and we don't care.	Can I take a message/let me connect you to someone who can take a message/that phone has an answering machine. I suggest you leave a message on it. Shall I transfer you?
Hang on, this pen doesn't work … no, this one doesn't either …	I don't actually need pens for my work. I just sit here and use telepathy.	(Have a number of pens available.)
All I can do …	You're not going to get what you want.	I can't do that, but here's what I can do …

Words/behaviour	Possible interpretation	Better approach
She's at the doctor's office …	… and you're not (useless personal information that can only frustrate).	She's unavailable at the moment. Can she ring you back, or can I perhaps help you?
She's gone home early …	… and you're still stuck at work (useless personal information that can only infuriate).	She's unavailable at the moment. Can she ring you back, or can I perhaps help you?
She's on vacation …	… and you're not (useless personal information that can only infuriate)/we are so disorganised that we haven't made provision for someone to do her work while she's gone.	She's unavailable until the 27th, I'm afraid. However, Mr Lars Hendle is familiar with these matters. May I transfer you?
If you've got any problems, get back to us and ask for Tania.	We think you operate as chaotically as we do.	If any problems occur, please contact me. My name is Tania Skotnicki — that's S-K-O-T-N-I-C-K-I — and my direct line is 220.1236 — that's 220.1236. I have voice-mail, so that you can leave a message if I'm not at my desk. I always try to return calls within two hours.
Your order should be there by Tuesday.	We all *should* be good, and we all *should* be paid more, but that's not reality at the moment, is it?(Often followed by 'hopefully'.)	Your order will be there by Tuesday. Should any problems arise before or on that date, please call me, Tania Skotnicki, that's S-K-O-T-N-I-C-K-I, on 220.1236.
Haven't Accounts been able to help you? This is the third call like this today.	We all hate each other in here and try and blame each other without investigating the situation/it's utter chaos here. Better get your business out of here while you can.	I'll just get through to Accounts for you and sort this out. Would you mind holding please?
Sorry, I just work here.	I am an idiot and your business with us is in serious jeopardy.	I'm not familiar with that area. Can I transfer you to someone who looks after those accounts?
Sorry, I don't know. I'm just new here.	We are in a state of chaos/we don't believe in training anyone in basic work procedures.	I'm not familiar with that area. Can I transfer you to someone who looks after those accounts?
I'll just transfer you … hope you don't get cut off … (muffled voice: How do I transfer this call to Carol?) (Clicks … silence … disconnect signal …)	We are in a state of chaos/we don't believe in training anyone in basic telephone procedures.	I'll just transfer you now. If by chance you are disconnected, Carol's direct number is 660.6163. Stand by, please.
Well love, it's like this …	I am unsophisticated and overly familiar.	Well, Ms Jenkins, the situation is …
No worries. See ya.	I am unsophisticated and possibly sloppy. You should worry. Best not to see me ever again.	That's fine/that's all under control now. I'll contact you tomorrow/I'll speak with you further. Goodbye.

(Source: adapted from Finch [1990], Anderson [1992], Broydrick [1994].)

ACTIVITIES

1. Consider the worst phone call you have ever made, and the best. What characterised them? Under what circumstances would they have been different? Write an analysis of these points, and/or discuss them with others.
2. Make a complete list of the features of the telephone system you work with. What are the strengths and weaknesses of such a system?
3. If you work in an organisation, make a chart of that organisation. Highlight the people on the chart you communicate with, or might need to communicate with, on the telephone. Make a list of such people, using these categories:

Extension no.	Name	Area of expertise

4. Create a chart showing at least another three things not to do or say on the telephone.

TALKING POINTS

A poem on loneliness

What do you see, stylist, what do you see?
Are you thinking when you are looking at me,
A crabby old woman, not very wise,
Uncertain of habit, with faraway eyes,
Who is late for appointments and makes no reply,
When you say in a loud voice, 'I do wish you'd try!'

I'll tell you who I am as I sit here so still,
As I rise at your bidding and I lift my head at your will.
I'm a small child of ten with a father and a mother,
With brothers and sisters who love one another.
A bride soon at twenty, my heart gives a leap,
Remembering the vows that I promised to keep.

At twenty-five now, I have young of my own,
Who need me to build a secure and happy home.
At fifty, once more babies round my knee,
Again we knew children, my loved one and me.

Dark days are upon me, my husband is dead.
I look to the future, I shudder with dread,
And I think of the years and the love that I've known.

I'm an old woman now and nature is cruel,
Tis her jest to make old age look like a fool.
This body it crumbles, grace and vigour depart,
There now is a stone where I once had a heart.

But inside this old carcass a young girl still dwells,
And now and again my bittered heart swells.
I remember the joys, I remember the pain,
I'm living and loving all over again.

And I think of the years all too few gone too fast,
And accept the stark fact that nothing will last.
So open your eyes, stylist, open and see,
Not a crabby old 9 o'clock, look closer, see me.

Anonymous

(Originally written to a nurse — rewritten as if from a client to a hair stylist)

How do you create a perceptible difference that sets your product above the rest? The key is service — not adequate customer service, but exemplary customer service! Extraordinary attention to the customer.

At American Express, service *is* our 'differentiator' — outstanding, superior, service quality. It's part of our contract with our customers. If something goes wrong, we view it as an opportunity to demonstrate our ability to exceed our customer's expectations. We don't want our customers to be simply satisfied. We want them to be delighted!

Terrence J. Smith
American Express Co.

And far beyond the level of executive behaviour, *everything you do communicates*. The look and feel of the operation, the pace of things, the way employees are treated by their bosses, the way bosses treat the customers they deal with, the importance attached to delivering the value package with style and quality — all of these are messages. Some of them are overt, conscious messages and some are unconscious messages. Every organisation has an implicit level of communication that either reinforces or counteracts the message of quality and customer value.

Karl Albrecht

COMMUNICATING WITH CUSTOMERS
THE OVERVIEW

MAKING COMMUNICATION EASIER

We have now considered a number of models of and approaches to the customer/service provider encounter. We should now have a better idea of just what goes on when a customer meets a provider. If you are a service provider, you should now have a better idea of what to do when meeting customers — whether they be customers from hell, or from other, more pleasant places. (Although as we have seen, customers from hell are often justified in behaving less than perfectly and, in fact, any complaints or negative feedback they might give us should be gratefully accepted, rather than aggressively rejected.)

Is the world then really populated with high- and low-context cultures, punishing Parent ego states, crossed transactions, manipulatives and passives, visual, auditory and kinaesthetic types? The answer is: we don't know. We're not dealing with physics or engineering here, but with complex human behaviour. Does this matter? Probably not. The models of behaviour we have considered are conjectural and suggestive, not factual and prescriptive. If, after studying them and putting them into practice, we are more sensitive communicators, then that's good enough.

Do active listening techniques, questioning techniques, assertiveness, non-verbal mirroring, rapport-building and telephone techniques work all the time, in every situation? No, they don't. But they work well enough much of the time to make communication just that much easier — and that, too, is good enough.

With these limitations in mind, let's recap on what is needed for service providers to be able to better communicate with customers (see table 9.1).

Table 9.1: How to better communicate with customers: an overview

Pay attention.	Acknowledge the customer, even if you can't attend to him or her right away. Say: 'Hello, I'll be with you in a minute', or simply nod, raise eyebrows, etc.
Welcome the customer.	Use the greetings you would give to a friend: 'Good morning', 'Hello'. Establish eye contact.
Personalise.	Use the customer's name. If the customer's name presents pronunciation difficulties for you, discreetly check: 'I'm not very good with names. Could you advise me as to how you would like your name pronounced?'

(*Continued*)

Identify yourself.	Tell the customer who you are.
Be polite.	Treat the customer as you would want to be treated. Use 'please' and 'thank you'.
Establish rapport.	Use NLP techniques to try and get a fix on verbal behaviour. Use NLP, assertiveness and transactional analysis models to try and 'read' the non-verbal behaviour of the customer.
Stay cool.	• Avoid game-playing. Wherever possible, try and operate from an Adult ego state position. • Resist aggressive, passive and manipulative ploys. Wherever possible, try and operate from an assertive position.
Listen, question, gather feedback.	Use active listening techniques, and ethical questioning techniques.
Give feedback.	Let personal and telephone customers know that you are alive, that you understand, and that you are there to help.
Know your stuff.	Be an expert. Know the products, services, procedures. Know the organisation. Know the competition. Derive satisfaction from being excellent.
Help.	Derive satisfaction from helping the customer to solve problems.
Strive for solutions.	Don't get bogged down in blaming — yourself, the organisation, the world in general or the customer. Apologise where necessary, and then get on with the job of fixing the problem.
Learn from previous experience and theory.	Stay cool, and analyse situations as they are happening. Can your understanding of human behaviour help you to make sense of what's happening?
Farewell the customer.	Close the encounter as you would with a friend: 'Goodbye', 'Good afternoon'. Give final eye contact.
Know when to quit.	You have rights too, and you do not have to take unrelenting insults or other types of negative feedback. Know when to walk away, delegate the problem to someone else, and expect backup. Know how, in extreme circumstances, your organisation can 'fire the customer'.
Expect backup.	Define what you need from the system in order to operate. You can deliver the smiles if the system delivers to you.

Much of this, of course, is just common sense. Much of it, indeed, is just good manners. Common sense, good manners, and a command of the more sophisticated models of communication in this book will help you to be a truly effective communicator with your customers.

ACTIVITIES

Consider an organisation with which you are familiar. Using your knowledge and skills in the area of customer/provider communication, write a proposal for improved customer service.

- Define at least three problems the organisation has in customer service. Propose solutions to each of these problems.
- Your final proposal should contain a master checklist of at least fifteen items which would help in the implementation and evaluation of your proposal.

TALKING POINTS

COMMENTS ABOUT CUSTOMER SERVICE

Haircutter (self-centred)	Psy-cosmetologist (client-centred)
Makes recommendations centred around personal knowledge and technical skills.	Makes recommendations centred around *client's* needs.
Has repertoire of few cuts.	Pictures as many different cuts as there are different clients.
Does robot-like cutting.	Believes in creativity, exploring alternatives, and encouraging new possibilities.
Cuts in mass production.	Individualises cut, perm and colour.
Sees all clients in the same way.	Sees clients in unique, special ways.
Focuses on hair.	Focuses on each client's total self — physical, emotional, educational, social, athletic, and lifestyle.
Dominates by talking and telling.	Harmoniously listens and dreams with clients.
Gives similar cut each time on the same client.	Always looks for ways to refine the cut in accordance with the client's changing life, needs, and goals.

Donald W. Scoleri and Lewis E. Losoncy
The New Psy-Cosmetologist

When your customer is the most anxious, you need to be at your best — most competent, confident, calmest, and in control of yourself.

Chip R. Bell

COMMUNICATING WITH CUSTOMERS: THE OVERVIEW   129

CUSTOMERS FROM HELL: SCENES FROM A NEWSAGENCY

Customer 1 brings a magazine to the counter and says: 'Here's my car keys, so you know I'll come back. I just want to take this to the library and photocopy a few pages'.

When it is pointed out that this violates copyright, and that lending magazines is not what a newsagency does, Customer 1 throws down the magazine and says, 'Well — a fat lot you know about customer service!'

Customer 2 brings her adult Rottweiler dog — with no lead attached — into the newsagency, and proceeds to browse through some magazines. Other customers are startled and frightened. When challenged (delicately), Customer 2 says: 'Oh, he won't hurt you — he's quite tame'.

Customer 3 picks up an interstate newspaper, and asks: 'Does this contain a local television guide magazine?' Answer: no, it doesn't. Customer 3 responds: 'Well, you think they'd give you one, wouldn't you?' (possibly implying that newsagent should supply a guide from a local paper, free of charge). No response from newsagent. Customer 3 (buys interstate paper): 'You're a real pig! As a matter of fact, you're all pigs in here! It's a wonder you're in business! But then again, I suppose it's money — you bought your way in!' (turns and strides out).

Customers 4-12 come up to counter, but stand back, and look down in a perplexed way, occasionally wrinkling up noses. Newsagent walks around counter to see what is going on, and sees *Customer 13* — an inebriated tramp — asleep against counter, near hot air vent.

ENDNOTES

1. Who is it who communicates with the customer? 'Provider' is almost so vague and bland as to be useless, but it seems to be the least worst term available. 'Salesperson' excludes not-for-profit transactions, and usually connotes the retail world, and not the realms of other transactions, such as those of doctor–patient and taxpayer–civil servant. 'Service provider' is marginally less general than 'provider', but excludes transactions involving tangible goods, and thus excludes people working in primary and secondary industries, who nevertheless need to communicate with their customers (p. 6). 'Vendor' is fairly general, but perhaps has a too-specific real estate connotation. So — unfortunately — 'provider' it is.

2. 'Customers' and 'clients' do not come from two different races of people. 'Client' tends to be a more upmarket way of saying 'customer', in much the same way as 'salary' is a more 'upmarket' way of saying 'pay'. Salary or pay, however, are both paid in the same type of money, and customers or clients need or want similar things. Semantics sometimes confuses more than it clarifies. Some organisations tend to take their customers for granted, and perhaps could benefit by reconceptualising or rethinking their customers as clients; some organisations, by contrast, tend to take too rarefied a view of reality, ignoring the competitive nature of the market they operate in: to avoid becoming client-less, they might well benefit by reconceptualising their clients as customers.

3. Baritz (1965) and others have criticised industrial psychologists for being 'servants of power' — for developing theories of motivation that have been used by authoritarian managers to better manipulate workers. See Eunson (1987: 37–38, 347–348). Note also the remarks of Steiner (1974: 11–12) re transactional analysis being taught as a customer relations technique:

    Transactional analysis is being used by banks and airlines and racetracks as a device taught to their employees to better deal with their customers. There might be nothing wrong with this if what was taught was, in fact, transactional analysis. But the fact is that transactional analysis is being corrupted and transformed to serve the needs of the banks, airlines and racetracks, not only in subtle ways which strip it of its basic principles, but even in the very crudest ways ... Briefly, transactional analysis was invented for use as a contractual therapeutic technique. (Transactional analysis founder Eric) Berne was very suspicious (of) and antagonistic to one-sided situations where one person held all the cards. Perhaps it was because of this that he enjoyed the game of poker where everyone starts with an even chance. In any case, transactional analysis was designed as a two-way, cooperative, transactional process; its one-sided use as a tool for behaviour control is an abuse of its potency, similar to slipping a customer a sedative in a coke so that he'll buy a used car.

4. Anonymous (b) (1994); Godbout (1993)
5. Lovelock (1994: 10-20)
6. ' "If you make a better mousetrap, the world will beat a path to your door." Yes, for about as long as it takes your neighbour to copy it, improve it, and offer it at half your price. IBM introduced the PC in late 1981 and the first "clones" were available in 1983. Today, clones account for half of all PCs sold ... New processes, incremental changes to old processes, investments in automation — none of these hold off the competition for long. Studies indicate that 60 to 90 per cent of all learning leaks away to competitors within a very short period of time.' (Lele and Sheth 1991: 2)
7. Davidow and Uttal (1989: 11)
8. Reich (1983). Note also Albrecht's analysis (Albrecht 1992: ix):

> Many executives have become confused by the welter of books, models, methods, and consultants telling them they must do 'quality'. The so-called quality movement is one of the most confusing and frustrating panaceas ever to hit the business scene.
>
> Other executives have fastened on the idea of 'customer service' as the holy grail of business success. In its most simple-minded form, the customer-service approach has become an undisciplined search for gimmicks to try and get the employees to 'be nice' and the customers to 'be happy'.
>
> Actually, neither 'quality' nor 'service' is the answer. There is no point in making 'quality' a thing unto itself, like a strange bump attached to the organisation. And there is no point in trying to love the customer to pieces if we don't make a profit or meet the related business objectives.
>
> The quality issue and the service issue are no longer two separate issues — they are now one and the same issue. Once we leave behind the archaic distinction between 'products' and 'services', we begin to understand that the only thing that really matters in business is delivering *customer value*, which is always a combination of tangibles and intangibles.

cf. Guaspari (1988: 111-12)

> It is commonly said: 'Fundamentally, all businesses are service businesses'. Although the idea is basically a correct one, I think that in practice its usefulness is limited, because to the extent it is so commonly accepted, it can become too familiar, too pat. People will stop noticing what's really being said. So I'd like to turn that notion around and suggest a different mind-set. I'd like to suggest that *all organisations are, fundamentally, factories* — to be more specific, *transaction factories*. Day in and day out, you build transactions for your customers. Their purchase decisions are based purely on the quality of those transactions, which they gauge in terms of their expectations. And all employees, in all departments, in all functions are direct assembly-line workers, adding their piece to the product being built, to the transaction.

9. See, for example, Carlzon (1987), Peters (1988).
10. For more on job and organisational design, see, for example, Eunson (1987), chapters 12-14.
11. See, for example, Eunson (1994b).
12. Desatnick (1987, chapter two), Peters (1988: 177-78). Note Peters' remarks:

> There are at least nine critical factors for enhancing attention to sales, service, and support people:
>
> 1. *Spend time with them*. If you're not visiting stores and distribution centres at 2 a.m., and dispatch offices very regularly, you don't care about these functions. It's that simple.

2. *Pay them well.* Are your distribution centre people paid well above the norm, with gain-sharing incentives to boot? If not, fix it now.

3. *Recognise them.* The boss's time counts. So do little things. A high-technology firm held a two-day offsite meeting for distribution people, looking for new opportunities. The firm was careful to make sure the setting and trappings were as lavish as those it provides for top-management affairs.

4. *Listen to them.* Like Toshiba ... provide regular senior management forums in which sales and service and support people can be heard.

5. *Make sales and service a feeder route to general management* and/or a necessary way-stop on the path to general management.

6. *Empower them.* Like Nordstrom or Federal Express, give the sales and service people wide latitude to act as 'the company' when they are in the field or on the phone, and especially when they are confronting a problem.

7. *Train them.* No firm I know has ever overtrained sales, service and support people. And make sure it's the right kind of training. One study of retail sales training revealed that twelve times as many hours were devoted to 'cash register techniques' and the policy manual as to selling skills and dealing with the problems of customers.

8. *Support them technically.* Make sure that the systems are in place which allow them to do their job to the fullest extent possible.

9. *Hire enough of them!* Think hard about the example of Buckman Labs, about Frito-Lay, BusinessLand and Nordstrom. All four have far too many salespeople, by industry standards. Seriously consider doubling or tripling your sales force (assuming minimal annual market growth) over the next three to five years.

13. How can you figure out who's who? At Dun & Bradstreet, the financial information company, people identify their customers, whether internal or external, by asking two simple questions:

1. Where does my work go?
2. Who is my work important to?

At Dun & Bradstreet, everybody has a customer, no matter where on the organisational ladder they may be. In your organisation, your customer is whoever benefits from the work you do, or, conversely, whoever suffers when your work is done poorly or not at all.

If, for example, you take customer orders at your company's telephone centre, obviously you are serving external customers directly. But you have internal customers, too. Who receives the orders you take from those external customers? What happens when necessary information is missing from those orders, or is entered incorrectly? The impact of what you do or don't do affects both your external customers, who may not receive what they ordered, and your internal customers in the warehouse, billing and shipping, who will have to deal with the complaint when the order isn't received. (Anderson and Zemke 1991: 33-34)

From the time your organisation starts producing its product or service, to the time you deliver it to your external customer, the product or service being changed for consumption goes through an internal chain of events.

In that chain, everybody is a customer, a producer and a supplier. When you accept the baton from a teammate, you are a customer. When you run with it for your leg of the relay, you are a producer — making some change or adding value to the baton. When you pass it off to the next member of the team, you become a supplier. (Chang and Kelly 1994: 41).

14. Lovelock (1994: 208) notes that high-income earners are more likely to complain than low-income earners, and younger people are more likely to complain than older people.

15. 'The irony is that when banks, airlines and telephone companies were regulated, their strategies were based on customer service. They were allowed to use no other competitive weapon. Once deregulated, however, they lost their focus on service and naively turned to competing on price. Their margins eroded. They began to disassemble service infrastructures that had taken years to build. They disenfranchised or got rid of employees who still believed in service. In short, they contributed heavily to the service crisis.' (Davidow and Uttal 1989: 7)

   Many Australian customers believe, however, that they have benefited from competition in some areas — for example, telecommunications.

16. 'Indeed, Stanley Marcus, the retailer who made Neiman-Marcus department stores legendary for service, once observed that publicly owned companies, constantly scrutinised by stockholders, have more difficulty giving good service than private firms that can spend money as they see fit. Public ownership, Marcus said, has a way of "turning corporations into commodities that are traded like pork bellies and soy beans", destroying managers' understanding of how important service is and their motivation to provide it'. (Davidow and Uttal 1989: 7–8)

   Note also Lele and Sheth (1991: 19–22).

17. 'Organisations will spend literally hundreds of millions of dollars to attract new customers while their old customers slip out the back door, never to return again. What drives people away is rude, discourteous, inept, incompetent service. It may simply be a matter of apathy or inattention.

   Now, it would seem logical that if an organisation is willing to spend $100 million or more annually on advertising and sales promotion, it should be willing to spend just about $20 million to keep its present customers. In fact, outstanding service and its ensuing word of mouth will not only keep present customers but attract new ones as well.

   If service is as important as chief executive officers claim it is, why is there not a vice-president of customer service, on the same level as the vice-president of sales and marketing?' (Desatnick 1987: 4)

18. Sewell and Brown (1990, chapter five).

   If customer service were a cake, the politeness, smiles, and being willing to go the extra mile would be the icing. The cake would be the systems that allow you to do a good job.

   Doing a good job has two parts:
   1. doing the job right the first time; and
   2. having a plan in place to deal with things when they go wrong.

   Having systems that allow you to do both these things is more important than all the warm and fuzzy feelings in the world. After all, it doesn't make any difference to our customers how nice we are if we don't do the job right or, at the very least, immediately take care of the problem when something goes wrong.

   It's like going to a restaurant. They can smile till their jaws ache, hold your chair for you when you sit down, and refold your napkin every time you leave the table, but if the food is no good, you're not likely to go back.

   What's needed in restaurants, car dealerships, department stores, and everyplace else is systems — not just smiles — that guarantee good service. (Sewell and Brown 1990: 23)

19. Quoted in Schlesinger and Heskett (1991).
20. See, for example, Jones (1989), Dupuy & Schweitzer (1994).
21. 'Greatgrandpa said to his son: If you are not careful, you could end up working in a factory. Is our generation saying to its offspring: if you are not careful, you could end up in a service industry?

    Industries are created to provide people and households with services as well as goods in greater abundance, cheaper and better than they can do themselves. We've done most of the "goods" bit; now it is the DIY services turn.' Ruthven (1994)

    The changing nature of customer relationships demands a new breed of service worker, folks who are empathetic, flexible, informed, articulate, inventive, and able to work with minimal levels of supevision. 'Rather than the service world being derided as having the dead-end jobs of our time, it will increasingly become an outlet for creativity, theatricality and expressiveness,' says Larry Keeley, president of Doblin Group, a Chicago management and design consulting firm. (Henkoff 1994)
22. Shamir (1980)
23. Hochschild (1983)
24. See, for example, Mehrabian (1971)
25. See, for example, McKinley (1984) and De Paulo and De Paulo (1989). Ekman (1992) suggests that deception can be detected if the two halves of a person's face are asymmetrical, that is, convey different emotions. This can be observed most precisely only by photographing a person's face, and then manipulating the image to create a double left-hand-side face and a double right-hand-side face.
26. For example, Beeler (1986) notes research which shows that computer professionals as a group often come across as unresponsive, expressionless, and extremely self-controlled. This makes it difficult for others to read them or to be comfortable in their presence. This immobile non-verbal behaviour, in fact, may act as a positive barrier to their career advancement in large companies.
27. Henley (1977)
28. Alper (1991)
29. Kennish (1989)
30. Henley (1977)
31. Abrams (1992)
32. Konopacki (1987a)
33. Cathcart and Allesandra (1985)
34. Chandler (1990)
35. Morris (1977)
36. Hall (1979)
37. Katz (1988)
38. Hall (1976)
39. Morris (1977)
40. Guthrie (1976)
41. Shreve, Harrigan, Kues and Kagas (1988)
42. Morris (1977)
43. Abrams (1992)
44. ' "Sorry, lady", the station attendant said, and shrugged his shoulders (shoulder shrugging is a certain clue that the curtain is about to go up on "It's not my department".)' (Glen 1990: 20)

45. In a recent study, waiters who squatted rather than stood when taking orders from customers in a restaurant got bigger tips. (Lynn and Minier 1993) What might this say about roles and perceptions of customers and service providers?
46. Waltman and Golen (1993), Nemec (1985)
47. Morris (1977)
48. Morris (1977)
49. Nierenberg and Calero (1971)
50. Model developed by Richard Heslin, Purdue University. Cited in Johnson (1988a).
51. Montagu (1971)
52. Simington (1993)
53. See, for example, Conway (1978), Canetti (1973).
54. Johnson (1988a), Hornik (1992)
55. Darwin, Charles (1872). If true, this gives an insight into why left-handers have often been unpopular throughout history.
56. Chandler (1990), Wesson (1992)
57. Fuller (1984)
58. Fuller (1984)
59. For a more extensive discussion of these functions, see examples in Morris (1977), Eunson (1987).
60. Peel (1987)
61. Rafaeli (1989)
62. For example, see Morris (1977), Thomas, Cassill and Forsythe (1991), Shim, Kotsiopulos and Knoll (1991).
63. Morris (1977), Cohen (1983), Pease (1981), Abrams (1992)
64. Henley (1977)
65. Pease (1981), Abrams (1992)
66. Church (1989)
67. Eroglu and Machleit (1990)
68. Bittner (1992)
69. Bellizi, Crowley and Hasty (1983)
70. Schiffman and Kanuk (1991: 107, 117)
71. Alpert and Alpert (1990), Donovan and Rossiter (1982)
72. Greene (1986), Bittner (1992)
73. See, for example, Sewell and Brown (1990: 124–125) and Chase and Stuart (1994). Note Sewell's remarks:
    > Signs say something about your organisation, your thought process, your taste, your attitude towards life, what kind of person you are, and what kind of business you're running. If you have signs screaming at you from all different angles, in all different typefaces and colours, I think it suggests to customers that they are visiting a zoo or circus, as opposed to a well-run business. (Sewell and Brown 1990: 125)
74. As Broydrick notes:
    > Retailers have discovered the value of making the first impression a personal impression. Tom Coughlin, senior vice president of Sam's Clubs, relates the following story in *Sam Walton: Made in America*:
    >> Back in 1990, Mr Walton and I went into a Wal-Mart in Crowley, Louisiana. The first thing we saw as we opened the door was this older gentleman standing there. The man didn't know me, and he didn't see Sam, but he said, 'Hi! How are ya? Glad you're here. If there's anything I can tell you about the store, just let me know'.

Sam Walton thought this was one of the best ideas he'd ever seen. After much cajoling and impassioned persuasion, he convinced his managers that every one of their stores should have a people greeter. Walk into any Wal-Mart today and chances are you'll be greeted by somebody like that older gentleman from that small town in Louisiana.

The larger the size of your retail store, the more valuable a greeter will be. Customers walking into a vast space can be overwhelmed and made to feel slightly insignificant. Seeing the warm smile of another human being helps provide some needed perspective...

The Towson Town Centre, a large shopping complex, helps its customers cope with the overwhelming scale of stores and floors by positioning shopper guides throughout the mall. 'We're approached by vendors trying to sell us automated directories but we think our customers appreciate being able to interact with a human being and get their questions asked', says the centre's marketing director... Broydrick (1994: 21-22)

75. Feinberg, Scheffler, Meoli and Rummel (1989)
76. Forman and Sriram (1991). Note also Ketrow (1991), where the author concludes that in many instances, customers prefer impersonal treatment from providers.
77. Anita Roddick, quoted in Fox (1994)
78. Donovan and Rossiter (1982)
79. Sewell and Brown (1990: 122, 155, 116)
80. For a large-scale and thought-provoking treatment of the perception of and use of time by customers and providers, see Lynch (1992).
81. Katz, Larson and Larson (1991)
82. Rohrer counsels salespeople never to send signals that they are in a hurry — the customer might take offence:

    To fidget, lose eye contact, drum fingers or constantly check the clock or watch is a sure symptom of inattentiveness. The buyer can sense it immediately. Buyers are not prone to give orders to impatient sales representatives, and impatience is contagious... take your time. Selling is a lot like fishing. Patience wins out in the end. (Rohrer 1990)

83. Maister (1985)
84. See, for example, Hall (1976), Hall (1989). Note also Kaufman, Lane and Lindquist (1991).
85. Hall (1976)
86. See, for example, Lill and Rose (1988); Park and Kline (1993); Nykodym, Longenecker and Ruud (1991); Hewson and Turner (1992).
87. 'Ego' in popular parlance suggests egotism or vanity, but Freud used the word more neutrally. *Ego* is Latin for 'I', while *superego* literally means 'that which is above the I or conscious self'. *Id* is Latin for 'it'. For a useful popular treatment of Freud's ideas, see Appignanensi and Zarato (1979).
88. See, for example, Freud 1964, Appignanensi and Zarato 1979, Eunson 1987, chapter 5. There is a family resemblance between Freud's ego defence mechanisms and Berne's games and other forms of time structuring.

    Freud's system depends heavily upon a sexual theory of human behaviour, and includes the concepts of the *Oedipus complex*, *penis envy* and the *castration complex*. Such theories are, to say the least, still controversial after many decades. Those who feel that Freud's theories are not shot though with fallacies, and would like to see their applications to the less exotic world of consumer behaviour, might be interested in Lawrence's notion of female compulsive shopping behaviour being explicable in terms of castration fears (the fears being allayed by purchasing of symbolically phallic objects). (Lawrence 1990)

89. Berne argued, nevertheless, that his system was different from Freud's in a number of ways. See, for example, Berne (1961: 243-244).
90. Berne (1983: 13)
91. Wagner (1981: 39)
92. Jongeward and Seyer (1978)
93. Wagner (1981: 35)
94. McDowell (1975) notes that the Persecutor role can have legitimate and illegitimate aspects. The legitimate aspect entails setting necessary limits on behaviour or enforcing rules, while the illegitimate aspect entails setting unnecessarily strict limits on behaviour or enforcing rules with sadistic brutality:

    > The officer who uses his position as a policeman to engage in an illegitimate persecutor role is quite a different story. His job becomes a licence to terrorise or harass others. The discretionary latitude available to the police officer permits him to become petty or tyrannical if he so desires and to pretty much get away with it. When an officer becomes overly harsh or petty he is no longer setting necessary limits or enforcing a rule; at this point, he is using his victims (p. 35).

95. Berne (1983: 44)
96. Berne notes the origin of this game:

    > White (the language or nomenclature is that of a chess game) needed some plumbing fixtures installed, and he reviewed the costs very carefully with the plumber before giving him the go-ahead. The price was set, and it was agreed that there would be no extras. When the plumber submitted his bill, he included a few dollars extra for an unexpected valve that had to be installed — about $4 on a $400 job. White became infuriated, called the plumber on the phone and demanded an explanation. The plumber would not back down. White wrote a long letter criticising his integrity and ethics and refused to pay the bill until the extra charge was withdrawn. The plumber finally gave in.
    >
    > It soon became obvious that both White and the plumber were playing games. In the course of their negotiations, they had recognised each other's potentials. The plumber made his provocative move when he submitted his bill. Since White had the plumber's word, the plumber was clearly in the wrong. White now felt justified in venting almost unlimited rage against him. Instead of merely negotiating in a dignified way that befitted the Adult standards he set for himself, perhaps with a little innocent annoyance, White took the opportunity to make extensive criticisms of the plumber's whole way of living. On the surface, their argument was Adult to Adult, a legitimate business dispute over a stated sum of money. At the psychological level it was Parent to (Child): White was exploiting his trivial but socially defensible objection (position) to vent the pent-up furies of many years on his cozening opponent, just as his mother might have done on a similar occasion. He quickly recognised his underlying attitude (NIGYSOB) and realised how secretly delighted he had been at the plumber's provocation. He then recalled (in a therapy session) that ever since early childhood he had looked for similar injustices, received them with delight, and exploited them with the same vigour. In many of the cases he recounted, he had forgotten the actual provocation, but remembered in great detail the course of the ensuing battle. The plumber, apparently, was playing some variation of 'Why does this always happen to me?' (WAHM). (Berne 1983: 74-75)

Note Beaumont's description of NIGYSOB in a sales situation:

> I recently saw (NIGYSOB) played to perfection by a woman shopper and a young, fairly inexperienced sales assistant (also female).
>
> The shopper had been in the store for some time, and had asked a variety of questions about prices and availability of certain lines of discounted cosmetics. As I was being served, she suddenly rushed up to the young assistant and said:
>
> 'Now did you say you don't carry Brand X moisturiser any more?'
>
> 'No', said the sales assistant. 'We haven't carried that brand for over a year.'
>
> 'Well', said the woman triumphantly, 'how come you've got this. I found a whole container under those shower caps over there in the corner. I can see you don't know your stock very well!'
>
> What could the assistant do? She mumbled something about only being on the job a couple of weeks, but to no avail. The woman shopper was extremely pleased and obviously felt she had won a major battle. (Beaumont 1989: 34)

97. Berne (1983: 98)

98. Note Hendricks' advice to police officers attempting to settle domestic disputes.

> Asking questions at this point can be inappropriate since a question may increase the emotional level of the husband. For example, 'What time does she come home at night?' or 'Don't you think we can handle this like adults?' The probability of the police officer getting involved in (Courtroom and) Uproar is increased by these questions, as the questions may elicit more negative feelings on the part of the husband or the wife. After separating the couple, the police officer may respond more appropriately by saying, 'You feel angry and upset to think she's messing around because it hurts a lot and you feel she doesn't care about you', or any response that tentatively labels the feeling and meaning expressed will serve well. This type of response allows the individual to release his tensions and pent-up feelings in an appropriate manner.
>
> After a few responses that indicate that the officer is really listening, the husband can then feel more comfortable to engage in a reasonable discussion. This can be a good learning experience for both the husband and the wife. The officer serves as a good role model of an active listener, and the experience demonstrates that discussion is a good method that may be used by the couple in future. (Hendricks 1977: 419)

99. See Berne (1983: 110–113).

100. Indeed, there are TA concepts we haven't had room to cover here, such as scripts and drivers. See, for example, Eunson (1987).

101. See, for example, at British Airways (Walker 1990) and at the New Jersey Division of Motor Vehicles (Forrest 1989).

102. For an overview of and critique of TA, see Eunson (1987), chapter 5.

103. Note the treatment of self-talk or styles of distorted thinking by psychologists of the rational-emotive therapy (RET) school (for example, McKay, Davis and Fanning 1981).

104. Adapted from Gerson (1992) and Gillen (1990).

105. See, for example, Laborde (1987), Zarro and Blum (1989), Woodsmall (1987), O'Connor and Seymour (1993), Madonik (1990), Gowens (1988), Johnson (1993), Bruce (1987), Weisburgh (1990), Goleman (1979).

> This system relates promptly to right-handed people and may not apply to left-handed people. (O'Connor and Seymour 1993)

106. Goleman (1979) tells the story of how some NLP practitioners were hired as consultants to determine why salespersons trained by one organisation were not as effective as their competitors. They found that the source of the problem was the man who hired the trainers. When participating in a simulated interview with the consultants, he responded positively to visual and kinaesthetic styles, but not to the auditory style. Why? Because he interpreted the sideways eye movements associated with the auditory style as 'shifty-eyed'. Consequently, he never hired trainers who could operate from that style, and thus the trainers he did hire were not able to train trainees in that style.

107. Laborde (1987: 206)

108. Laborde (1987: 33)

109. Critics of NLP — see comments in Goleman (1979). On NLP as a self-limiting system, note Laborde's comments:

> Determining outcomes, gaining rapport, matching representational systems, and using sensory acuity to gauge responses are extremely effective in sales presentations. They are also practically irresistible, so use them with extreme caution.
>
> A boutique's high-pressure salesperson once talked me into buying an expensive dress. I never liked wearing it, I discovered later: my curves turned into bulges in this particular style. I no longer shop at that boutique.
>
> So be sure the customer wants whatever you are selling. The three snakes of Remorse, Recrimination and Resentment and the dragon of Revenge will eat you alive unless you use these skills with integrity. (Laborde 1987: 142)

Note also the comments of John Grinder, who with Richard Bandler pioneered the basic NLP concepts:

> (In communicating with customers, all along you watch and listen carefully to tell whether this is appealing to them; you watch which systems they've gone into so you can track with them. You match systems, so you've got good rapport. Say I'm selling you a car. If you're auditory, I might talk about the purr of the motor, the squeal of those radial tyres. If you're kinaesthetic, the tight feel of the steering, the low centre of gravity, the comfort of the bucket seats. If you're visual, we'd be seeing eye-to-eye, have the same perspective.
>
> If you believe you've matched the person with the right product, then at the close, there's an inoculation against buyer's remorse. You're ready to sign — but if I'm really good, I'll say, 'Hold on a minute. We've been moving pretty fast. Maybe we ought to take a minute here and consider any other possibilities'. Then I'll direct the person into his or her other sensory systems, and get agreement on each one. If I do that, I'll never get buyer's remorse.
>
> My claim is that these techniques are good enough that I can sell most anything to anybody and have it be, in their best judgement, the product or service that best fills their needs. I have no interest in selling something that does not fit the person's needs, nor in teaching anyone else to. (quoted in Goleman 1979)

110. Iuppa (1985: 49)

111. Montgomery (1981: 6)

112. Wolvin and Coakley (1992: 9)

113. Peters (1988: 153)

114. Peters (1988: 150–151)

115. Peters (1988: 148)

116. Peters (1988: 145)

117. Huseman, Lahiff and Penrose (1991: 420)
118. Wolvin and Coakley (1992: 71-72)
119. Wolvin and Coakley (1992: 76-77)
120. See, for example, Burley-Allen (1982: 18-33); Bolton (1993: 30-31); Kotzman (1989: 57-59).
121. Kotzman (1989: 58-59)
122. Burley-Allen (1982: 30)
123. Rosenblatt, Cheatham and Watt (1982: 113)
124. Montgomery (1981: i)
125. Owen, Saunders and Dickson (1987: 173)
126. Hargie, Saunders and Dickson (1987: 173-174)
127. Atwater (1981: 24)
128. Atwater (1981: 24)
129. Hargie, Saunders and Dickson (1987: 172)
130. Hargie, Saunders and Dickson (1987: 181-182)
131. Anderson and Zemke (1991: 40)
132. Eunson (1944a: 37-39)
133. See, for example, Bell and Zemke (1992), chapter 6; Peters (1988), chapters C7, P3, L5; Flores (1993).
134. Note, for example, automatic call processing (Broydrick 1994) and voice-mail for customers, electronic bulletin boards, interactive radio, and fax response systems (Peppers and Rogers 1993).

    Note also Bly (1993), who discusses how the fax machine is useful (where face to face meetings, telephone and letter are not) in solving conflicts with customers.
135. Gillen (1990: 228)

REFERENCE LIST

Abrams, Arnold G. (1992). 'Body Language Speaks Louder than Words', *Life and Health Insurance Sales*, August.

Alberti, R. and Emmons, M. (1978). *Your Perfect Right* (New York: Impact).

Albrecht, Karl (1988). *At America's Service: How Corporations Can Revolutionise the Way They Treat Customers* (Homewood, Illinois: Dow Jones/Irwin).

Albrecht, Karl (1992). *The Only Thing That Matters: Bringing the Power of the Customer into the Center of Your Business* (New York: HarperCollins).

Albrecht, Karl and Bradford, Lawrence J. (1990). *The Service Advantage: How to Identify and Fulfill Customer Needs* (Homewood, Illinois: Dow Jones/Irwin).

Alessandra, T., Wexler, P. and Barrera, R. (1987). *Non-Manipulative Selling* (Second Edition) (New York: Prentice Hall Press).

Alper, Mort (1991). 'Reading Silent Signals from your Clients', *American Salesman*, June.

Alpert, Judy I. and Alpert, Mark I. (1990). 'Music Influences on Mood and Purchase Intentions', *Psychology and Marketing*, Summer.

Anderson, Kristin (1992). *Great Customer Service on the Telephone* (New York: Amacom).

Anderson, Kristin and Zemke, Ron (1991). *Delivering Knock Your Socks Off Service* (New York: Amacom).

Anonymous (a) (1991). 'Site Locations: Options and Advice', *Telemarketing Magazine*, June.

Anonymous (b) (1994). 'Schools Brief: The Manufacturing Myth', *The Economist*, March 19.

Appignanensi, F. and Zarato, O. (1979). *Freud for Beginners* (London: Writers and Readers Press).

Assael, Henry (1992). *Consumer Behavior and Marketing Action* (Boston: PWS-Kent).

Atwater, Eastwood (1981). *'I Hear You': Listening Skills to Make You a Better Manager* (Englewood Cliffs, New Jersey: Prentice-Hall).

Austin, Nancy K. (1991). 'The Subtle Signals of Success', *Working Woman*, April.

Baker, J., Levy, M. and Grewal, D. (1992). 'An Experimental Approach to Making Retail Store Environmental Decisions', *Journal of Retailing*, Winter.

Band, William A. (1991). *Creating Value for Customers: Designing and Implementing a Total Corporate Strategy* (New York: John Wiley & Sons).

Baritz, Leon (1965). *Servants of Power* (Middletown, Conn: Wesleyan University Press).

Barnes, Roger (1988). 'Body Language Can Say It All', *National Underwriter*, August 8.

Barnum, C. and Wolniansky, N. (1989). 'Taking Cues from Body Language', *Management Review*, June.

Baytosh, Christine M. and Kleiner, Brian H. (1989). 'Effective Business Communication for Women', *Equal Opportunities International*, Vol. 8, No. 4.

Beaumont, Jenny (1989). *The Australian Customer Relations Workbook* (Melbourne: Information Australia).

Beck, Ken and Beck, Kate (1989). *Assertiveness at Work: A Practical Guide to Handling Awkward Situations* (Second Edition) (London: McGraw-Hill).

Beeler, Jeffry (1986). 'Nonverbal Communication: DP Management Taken at Face Value', *Computerworld*, June 9.

Beisecker, Analee E. (1988). 'Aging and the Desire for Information and Input in Medical Decisions: Patient Consumerism in Medical Encounters'. *Gerontologist*, June.

Bell, Chip R. and Zemke, Ron (1992). *Managing Knock Your Socks Off Service* (New York: Amacom).

Bellizi, Joseph A., Crowley, Ayn E. and Hasty, Ronald W. (1983). 'The Effect of Color in Store Design', *Journal of Retailing*, Spring.

Bennett, Dudley (1978). *TA and the Manager* (New York: Amacom).

Bergadaa, Michelle M. (1990). 'The Role of Time in the Action of the Consumer', *Journal of Consumer Research*, December.

Berne, Eric (1961). *Transactional Analysis in Psychotherapy: A Systematic Individual and Social Psychiatry* (New York: Castle Books/Grove Press).

Berne, Eric (1983). *Games People Play: The Psychology of Human Relationships* (Harmondsworth: Penguin).

Berry, Leonard L., Bennett, David R. and Brown, Carter W. (1989). *Service Quality: A Profit Strategy for Financial Institutions* (Homewood, Illinois: Dow Jones/Irwin).

Bittner, Mary Jo (1992). 'Servicescapes: The Impact of Physical Surroundings on Customers and Employees', *Journal of Marketing*, April.

Blackwell, Stephen H. and Crihfield, Tara S. (1991). 'Controlling the Communications Impact', *Public Relations Journal*, June.

Bloom, Lynn, Coburn, Karen and Pearlman, B. (1975). *The New Assertive Woman* (New York: Delacorte).

Bly, Robert W. (1993). *Keeping Clients Satisfied: Make Your Service Business More Successful and Profitable* (Englewood Cliffs: New Jersey).

Bolton, Robert (1993). *People Skills: How to Assert Yourself, Listen to Others, and Resolve Conflicts* (Fourth Edition) (Englewood Cliffs, New Jersey: Prentice-Hall).

Booth-Butterfield, Melanie (1984). 'She Hears ... He Hears: What They Hear and Why', *Personnel Journal*, May.

Bowen, David E. and Lawler, Edward E. III (1992). 'The Empowerment of Service Workers: What, Why, How and When', *Sloan Management Review*, Spring.

Bozek, Phillip E. (1991). *50 One-Minute Tips to Better Communication* (Los Altos, California: Crisp Publications).

Brown, Andrew (1989). *Customer Care Management* (Jordan Hill, Oxford: Heinemann).

Broydrick, Stephen C. (1994). *How May I Help You? Providing Personal Service in an Impersonal World* (Burr Ridge, Illinois: Irwin).

Bruce, Leigh (1987). 'Mirror Behaviour Lends Wings to Better Understanding', *International Management*, June.

Buhler, Patricia (1991). 'Managing in the '90s: Are You Really Saying What You Mean?', *Supervision*, September.

Burley-Allen, Madelyn (1982). *Listening: The Forgotten Skill* (New York: John Wiley & Sons).

Burley-Allen, Madelyn (1983). *Managing Assertively: How to Improve Your People Skills* (New York: John Wiley & Sons).

Burnett, John M., Amason, Robert D. and Hunt, Shelby D. (1981). 'Feminism: Implications for Department Store Strategy and Salesclerk Behavior', *Journal of Retailing*, Winter.

Cameron, Jim (1991). 'For Claims Management, It's the Dawn of a New Era', *Canadian Insurance*, May.

Cannie, Joan Koob, with Caplin, Donald (1991). *Keeping Customers for Life* (New York: Amacom).

Carle, Gilda (1989). 'Handling a Hostile Audience — With Your Eyes', *IEEE Transactions on Professional Communication*, March.

Carlzon, Jan (1987). *Moments of Truth* (Cambridge, Massachusetts: Ballinger).

Caroselli, Marlene (1992). *Think on Your Feet — And Avoid Putting Them in Your Mouth!* (Los Altos, California: Crisp Publications).

Carr, Clay (1990). *Front-Line Customer Service: 15 Keys to Customer Satisfaction* (New York: John Wiley & Sons).

Cathcart, Jim and Alessandra, Tony (1985). 'Body Language: Selling Without Words', *Insurance Sales*, January.

Caudill, Donald W. (1986). 'Color Management: A Non-Verbal Communication Tool', *Journal of Systems Management*, January.

CERT/The State Training Agency for Hotels, Catering and Tourism in Ireland (1988). *A Practical Guide to Customer Relations* (Dublin: CERT).

Chandler, Robin (1990). 'Moving Towards Understanding', *Accountancy*, April.

Chang, Richard Y. and Kelly, P. Keith (1994). *Satisfying Internal Customers First! Improving Internal and External Customer Satisfaction* (Irvine, California: Richard Chang Associates).

Chase, Richard B. and Hayes, Robert H. (1991). 'Beefing Up Operations in Service Firms', *Sloan Management Review*, Fall.

Chase, Richard B. and Stewart, Douglas M. (1994) 'Make Your Service Fail-Safe', *Sloan Management Review*, Spring.

Chiu, Chi Yue, Tsang, Sai Chung and Yang, Chung Fang (1988). 'The Role of Face Situation and Attitudinal Antecedents in Chinese Consumer Complaint Behavior', *Journal of Social Psychology*, April.

Christopher, Martin (1992). *The Customer Service Planner* (Jordon Hill, Oxford: Butterworth-Heinemann).

Church, Wayne C. (1989). 'Keeping Crises Cool', *Security Management*, March.

Clutterbuck, David (1985). 'A Strange Body of Knowledge', *Chief Executive*, December.

Clutterbuck, David and Kernaghan, Susan (1991). *Making Customers Count: A Guide to Excellence in Customer Care* (London: Mercury Books).

Clynes, Geoff (1992). *Telephone Skill Builder for Sales and Service Professionals* (Sydney: Prentice-Hall/Australian Institute of Management).

Cohen, Lynn Renee (1983). 'Nonverbal (Mis)Communication Between Managerial Men and Women', *Business Horizons*, January/February.

Cohen, Lynn R. (1982). 'Minimizing Communication Breakdowns Between Male and Female Managers', *Personnel Administrator*, October.

Collis, Jack (1992). *Your Business is Your Customer* (Sydney: McGraw-Hill).

Conway, Ronald (1978). *Land of the Long Weekend* (Melbourne: Sun Books).

Conway, Ronald (1994). Personal communication.

Corporan, Chuck (1975). 'What Do You Say After You Say "Good Morning"?', *Training and Development Journal*, November.

Cowen, Emory L., Gesten, Ellis L., Boike, Mary, Norton, Pennie, Wilson, Alice B. and deStefano, Michael A. (1979). 'Hairdressers as Caregivers: A Descriptive Profile of Interpersonal Help-Giving Involvements', *American Journal of Community Psychology*, Vol. 7, No. 6.

Cowles, Deborah and Crosby, Lawrence A. (1990). 'Consumer Acceptance of Interactive Media in Service Marketing Encounters', *Service Industries Journal*, July.

Cyr, Robert (1990). 'Client Relations in Japan', *Training and Development Journal*, September.

Czepiel, John A., Solomon, Michael R. and Surprenant, Carol F. (eds). (1985). *The Service Encounter: Managing Employee/Customer Interaction in Service Businesses* (Lexington, Massachusetts: Lexington Books).

Danger, Eric P. (1968). *Using Colour to Sell* (London: Gower Press).

Darwin, Charles (1872). *The Expression of Emotion in Man and Animals* (London: John Murray).

Dastoor, Barbara (1993). 'Speaking Their Language', *Training and Development Journal*, June.

Davidow, William H. and Uttal, Bro (1989). *Total Customer Service: The Ultimate Weapon* (New York: Harper & Row).

Davidson, Jeffrey P. (1988). 'Shaping an Image that Boosts Your Career', *Marketing Communications*, November/December.

Dawson, Scott, Bloch, Peter H. and Ridgway, Nancy M. (1990). 'Shopping Motives, Emotional States, and Retail Outcomes', *Journal of Retailing*, Winter.

De Vrye, Catherine (1994). *Good Service is Good Business* (Sydney: Prentice-Hall).

Denton, D. Keith (1991). *Horizontal Management: Beyond Total Customer Satisfaction* (New York: Lexington Books).

DePaulo, Peter J. and DePaulo, Bella M. (1989). 'Can Deception by Salespersons and Customers Be Detected through Nonverbal Behavioral Cues?', *Journal of Applied Social Psychology*, December.

Desatnick, Robert L. (1987). *Managing to Keep the Customer: How to Achieve and Maintain Superior Customer Service Throughout the Organization* (San Francisco: Jossey-Bass).

Dickson, John P. and McLachlan, Douglas L. (1990). 'Social Distance and Shopping Behavior', *Journal of the Academy of Marketing Science*, Spring.

Dion, Paul A. (1987). 'Sales Objections as a Negotiation Tactic', *Journal of Behavioral Economics*, Spring.

Donatelli, Carlos (1976). 'TA and Collection of Delinquent Accounts', *Transactional Analysis Journal*, April.

Donovan, Robert J. and Rossiter, John R. (1982). 'Store Atmosphere: An Environmental Approach', *Journal of Retailing*, Spring.

Donnelly, James H. Jr (1992). *Close to the Customer: 25 Management Tips from the Other Side of the Counter* (Homewood, Illinois: Business One Irwin).

Dreyfack, Raymond (1988). 'Income Boosters for the Success-Minded Salesperson: The Selling Edge', *American Salesman*, August.

Dupuy, Max and Schweitzer, Mark E. (1994). 'Are Service Sector Jobs Inferior?' *Economic Commentary*, February 1.

Engel, James F., Blackwell, Roger D. and Miniard, Paul W. (1990). *Consumer Behavior* (Sixth Edition) (New York: Dryden Press).

Eroglu, Sevgin A. and Machleit, Karen A. (1990). 'An Empirical Study of Retail Crowding: Antecedents and Consequences', *Journal of Retailing*, Summer.

Eunson, Baden (1987). *Behaving: Managing Yourself and Others* (Sydney: McGraw-Hill).

Eunson, Baden (1994a). *Negotiation Skills* (Brisbane: John Wiley & Sons).

Eunson, Baden (1994b). *Communicating for Team Building* (Brisbane: John Wiley & Sons).

Evans, Martin (1989). 'Consumer Behaviour Towards Fashion', *European Journal of Marketing*, Vol. 23, No. 7.

Faber, Ronald J. (1992). 'Money Changes Everything: Compulsive Buying from a Biopsychological Perspective', *American Behavioral Scientist*, July–August.

Farber, Barry J. (1990). 'Have a Customer Run Your Next Sales Meeting', *Sales & Marketing Management*, April.

Feinberg, Richard A., Scheffler, Brent, Meoli, Jennifer and Rummel, Amy (1989). 'There's Something Social Happening at the Mall', *Journal of Business and Psychology*, Fall.

Fincanon, Bill W. (1990). 'Effective Customer Churn Control,' *Communications*, May.

Finch, Lloyd C. (1990). *Telephone Courtesy and Customer Service* (Los Altos, California: Crisp Publications).

Fischer, Eileen and Arnold, Stephen J. (1990). 'More Than a Labor of Love: Gender Roles and Christmas Gift Shopping', *Journal of Consumer Research*, December.

Flores, Fernando (1993). 'Innovation by Listening Carefully to Customers', *Long Range Planning*, June.

Forman, Andrew M. and Sriram, Ven (1991). 'The Depersonalization of Retailing: Its Impact on the "Lonely" Consumer', *Journal of Retailing*, Summer.

Forrest, David L. (1989). Training Helps Put New Jersey "On the Road"', *Training and Development Journal*, July.

Fox, Catherine (1994). 'Body Shop Ads Rethink', *Financial Review*, April 26, p. 47.

Francis, Bob (1993). 'The Battle Shifts to PC Services', *Datamation*, January 15.

Freud, Sigmund (1964). *An Outline of Psychoanalysis* (London: Hogarth Press).

Friend, William (1984). 'Reading Between the Lines', *Association Management*, June.

Fuller, Rex M. (1984). 'Know What You're Handing Them?', *American Salesman*, December.

Galassi, Merna D. and Galassi, John P. (1977). *Assert Yourself! How to Be Your Own Person* (New York: Human Sciences Press).

Galinat, Withold H. and Muller, Gunther F. (1988). 'Verbal Responses to Different Bargaining Strategies: A Content Analysis of Real-Life Buyer–Seller Interaction', *Journal of Applied Social Psychology*, February.

Gallie, Duncan (1991). 'Patterns of Skill Change: Upskilling, Deskilling, or the Polarization of Skills?' *Work, Employment and Society*, September.

Garfield, Maynard M. (1990). 'Reduce Customer Turnover for Long-Term Success', *Marketing News*, May 28.

Garrity, Kimberly and Degelman, Douglas (1990). 'Effect of Server Introduction on Restaurant Tipping', *Journal of Applied Social Psychology*, February.

Garside, Sandra G. and Kleiner, Brian H. (1991). 'Effective One-to-One Communication Skills', *Industrial and Commercial Training*, Vol. 23, No. 7.

Gerson, Richard F. (1992). *Beyond Customer Service: Keeping Customers for Life* (Los Altos, California: Crisp Publications).

Gerson, Richard F. (1993). *Measuring Customer Satisfaction* (Los Altos, California: Crisp Publications).

Gilbert, Evelyn (1991). 'Japanese Pose Unique Challenges to US Insurers', *National Underwriter*, July 22.

Gillen, Terry (1990). *20 Training Workshops for Customer Care* (Aldershot, Hants: Gower).

Glen, Peter (1990). *It's Not My Department! How to Get the Service You Want, Exactly the Way You Want It!* (New York: William Morrow and Company).

Godbout, Todd M. (1993). 'Employment Change and Sectoral Distribution in 10 Countries, 1979–90', *Monthly Labor Review*, October.

Goldzimer, Linda Silverman (1989). *Customer Driven* (London: Hutchinson).

Golis, Christopher C. (1991). *Empathy Selling: The New Sales Technique for the 1990s* (Port Melbourne: Lothian).

Gosselink, Carol A. and McKinley, Suzanne J. (1984). 'What You Don't Say: Nonverbal Telephone Tactics', *Communicator's Journal*, March/April.

Gouillart, Francis J. and Sturdivant, Frederick D. (1994). 'Spend a Day in the Life of Your Customer', *Harvard Business Review*, January/February.

Gowens, H. Philip (1988). 'Self-Programmed Perception: The Key to Mastering Stress', *Business Credit*, November.

Graham, Gerald H. (1991). 'The Impact of Nonverbal Communications in Organisations', *Journal of Business Communication*, Winter.

Granger, Russell H. (1988). 'Listen Your Way to Bigger and Better Sales', *Rough Notes*, October.

Greene, Alex (1986). 'The Tyranny of Melody', *Etc*, Fall.

Grewal, Dhruv and Sharma, Arun (1991). 'The Effect of Salesforce Behavior on Customer Satisfaction: An Interactive Framework', *Journal of Personal Selling and Sales Management*, Summer.

Griksheit, G. M., Cash, H. C. and Young, C. E. (1993). *The Handbook of Selling: Pyschological, Managerial and Marketing Dynamics* (Second Edition) (New York: John Wiley & Sons).

Guaspari, John (1991). *The Customer Connection: Quality for the Rest of Us* (New York: Amacom).

Guthrie, R. Dale (1976). *Body Hot Spots: The Anatomy of Human Social Organs and Behaviour* (New York: Van Nostrand Reinhold).

Hall, Edward T. (1966). *The Hidden Dimension* (New York: Doubleday).

Hall, Edward T. (1976). 'How Cultures Collide', *Psychology Today*, July.

Hall, Edward T. (1979). 'Learning the Arabs' Silent Language', *Psychology Today*, August.

Hall, Edward T. (1989). *Understanding Cultural Differences* (Greenwood, Maine: Intercultural Press).

Hall, Tim and Lloyd, Chris (1990). 'Non-Verbal Communication in a Health Care Setting', *British Journal of Occupational Therapy*, Vol. 59, No. 3.

Hamlin, Richard (1991). 'A Practical Guide to Empowering Your Employees', *Supervisory Management*, April.

Hargie, Owen, Saunders, Christine and Dickson, David (1987). *Social Skills in Interpersonal Communication* (Second Edition) (London: Croom Helm).

Harris, Thomas (1978). *I'm OK, You're OK* (London: Pan).

Harris, Thomas and Harris, Amy Bjork (1985). *Staying OK* (New York: Harper & Row).

Heintzman, Mark, Leathers, Dale G., Parrott, Roxanne L. and Cairns, Adrian Bennett III (1993). 'Nonverbal Rapport-Building Behaviors' Effects on Perceptions of a Supervisor', *Management Communication Quarterly*, November.

Henderson, Pauline E. (1989). 'Communication Without Words', *Personnel Journal*, January.

Hendricks, Jim (1977). 'Transactional Analysis and the Police: Family Disputes', *Journal of Police Science and Administration*, December.

Henkoff, Ronald (1994). 'Service is Everybody's Business', *Fortune*, June 27.

Henley, Nancy M. (1977). *Body Politics: Power, Sex and Non-Verbal Communication* (Englewood Cliffs, New Jersey: Prentice-Hall).

Herbig, Paul A. and Kramer, Hugh E. (1992). 'Do's and Don'ts of Cross-Cultural Negotiations', *Industrial Marketing Management*, November.

Heskett, James L. (1986). *Managing in the Service Economy* (Boston, Massachusetts: Harvard Business School Press).

Heskett, James L., Sasser, W. Earl Jr and Hart, Christopher W. L. (1990). *Service Breakthroughs: Changing the Rules of the Game* (New York: Free Press).

Heskett, James L., Jones, Thomas O., Loveman, Gary W., Sasser, W. Earl Jr and Schlesinger, Leonard A. (1994). 'Putting the Service–Profit Chain to Work', *Harvard Business Review*, March–April.

Hewson, Julie and Turner, Colin (1992). *Transactional Analysis in Management* (London: The Staff College).

Higie, Robin A., Feick, Lawrence F. and Price, Linda L. (1987). 'Types and Amount of Word-of-Mouth Communications About Retailers', *Journal of Retailing*, Fall.

Hobler, Randy (1993). 'From Gutenberg to Spielberg: How Not to Be "The Client from Hell" (Part II)', *Communication World*, November.

Hochschild, Arlie Russell (1983). *The Managed Heart: Commercialisation of Human Feeling* (Los Angeles: University of California Press).

Hoffman, Gail (1993). 'Customers Can Hone Mystery Shopping', *Bank Marketing*, August.

Hoffman, K. Douglas and Ingram, Thomas N. (1991). 'Creating Customer-Oriented Employees: The Case in Home Health Care', *Journal of Health Care Marketing*, June.

Hornik, Jacob (1992). 'Tactile Stimulation and Consumer Response', *Journal of Consumer Research*, December.

Howard, James S. (1992). 'Customers Send a Wake-Up Call', *D&B Reports*, January/February.

Howard, John A. (1989). *Consumer Behavior in Marketing Strategy* (Englewood Cliffs, New Jersey).

Hui, Michael K. and Bateson, John E. (1991). 'Perceived Control and the Effects of Crowding and Consumer Choice on the Service Experience', *Journal of Consumer Research*, September.

Hunsaker, Johanna S. (1982). 'Eye Language: Implications and Applications for the Effective Manager', *Industrial Management*, January/February.

Hunt, H. Keith (1991). 'Consumer Satisfaction, Dissatisfaction, and Complaining Behavior', *Journal of Social Issues*, Spring.

Huseman, Richard C., Lahiff, James M. and Penrose, John M. Jr (1991). *Business Communication: Strategies and Skills* (Fourth Edition) (Chicago: Dryden Press).

Iuppa, Nicholas V. (1985). *Management by Guilt, and Other Uncensored Tactics* (Belmont, California: Pitman Books).

Izard, Carroll E. (1990). 'Personality, Emotional Expressions, and Rapport', *Psychological Inquiry*, Vol. 1, No. 4.

Jacobs, Russell (1988). 'Do You Have "Busy-Bodies" for Prospects?', *American Salesman*, February.

Johnson, Kerry L. (1988a). 'The Touch of Persuasion', *Broker World*, April.

Johnson, Kerry L. (1988b). 'How to Interview for the Truth', *Broker World*, July.

Johnson, Kerry L. (1991). 'The Gender Gap: How to Sell to the Opposite Sex', *Broker World*, June.

Johnson, Kerry L. (1993). 'How to Gain your Client's Trust — Fast', *CPA Journal*, September.

Jolley, Dave (1989). 'Barriers to Communication', *American Salesman*, September.

Jones, Barry (1989). *Sleepers, Wake! Technology and the Future of Work* (Melbourne: Oxford University Press).

Jongeward, Dorothy and James, Muriel (1976). *Winning with People: Group Exercises in Transactional Analysis* (Reading, Mass: Addison-Wesley).

Jongeward, Dorothy and Seyer, Phillip (1978). *Choosing Success: Transactional Analysis on the Job* (New York: John Wiley & Sons).

Juni, Samuel, Brannon, Robert and Roth, Michelle M. (1988). 'Sexual and Racial Discrimination in Service-Seeking Interactions: A Field Study in Fast-Food and Commercial Establishments', *Psychological Reports*, August.

Karrass, Chester L. (1992). 'Body Language: Beware the Hype', *Traffic Management*, Jan.

Katz, Bernard (1988). *How to Turn Customer Service Into Customer Sales* (Lincolnwood, Illinois: NTC Business Books).

Katz, Karen L., Larson, Blaire M. and Larson, Richard C. (1991). 'Prescription for the Waiting-in-Line Blues: Entertain, Enlighten and Engage', *Sloan Management Review*, Winter.

Kaufman, Carol F., Lane, Paul M. and Lindquist, Jay D. (1991). 'Exploring More than 24 Hours a Day: A Preliminary Investigation of Polychronic Time Use', *Journal of Consumer Research*, December.

Kearney, Elizabeth I., Bandler, Michale J., Anderson, Barbra C. and Tellin, Mary Jo (1990). *Customers Run Your Company: They Pay the Bills!* (Provo, Utah: Kearney/Bandler).

Kelley, Alison (1977). *Assertion: A Trainer's Guide* (San Diego, California: University Associates).

Kennish, John W. (1989). 'Finding the Truth', *Internal Auditor*, December.

Ketrow, Sandra M. (1991). 'Nonverbal Communication and Client Satisfaction in Computer-Assisted Transactions', *Management Communication Quarterly*, November.

Kharbanda, Om P. and Stallworthy, Ernest A. (1991). 'Verbal and Non-Verbal Communication', *Journal of Managerial Psychology*, Vol. 6, No. 4.

Kinsella, Edward M. (1990). 'Achieving First-Class Customer Service', *Small Business Reports*, August.

Kleiner, Brian H. (1983). 'Dress Management: Applied Nonverbal Communication for Career Development', *Journal of Systems Management*, March.

Knapp, Mark L. (1978). *Nonverbal Communication in Human Interaction* (New York: Holt, Rinehart and Winston).

Konopacki, Allen (1987a). 'How to Use Eye Language to Succeed in Selling Your Ideas', *Agency Sales Magazine*, July.

Konapacki, Allen (1987b). 'Eye Language: Clues to Your Prospect's Thoughts', *Medical Marketing & Media*, June.

Kotzman, Ann (1989). *Listen to Me, Listen to You* (Ringwood, Victoria: Penguin Books).

Krapfel, Robert E. (1988). 'Customer Complaint and Salesperson Response: The Effect of the Communication Source', *Journal of Retailing*, Summer.

Kroeger, Lin J. (1989). 'Communication: Clarity and Style', *Internal Auditor*, December.

Laborde, Genie Z. (1987). *Influencing with Integrity: Management Skills for Communication and Negotiation* (Palo Alto, California: Syntony Publishing).

Lash, Linda M. (1989). *The Complete Guide to Customer Service* (New York: John Wiley & Sons).

Lawrence, Lauren (1990). 'The Psychodynamics of the Compulsive Female Shopper', *American Journal of Psychoanalysis*, March.

Le Roux, Paul (1984). 'Managers: Nerving Up the Right Way for that Major Presentation', *Successful Meetings*, August.

Leader, Gerald C. (1973). 'Interpersonally Skilful Bank Officers View Their Behavior', *Journal of Applied Behavioural Science*, July.

Leeds, Dorothy (1992). 'Increase Sales without Saying a Word', *National Underwriter*, Sept. 7.

Lehman, Carol M. and Lehman, Mark W. (1989). 'Effective Nonverbal Communication Techniques: Essential Element in the Promotional Strategies of Professional Service Firms', *Journal of Professional Services Marketing*, Vol. 5, No. 1.

Lele, Milind M., with Sheth, Jagdish N. (1991). *The Customer is Key: Gaining Unbeatable Advantage Through Customer Satisfaction* (New York: John Wiley & Sons).

Lewis, Herschell Gordon (1993). '100 of the Easiest Ways to Begin an Effective Sales Letter', *Direct Marketing*, July.

Lill, David J. and Rose, John T. (1988). 'Transactional Analysis and Personal Selling: A Primer for Bankers', *Journal of Commercial Bank Lending*, February.

Long, Charles F. and Caudill, Donald W. (1989). 'Ten Practical Tips for the Manufacturer's Agent', *Agency Sales Magazine*, April.

Loudon, David L. and Della Bitta, Albert J. (1988). *Consumer Behavior: Concepts and Applications* (Third Edition) (New York: McGraw-Hill).

Lovelock, Christopher (1994). *Product Plus: How Product + Service = Competitive Advantage* (New York: McGraw-Hill).

Lusardi, Lee A. (1990). 'Power Talk: When a Woman Speaks, Does Anybody Listen?', *Working Woman*, July.

Lusteberg, Arch (1984). 'Turning Confrontation into Communication', *Nation's Business*, June.

Luthans, Fred (1991). 'Improving the Delivery of Quality Service: Behavioral Management Techniques', *International Journal of Bank Marketing*, Vol. 9, No. 3.

Lynch, James J. (1992). *The Psychology of Customer Care: A Revolutionary Approach* (London: Macmillan).

Lynn, Michael and Mynier, Kirby (1993). 'Effect of Server Posture on Restaurant Tipping', *Journal of Applied Social Psychology*, April.

Lytle, John F. (1993). *What Do Your Customers Really Want?* (Chicago, Illinois: Probus Publishing).

McPhee, Joan and McNicol, Bruce (1992). 'New Directions for Supervisor Training', *Training Australia*, March.

Madonik, Barbara Haber (1990). 'I Hear What You Say, But What Are You Telling Me?', *Canadian Manager*, March.

Maister, David H. (1985). 'The Psychology of Waiting Lines', in Czepiel, Solomon and Surprenant (eds).

Makens, James C. (1991). 'Hotel Salespersons: Enhancing Their Creativity and Efficiency', *Cornell Hotel & Restaurant Administration Quarterly*, May.

March, Robert M. (1990). *The Honourable Customer: Marketing and Selling to the Japanese in the 1990s* (Melbourne: Longman).

Marcus, Eric H. (1983). 'Neurolinguistic Programming', *Personnel Journal*, December.

Margerison, Charles J. (1987). *Conversational Control Skills for Managers* (London: Mercury Books).

Marken, G. A. 'Andy' Marken (1992). 'Telephone Hurdles Kill Companies', *Public Relations Quarterly*, Fall.

Mars, Gerald and Nicod, Michael (1984). *The World of Waiters* (London: Allen & Unwin).

Martin, William B. (1989a). *Managing Quality Customer Service* (Los Altos, California: Crisp Publications).

Martin, William B. (1989b). *Quality Customer Service* (Revised Edition) (Los Altos, California: Crisp Publications).

Martinko, Mark J., White, J. Dennis and Hassell, Barbara (1989). 'An Operant Analysis of Prompting in a Sales Environment', *Journal of Organizational Behavior Management*, Vol. 10, No. 1.

Martinko, Mark J. (1986). 'An O.B. Mod. Analysis of Consumer Behavior', *Journal of Organizational Behavior Management*, Spring–Summer.

Mayers, Kathleen S. (1993). 'When Residents Refuse to Take Their Medications', *Nursing Homes*, April.

McDowell, Charles P. (1975). 'Victims, Persecutors and Rescuers: A Challenge to Police Performance', *Journal of Police Science and Administration*, March.

McKenzie, Cheryl L. and Qazi, Carol J. (1983). 'Communication Barriers in the Workplace', *Business Horizons*, March/April.

McKinley, Suzanne J. and Gosselink, Carol A. (1984). 'I Don't Believe a Word of It', *Communicator's Journal*, Vol. 2, No. 4.

McNally, Kathleen A. and Abernathy, William B. (1989). 'Effects of Monetary Incentives on Customer Behavior: Use of Automatic Teller Machines (ATMs) by Low Frequency Users', *Journal of Organisational Behavior Management*, Vol. 10, No. 1.

McNeilage, Linda A. and Adams, Kathleen A. (1982). *Assertiveness at Work: How to Increase Your Personal Power on the Job* (Englewood Cliffs, New Jersey: Prentice-Hall).

McPhee, Joan and McNicol, Bruce (1992). 'New Directions for Supervisor Training', *Training Australia*, March.

Mendez, Antonio, Shymansky, J. A. and Wolraich, M. (1986). 'Verbal and Non-Verbal Behavior of Doctors While Conveying Distressing Information', *Medical Education*, September.

Mehrabian, Albert (1971). *Silent Messages* (Los Angeles: Wadsworth).

Mick, David Glen and DeMoss, Michelle (1990). 'Self-Gifts: Phenomenonological Insights from Four Contexts', *Journal of Consumer Research*, December.

Milliman, Ronald E. and Decker, Phillip J. (1990). 'The Use of Post-Purchase Communication to Reduce Dissonance and Improve Direct Marketing Effectiveness', *Journal of Business Communication*, Spring.

Montagu, Ashley (1971). *Touching: The Human Significance of the Skin* (New York: Harper & Row).

Montgomery, Robert L. (1981). *Listening Made Easy* (New York: Amacom Books).

Moore, Chris (1975). *How to Handle Customer Complaints: A Company Guide to Customer Relations and Consumer Rights* (Westmead, Farnborough, Hampshire: Gower Press).

Morgan, Rebecca L. (1989). *Calming Upset Customers: Staying Effective During Unpleasant Situations* (Los Altos, California: Crisp Publications).

Morris, Desmond (1977). *Manwatching: A Field Guide to Human Behaviour* (London: Jonathan Cape).

National Training Council (1986). *Interpersonal Skills As a Critical Component in Customer Service* (Canberra: Australian Government Publishing Service).

Nemec, John (1985). 'Use Non-Verbal Signals to Sell More', *American Salesman*, February.

Neu, Joyce, Graham, John L. and Gilly, Mary C. (1988). 'The Influence of Gender on Behaviors and Outcomes in a Retail Buyer–Seller Negotiation Simulation', *Journal of Retailing*, Winter.

Nierenberg, G. I. and Calero, H. H. (1971). *How to Read a Person Like a Book* (New York: Hawthorn Books).

Noonan, Bob (1985–1986). ' "Nothing Happens Unless Someone Buys Something": Identifying and Responding to your Customers' Communication Style', *Health Marketing Quarterly*, Winter–Spring.

Nord, Walter R. and Peter, J. Paul. (1980). 'A Behavior Modification Perspective on Marketing', *Journal of Marketing*, Spring.

Notarantonio, Elaine M. (1990). 'The Effects of Open and Dominant Communication Styles on Perceptions of the Sales Interaction', *Journal of Business Communication*, Spring.

Novak, Thomas P. and McEvoy, Bruce (1990). 'On Comparing Alternative Segmentation Schemes: The List of Values (LOV) and Values and Life Styles (VALS)'. *Journal of Consumer Research*, June.

Nykodym, Nick, Longenecker, Clinton O. and Ruud, William N. (1991). 'Improving Quality of Work Life with Transactional Analysis as an Intervention Change Strategy', *Applied Psychology: An International Review*, October.

Nyquist, Jody D., Bittner, Mary J. and Booms, Bernard H. (1985). 'Identifying Communication Difficulties in the Service Encounter: A Critical Incident Approach', in Czepiel et al. (eds).

O'Connor, Joseph and Seymour, John (1993). *Introducing Neuro-Linguistic Programming* (Revised Edition) (London: Aquarian/Harpercollins).

Palleschi, Patricia D. (1981). 'The Hidden Messages Managers Send', *Manage*, July.

Parasuraman, A., Berry, Leonard L. and Zeithaml, Valerie A. (1991). 'Understanding Customer Expectations of Service', *Sloan Management Review*, Spring.

Park, Hoon and Harrison, J. Kline (1993). 'Enhancing Managerial Cross-Cultural Awareness and Sensitivity: Transactional Analysis Revisited', *Journal of Management Development*, Vol. 12, No. 3.

Parlee, Mary Brown (1984). 'Getting a Word in Sex-Wise', *Across the Board*, September.

Pearl, Lynn (1992). 'Opening the Door to Rapport', *Agri Marketing*, April.

Pease, Alan (1981). *Body Language* (Sydney: Camel Publishing).

Peel, Malcolm (1987). *Customer Service: How to Achieve Total Customer Satisfaction* (London: Kogan Page).

Peoples, Edward E. (1977). 'Analyzing Police–Citizen Transactions: A Model for Training in Communications', *Journal of Police Science and Administration*, June.

Peppers, Don and Rogers, Martha (1993). *The One to One Future: Building Relationships One Customer at a Time* (Englewood Cliffs: Prentice-Hall).

Peter, J. Paul and Olsen, Jerry C. (1987). *Consumer Behavior: Marketing Strategy Perspectives* (Homewood, Illinois: Irwin).

Peters, Tom (1988). *Thriving on Chaos: A Handbook for a Management Revolution* (London: Macmillan).

Peters, Tom (1991). 'Twenty Ideas on Service', *Executive Excellence*, July.

Peters, Tom (1992). *Liberation Management* (London: Pan Books).

Peters, Tom (1994). *The Tom Peters Seminar: Crazy Times Call for Crazy Organisations* (London: Macmillan)

Phelps, Stanlee and Austin, Nancy (1988). *The Assertive Woman* (Second Edition) (San Osbispos, California: Impact Press).

Phillips, Hugh and Bradshaw, Roy (1993). 'How Customers Actually Shop: Customer Interaction with the Point of Sale', *Journal of the Market Research Society*, January.

Pizzano, Joan S. and Pizzano, Richard G. (1988). 'Empathy: The Key to an Effective Client Interview', *Legal Assistant Today*, May/June.

Pratkanis, Anthony R. and Greenwald, Anthony G. (1993). 'Consumer Involvement, Message Attention, and the Persistence of Persuasive Impact in a Message-Dense Environment', *Psychology and Marketing*, July/August.

Pryor, Fred (1986). 'Communications: It's a Two-Way Contract Between Sender & Receiver', *Agency Sales Magazine*, April.

Quinto, Louis B. (1993). 'How to Communicate with Your Donors', *Fund Raising Management*, September.

Rafaeli, Anat (1989a). 'When Cashiers Meet Customers: An Analysis of the Role of Supermarket Cashiers', *Academy of Management Journal*, June.

Rafaeli, Anat (1989b). 'When Clerks Meet Customers: A Test of Variables Related to Emotional Expressions on the Job', *Journal of Applied Psychology*, June.

Rafaeli, Anat and Sutton, Robert I. (1990). 'Busy Stores and Demanding Customers: How Do They Affect the Display of Positive Emotion?' *Academy of Management Journal*, September.

Ralis, Michael T. and O'Brien, Richard M. (1986). 'Prompts, Goal-Setting and Feedback to Increase Suggestive Selling', *Journal of Organizational Behavior Management*, Spring–Summer.

Reardon, Kathleen K. and Enis, Ben (1990). 'Establishing a Companywide Customer Orientation Through Persuasive Internal Marketing', *Management Communication Quarterly*, February.

Reekie, Gail (1993). *Temptations: Sex, Selling and the Department Store* (Melbourne: Allen & Unwin).

Reich, Robert (1983). *The Next American Frontier* (New York: Times Books).

Remland, Martin (1981). 'Developing Leadership Skills in Nonverbal Communication: A Situational Perspective', *Journal of Business Communication*, Summer.

Richins, Marsha L. and Verhage, Bronislaw J. (1987). 'Assertiveness and Aggression in Marketplace Exchanges: Testing Measure Equivalence', *Journal of Cross-Cultural Psychology*, March.

Roddick, Anita, with Miller, Russell (1992). *Body and Soul* (London: Vermilion).

Rohrer, Robert (1990). 'What's Your Hurry?' *American Salesman*, November.

Rosen, R. D. (1977). *Psychobabble: Fast Talk and Quick Cure in the Era of Feeling* (New York: Athenaeum).

Rothlach, Roswitha (1991). 'Anglo-German Misunderstandings in Language and Behaviour', *Industrial and Commercial Training*, Vol. 23, No. 3.

Ruben, Brent D. (1992). *Communication and Human Behaviour* (Third Edition) (Englewood Cliffs, New Jersey: Prentice-Hall).

Ruth, William J. (1990). 'Effects of Freudian Sexual Symbolism in Advertising on Self-Reported Purchasing Tendencies: A Preliminary Intrabrand Analysis', *Psychological Reports*, December.

Safer, David Alan (1985). 'Institutional Body Language', *Public Relations Journal*, March.

Salomon, Ilan and Koppelman, Frank S. (1992). 'Teleshopping or Going Shopping? An Information Acquisition Perspective', *Behaviour and Information Technology*, July–August.

Schiffman, Leon G. and Kanuk, Leslie Lazar (1991). *Consumer Behavior* (Fourth Edition) (Englewood Cliffs, New Jersey: Prentice-Hall).

Schillios, Carol (1987). 'Member Relations: Sharpen Employees' Communication Skills', *Credit Union Executive*, Spring.

Schlesinger, Leonard L. and Heskett, James L. (1991). 'Breaking the Cycle of Failure in Services', *Sloan Management Review*, Spring.

Schul, Patrick L. and Lamb, Charles W. (1982). 'Decoding Nonverbal and Vocal Communications: A Laboratory Study', *Journal of the Academy of Marketing Science*, Winter/Spring.

Scoleri, Donald W. and Losoncy, Lewis E. (1985). *The New Psy-Cosmetologist* (Reading, Pennsylvania: People-Media, Inc.).

Scott, Dru (1991). *Customer Satisfaction: The Other Half of Your Job* (Los Altos, California: Crisp Publications).

Seeley, Eric (1992). 'Human Needs and Consumer Economics: The Implications of Maslow's Theory of Motivation for Consumer Expenditure Patterns', *Journal of Socio-Economics*, Winter.

Sewell, Carl and Brown, Paul B. (1991). *Customers for Life: How to Turn that One-Time Buyer into a Lifetime Customer* (New York: Doubleday/Currency).

Shamir, B. (1980). 'Between Service and Servility: Role Conflict in Subordinate Service Roles', *Human Relations*, Vol. 33: 741–756.

Shapley, C. (1987). 'Research Findings on Neurolinguistic Programming: Non-supportive Data or Untestable Theory?' *Journal of Counselling Psychology*, pp. 34, 103–107.

Sheppard, I. Thomas (1986). 'Silent Signals', *Supervisory Management*, March.

Shreve, Elizabeth G., Harrigan, Jinni A., Kues, John R. and Kagas, Denise K. (1988). 'Nonverbal Expressions of Anxiety in Physician–Patient Interactions', *Psychiatry*, November.

Siehl, Caren, Bowen, David E. and Pearson, Christine M. (1992). 'Service Encounters as Rites of Integration: An Information Processing Model', *Organization Science*, November.

Simington, Jane A. (1993). 'The Elderly Require a "Special Touch"', *Nursing Homes*, April.

Singh, Jagdip (1990a). 'A Typology of Consumer Dissatisfaction Response Styles', *Journal of Retailing*, Spring.

Singh, Jagdip (1990b). 'Voice, Exit and Negative Word-of-Mouth Behaviors: An Investigation Across Three Service Categories', *Journal of the Academy of Marketing Science*, Winter.

Siomkos, George J. and Malliaris, Peter G. (1992). 'Consumer Response to Company Communications During a Product Harm Crisis', *Journal of Applied Business Research*, Fall.

Slesinksi, Raymond (1986). 'Reading Nonverbal Signals', *Agency Sales Magazine*, December.

Smith, Manuel J. (1975). *When I Say No, I Feel Guilty* (New York: Bantam).

Smith, Rich and Ross, Rachel (1989). 'Learning to be a Great Communicator', *Journal of Property Management*, January/February.

Snader, Jack R. (1984/1985). 'A Strategy for Selling Consulting Services', *Journal of Management Consulting*, Winter.

Sommers, M. S., Greeno, D. W. and Boag, D. (1989). 'The Role of Non-Verbal Communication in Service Provision and Representation', *Service Industries Journal*, October.

Sorensen, Richard C. (1988). 'Interviewing Techniques for Appraisers', *Appraisal Journal*, October.

Spivak, Helayne (1991). 'The Art of Standing Out in a Crowd', *Working Woman*, June.

Steckler, Nicole A. and Rosenthal, Robert (1985). 'Sex Differences in Nonverbal and Verbal Communication with Bosses, Peers, and Subordinates', *Journal of Applied Psychology*, February.

Steiner, Claude (1974). *Scripts People Live* (New York: Bantam).

Stern, Gary M. (1993). 'Improving Verbal Communications', *Internal Auditor*, August.

Stoneall, Linda (1988). 'Open Your Eyes: Observation Skills', *Personnel Journal*, October.

Street, Richard L. and Buller, David B. (1988). 'Patients' Characteristics Affecting Physician–Patient Nonverbal Communication', *Human Communication Research*, Fall.

Sumutka, Alan R. (1983). 'Client Body Language', *Massachusetts CPA Review*, Winter.

Swan, John E. and Oliver, Richard L. (1989). 'Postpurchase Communications by Consumers', *Journal of Retailing*, Winter.

Szymanski, David M. and Churchill, Gilbert A. (1990). 'Client Evaluation Cues: A Comparison of Successful and Unsuccessful Salespeople', *Journal of Marketing Research*, May.

Tack, Alfred (ed.) (1992). *Profitable Customer Care* (Jordon Hill, Oxford: Butterworth-Heinemann).

Tansik, David A. (1985). 'Nonverbal Communication and High-Contact Employees', in Czepiel et al. (eds).

Taylor, Christina J. and Dawid, Sharon M. (1986). 'Bargaining for a New Car: The Knowledgeable versus the Naive Consumer', *Psychological Reports*, August.

Taylor, Lynda King (1993). *Quality: Sustaining Customer Service* (London: Century Business/The *Sunday Times* 'Business Skills' Series).

Thomas, Jane B., Cassill, Nancy L. and Forsythe, Sandra M. (1991). 'Underlying Dimensions of Apparel Involvement in Consumers' Purchase Decisions', *Clothing and Textiles Research Journal*, Spring.

Townsend, John (1988). 'Paralinguistics: It's Not What You Say, It's the Way That You Say It', *Management Decision*, Vol. 26, No. 3.

Tschohl, John, with Franzmeier, Steve (1991). *Achieving Excellence Through Customer Service* (Englewood Cliffs, New Jersey: Prentice Hall).

Trimby, Madeleine M. (1988). 'What Do You Really Mean?', *Management World*, July/August.

Urqhart, Barry (1991). *'Serves You Right!' You Are Responsible for Customer Service* (Kalamunda, Western Australia: Marketing Focus).

Velardi, Peter J. (1990). 'Communicating with the Corner Office', *Chief Executive*, May.

Video Arts (1989). *So You Think You Can Cope With Customers?* (London: Mandarin/Methuen).

Walker, Denis (1990). *Customer First: A Strategy for Quality Service* (Aldershot, Hants: Gower).

Waltman, John L. and Golen, Steven P. (1993). 'Detecting Deception during Interviews', *Internal Auditor*, August.

Watzlawick, Paul, Bavelas, Janet Beavin, and Jackson, Don (1967). *Pragmatics of Human Communication: A Study of Interactional Patterns, Pathologies and Paradoxes* (New York: W. W. Norton).

Wertheim, E. H., Habib, C. and Cumming, B. (1986). 'Test of the Neurolinguistic Programming Hypothesis that Eye Movements Relate to Processing Imagery', *Perceptual and Motor Skills*, pp. 62, 523–29.

Weisburgh, Mitchell (1990). 'Using NLP to Focus on Learners', *Training and Development Journal*, November.

Weitzel, William, Schwarzkopf, Albert B. and Peach, E. Brian (1989). 'The Influence of Employee Perceptions of Customer Service on Retail Store Sales', *Journal of Retailing*, Spring.

Wesson, David A. (1992). 'The Handshake as Non-Verbal Communication in Business', *Marketing Intelligence and Planning*, Vol. 10, No. 9.

White, Bobby E. (1989). 'Communication and Member Enquiries', *Management Quarterly*, Fall.

Wilcock, Keith D. (1989). 'Customer Service Behavior Spelled Out', *Training and Development Journal*, November.

Wilkie, William L. (1994). *Consumer Behavior* (Third Edition) (New York: John Wiley & Sons).

Williams, Terrell G. (1982). *Consumer Behavior: Fundamentals and Strategies* (St Paul, Minnesota: West Publishing).

Winett, Richard A., Kramer, Kathryn D., Walker, William B. and Malone, Steven W. (1988). 'Modifying Food Purchases in Supermarkets with Modelling, Feedback, and Goal-Setting Procedures', *Journal of Applied Behavior Analysis*, Spring.

Wing, Michael (1993). *Talking With Your Customers: What They Will Tell You About Your Business — When You Ask the Right Questions* (Chicago, Illinois: Dearborn).

Wolvin, Andrew and Coakley, Carolynn Gwynn (1992). *Listening* (Dubuque, Iowa: Wm. C. Brown).

Woollams, Stan and Brown, Michael (1979). *T.A. — The Total Handbook of Transactional Analysis* (Englewood Cliffs, New Jersey: Prentice Hall).

Woodsmall, Wyatt (1988). *Business Applications of Neurolinguistic Programming* (Toorak, Victoria: Maxxum).

Yau, Oliver H. M. (1988). 'Chinese Cultural Values: Their Dimensions and Marketing Implications', *European Journal of Marketing*, Vol. 22, No. 5.

Zaltman, Gerald and Wallendorf, Melanie (1983). *Consumer Behavior: Basic Findings and Management Implications* (New York: John Wiley & Sons).

Zarro, Richard A. and Blum, Peter (1989). *The Phone Book: Breakthrough Neurolinguistic Phone Skills for Profit and Enlightenment* (Portland, Oregon: Metamorphous Press).

Zeithaml, Valerie A., Parasuraman, A. and Berry, Leonard L. (1990). *Delivering Quality Service: Balancing Customer Perceptions and Expectations* (New York: Free Press).

Zemke, Ron and Anderson, Kristin (1990). 'Customers from Hell', *Training*, February.

INDEX

active listening   103
activities   60
adaptive Child ego state (*see* transactional analysis)
Adult ego state (*see* transactional analysis)
aggression (*see* assertiveness)
agricultural society   4-5
Ain't It Awful   59
anger, expressing   74
answering machines   115, 118-19
Apple computers   96
assertiveness   70-84
auditory style, neurolinguistic programming   87-93
Australian saleswomen, early twentieth century   18
Australian Mutual Provident (AMP) Society   108

barrier cross   25
Berne, Eric   38-69, 131, 137, 139
Blemish, game   56
body language (*see* non-verbal communication)
Body Shop, The   19, 23
body-lowering   26
British Airways   18
British Rail   86
broken record   79-81, 84

Child ego state (*see* transactional analysis)
chronicity (*see* time and cultural context)
chunking, neurolinguistic programming   91
clarifying (*see* active listening)
clothing and adornment   27-28
cocktail party effect   97
co-destiny, strategic alliances   7
cold prickly (*see* strokes)
colour   31-32
communication
   models   2-3
   channels   2
competitive pressure   11
complaints (*see* customer complaints)
compliments   72
consumer activism   11
convergence of products   7
conversation, initiating and maintaining   73
Conway, Ronald   93-94
Cops and Robbers, game   58
Courtroom, game   57, 103
crowding (*see* personal space, territoriality)
customer complaints   8, 9, 106-107, 109
customers from hell   3, 127, 129
customers versus clients   1, 131
customers, internal   1, 10, 133
cycle of success   14
cycle of failure   13

Debtor, game   57
deregulation   11
differentiation of products   6-7
discounting   65-66
downsizing   10
drama triangle   61-63

ego, Freudian   38-38
emotional labour   15
employee relations, mirror of customer relations   10-11
environment   31-33
extractive industry (*see* agricultural society)
eye contact   23, 87-93

face-to-face interaction, versus telephone interaction   112-14
facial behaviour   22
feedback   106-107
firing the customer   128
flat structure, organisational design   9-10
fogging   79-81, 84
free information   79-81, 84
Freud, Sigmund   38-39, 137

games people play — transactional analysis   52-60
Gee, You're Wonderful, Professor   54
gender   23, 99-100
gestures   24-25
Ginger and Pickles   85
goods and services, blurring of distinction   7, 133
greetings, on telephone   116-117

Hall, Edward T.   29, 35-36
handshakes   27
Happy to Help, game   59
Harried, game   56-57
head movements   21
help, asking for   72
high context culture   35-36

iceberg, service   15-16
Id (Freudian)   38-39, 137
I'm OK, You're OK (*see* life positions)
I'm Only Trying to Help You   54
Industrial Revolution   4-5
intimacy   60
inverted pyramid model of organisational design   9-10

Just In Time (JIT) manufacturing   7

Kick Me, game   55
kinaesthetic style, neurolinguistic programming   87-93

Let's You and Him Fight, game 58
life positions 64
liking, expressing 73
listening 95-108
love, expressing 73
low context cultures 27, 35-36

manufacturing society 4-5
malls 32
manipulativeness (*see* assertiveness)
McJobs 14
moments of truth 8

Natural Child ego state (*see* transactional analysis)
negative enquiry 79-81, 84
negotiation 102
neurolinguistic programming 87-93
NLP (*see* neurolinguistic programming)
non-verbal communication (*see also* separate aspects) 20-36, 40, 49, 75-77, 89-91, 100, 113, 120, 128)
Now I've Got You, You Son of a Bitch 55-56, 139
Nurturing Parent ego state (*see* transactional analysis)

Ohmae, Kenichi 96
oral gratification (*see* gestures)
orientation 26

paraphrasing (*see* active listening)
Parent ego state (*see* transactional analysis)
passivity (*see* assertiveness)
pastimes 59
persecutor (*see* drama triangle)
personal opinions, expressing 74
personal space, territoriality 29-30
Pinocchio syndrome 25
police, and transactional analysis 50-52
positive enquiry 79-81, 84
postural echo 26, 89-91
posture 26
primary industry (*see* agricultural society)
proactive approach 9, 12
providers 1, 131
psychobabble 3
punishing/Critical Parent ego state (*see* transactional analysis)
pyramid design of organisations 9-10

questioning 105-106
queuing (*see* waiting)
quick fix, in listening 101-102

Rapo, game 58
rapport, neurolinguistic programming 89-91, 128
reactive approach 12
Remington Shaver Company 19
representational systems 87-93
requests 72
    refusing 73-74
rescuer (*see* drama triangle)
rights, assertive 73, 82-83
rituals 59
Roddick, Anita (*see* Body Shop)

roles (*see* drama triangle)
rural versus urban space needs (*see* personal space)

Schlemiel, game 55
secondary industry (*see* manufacturing society)
security guards 30
self-disclosure 79-81, 84
self-talk 78-79
service society 4-17
service factories 5
servicescape (*see* environment)
servility versus service 15
Sewell, Carl 33, 134
sex roles 28
short-term, financial planning approach 11
Siberia, organisational 12
signalling, in negotiation 102
smell 24, 31
smile burnout 15, 23
smiles, not systems approach 12, 134
smiling 23
Sony 96
span of control 10
strategic listening 106-107
strokes, transactional analysis 43-46, 68-69
subliminal perception 97-98
superego (Freudian) 38-39
Sweetheart, game 58
Swissair 37
systems backup 12, 16

TA (*see* transactional analysis)
tall structure, organisational design 9-10
technical backup (*see* systems backup)
telephone communication 112-124
tertiary sector (*see also* service society) 4-5
time structuring 59-61
time and cultural context 33-36
too much growth, too little maintenance approach 11-12, 134
touching 26-27
transactional analysis 38-69, 70, 128
transactions (transactional analysis) 46-52
transferring telephone calls 114, 122

uniforms 28
Uproar, game 59

victim (*see* drama triangle)
visual style, neurolinguistic programming 87-93
voice 24
    on telephone 120

waiting 33-34
warm fuzzy (*see* strokes)
Why Don't You — Yes, But . . ., game 53-54
win-win solution 26, 75
Wish List 17
withdrawal 59
workable compromise 79-81, 84